Sanity, Madness, and the Family

Sanity, Madness, and the Family

Families of Schizophrenics

Second Edition

R. D. Laing
A. Esterson

BASIC BOOKS, Inc., Publishers
New York

RC
514
L274
1971

Contents

Preface to Second Edition

There have been many studies of mental illness and the family. This book is not of them, at least in our opinion. But it has been taken to be so by many people.[1] The result is that much of the considerable controversy that the first edition of this book has occasioned is entirely irrelevant to our own stated aims and method.

When a psychiatrist diagnoses schizophrenia, he means that the patient's experience and behaviour are disturbed *because* there is something the matter with the patient that causes the disturbed behaviour he observes. He calls this something schizophrenia, and he then must ask what causes the schizophrenia.

We jumped off this line of reasoning at the beginning. In our view, it is an assumption, a theory, a hypothesis, but not a *fact*, that anyone suffers from a condition called 'schizophrenia'. No one can deny us the right to disbelieve in the fact of schizophrenia. We did not say, even, that we do *not* believe in schizophrenia.

If anyone thinks that 'schizophrenia' is a fact, he would do well to read critically the literature on 'schizophrenia' from its inventor Bleuler to the present day. After much disbelief in the new disease, more and more psychiatrists adopted the term, though few English or American psychiatrists knew what it meant, since Bleuler's monograph, published in 1911, was not available in English till

---

[1] An exception is Bannister, D. (1968), 'Logical Requirements of Research into Schizophrenia'. *Brit. J. Psychiat.* Vol. 114, pp. 181–188. Bannister argues that schizophrenia is so diffuse and confused a concept as to be scientifically unusable and hence that 'research into schizophrenia, as such, should not be undertaken'.

1950. But though the term has now been generally adopted and psychiatrists trained in its application, the fact it is supposed to denote remains elusive. Even two psychiatrists from the same medical school cannot agree on who is schizophrenic independently of each other more than eight out of ten times at best; agreement is less than that between different schools, and less again between different countries. These figures are not in dispute. But when psychiatrists dispute the diagnosis, there is no court of appeal. There are at present no objective, reliable, quantifiable criteria—behavioural or neurophysiological or biochemical—to appeal to when psychiatrists differ.

We do not accept 'schizophrenia' as being a biochemical, neurophysiological, psychological fact, and we regard it as palpable error, in the present state of the evidence, to take it to be a fact. Nor do we assume its existence. Nor do we adopt it as a hypothesis. We propose no model of it.

This is the position from which we start. Our question is: are the experience and behaviour that psychiatrists take as symptoms and signs of schizophrenia more socially intelligible than has come to be supposed?

This is *what* we are asking. Is this a reasonable question?

In the Introduction we describe *how* we set about contributing towards an answer. Is our way of contributing towards an answer valid?

A common reaction has been to forget *our* question, and then to accuse us of not going about answering other questions adequately. Eleven cases, it is said, all women, prove nothing. There are no controls. How do you sample your data? What objective, reliable rating scales have you employed? And so on. Such criticism would be justified if we had set out to test the hypothesis that the family is a pathogenic variable in the genesis of schizophrenia. But we did not set out to do this, and we have not claimed to have done so. We set out to illustrate by eleven examples that, if we look at some experience and behaviour without reference to family interactions, they may appear com-

viii

PREFACE TO SECOND EDITION

paratively socially senseless, but that if we look at the same experience and behaviour in their original family context, they are liable to make more sense.

This average-size book contains eleven studies. That seems to us enough to make our point. Would a control group help us to answer our question? After much reflection, we came to the conclusion that a control group would contribute nothing to an answer to *our* question. We have not tried to quantify our data, because we could not see how this would help us to answer our question. We have done reliability studies, but they add nothing relevant to this particular study, so they are not included.

We alone cannot answer our question. We can put to you, however, the distillations of our investigation of eleven families, and say: this is the sort of thing we have found *every time* we have taken the trouble to do so (now over two hundred times). Is it what you already knew, expected, suspected? Do these things go on in all sorts of families? Possibly. They go on in these families, at any event, and if one looks, in the way we have, at the experiences and behaviour of the person whose experience and behaviour are invalidated, they take on a complexion very different from that seen from the usual clinical psychiatric vantage point, or dis-vantage point. Those psychiatrists who are not prepared to get to know for themselves what goes on outside their clinics and hospitals simply do not know what goes on, and those sociologists who think they can find out what goes on by analysing medical records are merely trying to turn clinical sows' ears into statistical silk purses. If they think they are studying anything other than pieces of paper, they are only making fools of themselves.[1] Most research into social processes and 'schizophrenia' begs all the questions begged by mental hospital and clinic case histories.

No devices are employed here that do not help us to discover social intelligibility as such. We have even been accused of

---

[1] See Garfinkel, H. (1967). 'Good Organizational Reasons for Bad Clinical Records.' *In Studies in Ethnomethodology.* New York: Prentice-Hall.

finding too much of it. What is the social intelligibility of the fact that not one study has been published, so far as we know, of a comparable kind before and since this one?[1]

Surely, if we are wrong, it would be easy to show that we are, by studying a few families and revealing that 'schizophrenics' really are talking a lot of nonsense after all.

R. D. LAING
A. ESTERSON

London

---

[1] Although, of course, there have been many valuable studies of a different kind into schizophrenia and families, before and since this study was published. See, for example, Boszormenyi-Nagy, I. and Framo, James L., Eds. (1965). *Intensive Family Therapy.* New York: Hoeber; and Rosenthal, D. and Kety, S. S., Eds. (1968). *The Transmission of Schizophrenia.* London: Pergamon.

Preface to First Edition

The data presented in the following pages is part of an investigation into the families of schizophrenics which the authors began in 1958. During this time Dr. R. D. Laing was a member of the Tavistock Institute of Human Relations and the Tavistock Clinic, and since 1960 he has been a Fellow of the Foundations' Fund for Research in Psychiatry. Dr. A. Esterson was on the staff of two mental hospitals, referred to as East Hospital and West Hospital, where most of the interviewing was conducted.

Others who have intensively participated in the research have been Dr. A. Russell Lee, Miss Marion Bosanquet, Psychiatric Social Worker, Mr. H. Phillipson, Principal Psychologist, Tavistock Clinic. Dr. A. Russell Lee's participation was made possible through a grant from the National Institute of Mental Health, Bethesda (MF—10579). This investigation was further aided by a grant from the Foundations' Fund for Research in Psychiatry.

Detailed and helpful discussions of this work have been conducted at a research seminar at the Tavistock Clinic in the last three years, of which Dr. Marie Jahoda has been Chairman. The authors would like to thank members of this seminar for their constructive criticisms: Mr. A. Ambrose, Dr. J. Bowlby, Professor Janis, Mrs. Janis, Dr. Michell, Mr. J. Robertson, Mrs. E. Spillius, Dr. J. D. Sutherland. We wish to thank particularly Paul Senft for his detailed criticisms of the text and our discussions with him.

Through the Foundations' Fund for Research in Psychiatry, Dr. Laing visited the United States in 1962, and discussed this research with a number of investigators there: to name only some of those with whom he had valuable exchanges: Gregory Bateson, Ray Birdwhistell, Erving Goffman, Don Jackson, John Romano, Roger Shapiro, Albert Scheflen, Ross Speck, Lyman Wynne.

Our gratitude is due to the respective superintendents and consultants at the two mental hospitals for the facilities they made available, and for their permission to publish certain clinical data. We are also indebted to members of the nursing staff of these two hospitals.

Our greatest debt is to the persons, patients and family members, whom this book is about, who so generously consented to being studied, and to the results of our research being published.

We have taken every care to preserve the anonymity of all persons involved.

R. D. LAING
A. ESTERSON

London, August 1963

Sanity, Madness, and the Family

Introduction

For five years now we have been studying the families of schizophrenic patients. This book is our first report on this research.
It contains accounts of the first eleven of a series of twenty-five
families of female patients studied at two mental hospitals.

These eleven comprise the families of three patients from East
Hospital, where our investigation began, and eight from West
Hospital, where it was continued.

CRITERIA FOR SELECTION OF FAMILIES

We wished to investigate the families of (i) women (ii) between
the age of fifteen and forty, (iii) who had been diagnosed as
'schizophrenic' by at least two senior psychiatrists and who were
regarded as such by the staff; (iv) who were not and who had
not been subject to any organic condition (e.g. brain injury,
epilepsy) that might have affected those functions regarded as
disturbed in schizophrenia; (v) who were not of obviously sub-
normal intelligence; (vi) who had not been subjected to brain
surgery of any kind; and (vii) who had not received more than
fifty electro-shocks in the year before the investigation began,
and not more than one hundred and fifty in all.

As for the family, we wished to know only if at least one
parent was alive and resident in the United Kingdom. Patients
could be with or without brothers or sisters, married or single,
and with or without children. They could be living with their
families or on their own.

In East Hospital these criteria were applied to all those female patients who had been admitted to hospital for one year or more before the beginning of our investigation.

In West Hospital, the same criteria were applied to each third woman to be admitted after the investigation began.

Three patients from the 'chronic' population of East Hospital satisfied our criteria, and their families are the first three reported on here. The remaining studies presented are the first eight of the series investigated at West Hospital. As it happened, none of the families chosen refused their co-operation, and none asked for the investigation to be stopped. We are still in touch with all of them.

We do not wish to enter into an extended theoretical discussion here on the nature of schizophrenia or of the family, but a brief statement of some of the theoretical background of this work in relation both to schizophrenia and to the family is necessary to an adequate appreciation of the rationale of our methodology.

Despite the prevalence of the diagnosis of schizophrenia, there is no condition over which there is more dispute in the whole field of medicine.

Psychiatry has been particularly concerned with individual experiences and behaviour regarded in our society as 'abnormal'.

In an effort to bring psychiatry into line with neurology and medicine in general, attempts have been made to categorize such experience and behaviour into 'symptoms' and 'signs' of supposedly pathological syndromes or illnesses.

Probably the most common though by no means undisputed view among psychiatrists in Britain and America at the time of writing is that there exists a condition, or group of conditions, usually termed, since Bleuler, schizophrenia, characterized by certain forms of experience and certain ways of behaving, that are taken to be the symptoms and signs of some disease or group of diseases of unknown origin, but largely genetic-constitutionally determined. Investigations of the family environments of people suffering from this illness are seen as studies of the ways in which the advent of such a pathological condition influences the family, and the influence the family in its turn may have on its onset and on its course.

Although the reader is free, of course, to take this clinical point of view on schizophrenia as his starting-point in approaching the following accounts of the families of persons diagnosed as schizophrenics, we recommend that this book be read with the very minimum of presuppositions.

We shall use the expression 'schizophrenic' for a person or for his experience or behaviour in so far as he, his experience, or his behaviour, is clinically regarded as betokening the presence of 'schizophrenia'. That is, this person has come to have attributed to him behaviour and experience that are not simply human, but are the product of some pathological process or processes, mental and/or physical, nature and origin unknown.

Now, it is clear that 'schizophrenia' is a social event in so far as something like one per cent of the population can be expected to be diagnosed as 'schizophrenic' if they live long enough. Psychiatrists have struggled for years to discover what those people who are so diagnosed have or have not in common with each other. The results are so far inconclusive.

No generally agreed objective clinical criteria for the diagnosis of 'schizophrenia' have been discovered.

No consistency in pre-psychotic personality, course, duration, outcome, has been discovered.

Every conceivable view is held by authoritative people as to whether 'schizophrenia' is a disease or a group of diseases; whether an identifiable organic pathology has been, or can be expected to be, found.

There are no pathological anatomical findings *post mortem*. There are no organic structural changes noted in the course of the 'illness'. There are no physiological-pathological changes that can be correlated with these illnesses. There is no general acceptance that any form of treatment is of proven value, except

3

perhaps sustained careful interpersonal relations and tranquil-
lization. 'Schizophrenia' runs in families, but observes no
genetically clear law. It appears usually to have no adverse
effect on physical health, and given proper care by others it does
not cause death or foreshorten life. It occurs in every constitutional
type. It is not associated with any other known physical mal-
functions.

It is most important to recognize that the diagnosed patient is
not suffering from a disease whose aetiology is unknown, unless
he can prove otherwise.[1] He is someone who has queer experiences
and/or is acting in a queer way, from the point of view usually
of his relatives and of ourselves. Whether these queer experiences
and actions are constantly associated with changes in his body is
still uncertain, although it is highly likely that relatively enduring
biochemical changes may be the consequence of relatively
enduring interpersonal situations of particular kinds.

That the diagnosed patient is suffering from a pathological
process is either a fact, an hypothesis, an assumption, or a judgement.

To regard it as fact is unequivocally false. To regard it as an
hypothesis is legitimate. It is unnecessary either to make the
assumption or to pass the judgement.

Now, the psychiatrist adopting his clinical stance in the presence
of the pre-diagnosed person, whom he is already looking at and
listening to as a patient, has too often come to believe that he is
in the presence of the 'fact' of 'schizophrenia'. He acts 'as if' its
existence were an established fact. He then has to discover its
'cause' or multiple 'aetiological factors', to assess its 'prognosis',
and to treat its course. The heart of the 'illness', all that is the
outcome of process, then resides outside the agency of the person.
That is, the illness, or process, is taken to be a 'fact' that the person
is subject to, or undergoes, whether it is supposed to be genetic,
constitutional, endogenous, exogenous, organic or psychological,

---

[1] For the development of this argument see, Szasz, Thomas S. (1961), *The Myth of
Mental Illness*. New York: Hoeber; London: Secker & Warburg, 1962.

4

or some mixture of them all. This, we submit, is a mistaken starting-point.

The judgement that the diagnosed patient is behaving in a biologically dysfunctional (hence pathological) way is, we believe, premature, and one that we shall hold in parenthesis.

Although we ourselves do not accept the validity of the clinical terminology, it is necessary to establish the fact that the persons whose families we are describing are as 'schizophrenic' as anyone is. By 'schizophrenic' we mean here a person who has been diagnosed as such and has come to be treated accordingly. Thus we have begun each account by a description, couched in clinical terms, of the experience and behaviour of the person to whom 'schizophrenia' is attributed. We reiterate that we ourselves are not using the term 'schizophrenia' to denote any identifiable condition that we believe exists 'in' one person. However, in so far as the term summarizes a set of clinical attributions made by certain persons about the experience and behaviour of certain others, we retain the term for this set of attributions. We put in parenthesis any judgement as to the validity or implications of such a set of attributions.

After recording these attributions we have then described the family relationships phenomenologically. Neither *organic* pathology, nor *psycho*pathology, nor for that matter *group* pathology (see below) is assumed to be or not to be in evidence. This issue is simply bracketed off. Whenever we use such judgemental clinical terminology outside the clinical section at the beginning of each chapter, the reader should bear in mind the parenthesis or suspension of judgement that all such terms are placed in.

We are concerned with persons, the relations between persons, and the characteristics of the family as a system composed of a multiplicity of persons. Our theoretical position, with particular respect to our method, is as follows.

Each person not only is an object in the world of others but is a position in space and time from which he experiences, constitutes, and acts in *his* world. He is his own centre with his own point of view, and it is precisely each person's *perspective* on the situation that he shares with others that we wish to discover.

However, each person does not occupy a single definable position in relation to other members of his or her own family.

The one person may be a daughter and a sister, a wife and a mother. There is no means of knowing *a priori* the relation between: the dyadic set of reciprocals she has with her father, the dyadic set with her mother, and the triadic set she has in the trio of them all together, and by the same token, she may be a sister to her brother, and to her sister, and, in addition, she may be married with a son or daughter.

Let us suppose that Jill has a father and mother and brother, who all live together. If one wishes to form a complete picture of her as a family person, let alone as a person outside the family, it will be necessary to see how she experiences and acts in all the following contexts:

Jill alone
Jill with mother
Jill with father
Jill with brother
Jill with mother and father
Jill with mother and brother
Jill with father and brother
Jill with mother, father, and brother.

One sees that it is a fairly crude differentiation of the various positions that Jill has to adopt to characterize them as daughter or sister.

Samples of behaviour require to be taken of each person in the family in turn in the same way. People have identities. But they may also change quite remarkably as they become different others-to-others. It is arbitrary to regard any one of these transformations or *alter*ations as basic, and the others as variations.

Not only may the one person behave differently in his different alterations, but he may experience himself in different ways. He is liable to remember different things, express different attitudes, even quite discordant ones, imagine and phantasize in different ways, and so on.

Our interest is in persons always in relation either with us, or with each other, and always in the light of their group context, which in this work is primarily the family, but may include also the extra-familial personal networks of family members if these have a specific bearing on the issues we are trying to illumine. In other words, we are interested in what might be called the family *nexus*, that multiplicity of persons drawn from the kinship group, and from others who, though not linked by kinship ties, are regarded as members of the family. The relationships of persons in a nexus are characterized by enduring and intensive face-to-face reciprocal influence on each other's experience and behaviour.

We are studying the persons who comprise this nexus, their relationships, and the nexus itself, in so far as it may have structures, processes, and effects as a system, not necessarily intended by its members, nor necessarily predictable from a knowledge of its members studied out of context.

If one wishes to know how a football team concert or disconcert their actions in play, one does not think only or even primarily of approaching this problem by talking to the members individually. One watches the way they play together.

Most of the investigations of families of 'schizophrenics', while contributing original and useful data to different facets of the problem, have not been based on direct observation of the members of the family *together* as they actually interact with each other.

The way in which a family deploys itself in space and time, what space, what time, and what things are private or shared, and by whom—these and many other questions are best answered by seeing what sort of world the family has itself fleshed out for itself, both as a whole and differentially for each of its members.

One does not wish, however, to study the system-properties of a family abstracted from the experience and actions of the individuals whose continued living together in a particular way alone guarantees the continuance of the system.

The relation between persons, their relationships, and the group they comprise continues to present conceptual and methodological difficulties.

Part of the problem is the apparent discontinuity between the processes of the system and the actions of the agents who comprise the system. Here we have found it useful to utilize the concepts of praxis, process, and intelligibility, as developed recently by Sartre.[1]

Events, occurrences, happenings, may be deeds done by doers, or they may be the outcome of a continuous series of operations that have no agent as their author.

In the first case, we shall speak of such events as the outcome of praxis; in the second case, as the outcome of process.

When what is going on in any human group can be traced to what agents are doing, it will be termed *praxis*. What goes on in a group may not be intended by anyone. No one may even realize what is happening. But what happens in a group will be *intelligible* if one can retrace the steps from what is going on (process) to who is doing what (praxis).

Phenomenologically, a group can feel to its members to be an organism; to those outside it, it can appear to act like one. But to go beyond this, and to maintain that, *ontologically*, it *is* an organism, is to become completely mystified. Just when the sociologists have all but completely abandoned organicism, a new medical sociology is arising, as the clinician, abandoning his position of a one-person medical psychologist, is beginning to

---

[1] For extended expositions of these concepts, see Sartre, J-P. (1960). *Critique de la raison dialectique*. Paris: Gallimard; and Laing, R. D. & Cooper, D. G. (1964). *Reason and Violence: A Decade of Sartre's Philosophy (1950–1960)*. London: Tavistock Publications.

occupy the old positions of the sociologist with a curious type of medical organicism.

The concept of family *pathology* is therefore, we believe, a confused one. It extends the unintelligibility of individual behaviour to the unintelligibility of the group. It is the *biological analogy*[1] applied now not just to one person, but to a multiplicity of persons. This instance of the transference of concepts derived from clinical biology into the realm of multiplicities of human beings is, in our view, unfruitful. Its initial impact is seductive, but it creates ultimately even greater difficulties than the biological analogy as applied to the one person. Not the individual but the family is the unit of illness: not the individual but the family, therefore, needs the clinician's services to 'cure' it: the family (or even society at large) is now a sort of hyperorganism, with a physiology and pathology, that can be well or ill. One arrives at a pan-clinicism, so to say, that is more a system of values than an instrument of knowledge.

The group is *not* to the individual as whole to part, as hyper-organism to organism. It is not a mechanism, except in the sense that the mechanical action of the group may be constituted as such in and through the praxes of each and all of its members, and is the intelligible outcome of such praxes and can be elucidated by the use of an appropriate methodology.

We have tried to develop a method, therefore, that enables us to study at one and the same time (i) each person in the family; (ii) the relations between persons in the family; (iii) the family itself as a system.

We have followed the same general plan with each family. Details of the structure of each investigation are given at the beginning of our account of each family and in the appendix.

The first step in each case was to tell the patient that we wished

[1] See MacMurray, John (1957). *The Self as Agent.* London: Faber; and Chapter 1 of Laing, R. D. (1960). *The Divided Self.* London: Tavistock Publications; New York: Pantheon.

to have interviews with her and the members of her family. Some expressed initial anxiety, but none refused.

Usually the first relatives we contacted were the patient's parents. It was explained that we were trying to find more facts that would help us understand why the patient was a patient and in hospital. In every case the response was virtually the same. They would do anything if it would help us help the patient. We then said we would like to know more about her family life, and that the way we wished to do this was to meet with them, singly and together, with the patient present, and without, and that we would like to meet them in their homes, because then things would become more vivid for us. These initial exchanges were made with the tape-recorder on in the same room, in full view. This, we explained, was our memory. With it, we could attend to what was said without simultaneously trying to remember everything. No objections were made to this.

After one or two interviews with the initial relatives, we suggested that we meet and similarly interview other members of the family. Sometimes reasons were given why this should not be done. We did not press the point when children under twelve were in question, but otherwise we tried to overcome these objections, usually successfully. But in some families we could not interview every relevant person, sometimes because of a veto from one of the initially consenting relatives, sometimes because the relative in question refused his or her co-operation. The details of these lacunae are given in each of the studies reported here. The reader will see that we were generally successful in interviewing all the persons we wished.

We have seen all these families at different times of the day. We have seen them when the patient was acutely psychotic, and apparently well: we have seen the reactions of the family as a total system, of each of its sub-systems, and of each of its members, to the patient's recovery, and to further threatened or actual breakdowns. We have known all the families reported here for more than three years at the time of writing.

Having gathered our data in the form of notes and sound-recordings, complete transcriptions were made of the latter, all of which have been retained.

From each set of recordings and transcriptions, we made a concordance-index, and from these dossiers the eleven following accounts were distilled. In the eleventh we give the reader a closer look at the chronological unfolding of the actual course of an investigation. In this case we have put the data before the reader at a half-way stage, as it were, between the primary data and the finished stories.

We have of course substituted names, and taken every care to ensure complete anonymity of the persons concerned. Except for changes of name, place, and occupation, all conversations reproduced are strictly verbatim.

Within the terms of phenomenology itself, this study is limited methodologically and heuristically.

Most of our data is in the form of interviews. Despite the relatively systematic nature of our sampling of the family by such interviews, our study of these families is of course far from complete, in that, firstly, the majority of these interviews were conducted in our own consulting-rooms, and not in the family homes, and second, and more serious, an interview is itself not a naturally occurring family situation.

We are also dissatisfied with our method of recording. Its main limitation is that all our permanent records are restricted to the auditory transactions of the family members in our presence. Although such a permanent library of magnetic recordings is an advance on clinical notes made during or after interviews, it can be regarded only as a stepping-stone to permanent audio-visual records.

Our findings are presented with very few interpretations, whether existential or psycho-analytic. Psycho-analysis has largely concerned itself with the relation of the unconscious to manifest behaviour. The psycho-analyst frequently makes attributions about the analysand's motives, experiences, actions, intentions, that the analysand himself disavows or is unaware of. The reader will see that we have been very sparing about making attributions of this kind in respect to the members of these families.

Undoubtedly, in our view, in all these families the phantasy experiences of the family members and the motives, actions, intentions, that arise on the basis of such experience, are mostly unknown to the persons themselves. Thus, it is not possible to deal adequately with such a central issue, for instance, as sexuality in these families without being prepared to attribute to the agents involved phantasies of which they are themselves unconscious. However, in this volume, we have not undertaken to do this.

Our discussion and comments on each family are pared down to what seems to us to be an undeniable bedrock.

Inferences about experiences that the experiencers themselves deny, and about motives and intentions that the agent himself disavows, present difficulties of validation that do not arise at that phenomenological level to which we have restricted ourselves.

It has seemed to us on the whole desirable to limit this volume in this way, even sometimes at the price of not being able to state what we regard as basic elements of the family dynamics.

Here, then, the reader will find documented the quite manifest contradictions that beset these families, without very much exploration of the underlying factors which may be supposed to generate and maintain them. Subsequently we hope to go much further in interpreting data.

Another limitation, and one that we feel is necessary in the transition from a clinical to a social phenomenological perspective, is that our *totalization*[1] of the family itself as a system is incomplete. Our account of each family is to a considerable degree polarized around the intelligibility of the experience and behaviour of the

[1] See Sartre, J-P. (1960); and Laing, R. D. & Cooper, D. G. (1964) op. cit.

person who has already begun a career[1] as a schizophrenic. As such, the focus remains somewhat on the identified patient, or on the mother-daughter relationship, on the person-in-a-nexus, rather than on the nexus itself. This we believe to be historically unavoidable. That this study is transitional is both its weakness and its strength, in that we hope it will constitute a bridge between past and future efforts in the understanding of madness.

In this book, we believe that we show that the experience and behaviour of schizophrenics is much more socially intelligible than has come to be supposed by most psychiatrists.

We have tried in each single instance to answer the question: to what extent is the experience and behaviour of that person, who has already begun a career as a diagnosed 'schizophrenic' patient, intelligible in the light of the praxis and process of his or her family nexus?

We believe that the shift of point of view that these descriptions both embody and demand has an historical significance no less radical than the shift from a demonological to a clinical viewpoint three hundred years ago.

[1] See Goffman, Erving (1961). *Asylums.* New York: Doubleday Anchor.

FAMILY 1

The Abbotts

Maya is a tall, dark, attractive woman of twenty-eight. She is an only child. Until she was eight she lived with her mother and father, the manager of a general store. From then until fourteen she was an evacuee with an elderly childless couple and from fourteen to eighteen when she was first admitted to hospital, she was once again with her parents.

She has spent nine of her last ten years in West Hospital.

CLINICAL PERSPECTIVE

Maya's 'illness' was diagnosed as paranoid schizophrenia. It appeared to come out of the blue. A report by a psychiatric social worker based on interviews with her mother and father described the onset in the following way:

'Patient did not seem to be anything other than normal in her behaviour until about a month before her admission to hospital. She had of course been worrying about her school work, but the parents were used to this, and from past experience regarded her fears as quite groundless. One afternoon she came home from school and told her parents that the headmistress wished her to leave the school. Parents were immediately worried as they knew this was not right. Further, the patient reiterated this on other occasions. She then said that she could not sleep, and

15

shortly afterwards became convinced that burglars were breaking into the house. A sedative was prescribed but the patient at
first refused to take this. One night when she did so, she sat bolt
upright in bed, and managed to stay awake in spite of the drug.
She then decided her father was poisoning her, and one day ran
out of the house and told a neighbour that her father was
trying to poison her. Parents eventually found her and brought
her home. She did not seem frightened of her father and
discussed the matter quite calmly with him, but refused to be
convinced that he was not trying to get rid of her. A doctor
was called and advised that she have treatment immediately.
Patient was more than willing to have treatment, and entered
hospital as a voluntary patient.'

Ten years later her parents gave us the same report.

In the past ten years her behaviour has given rise to clinical
attributions that she had auditory hallucinations and was de-
personalized; showed signs of catatonia; exhibited affective
impoverishment and autistic withdrawal. Occasionally she was
held to be 'impulsive'.

Expressed more phenomenologically, she experienced herself
as a machine, rather than as a person: she lacked a sense of her
motives, agency, and intentions belonging together: she was very
confused about her autonomous identity. She felt it necessary to
move and speak with studious and scrupulous correctness. She
sometimes felt that her thoughts were controlled by others, and
she said that not she but her 'voices' often did her thinking.

In our account, as we are not approaching our study from a
clinical but from a social phenomenological perspective, we shall
not be able to compartmentalize our inquiry in terms of clinical
categories. Clinical signs and symptoms will become dissolved in
the social intelligibility of the account that follows.

What we are setting out to do is to show that Maya's experiences
and actions, especially those deemed most schizophrenic, become
intelligible as they are seen in the light of her family situation.

This 'situation' is not only the family seen by us from without, but the 'family' as experienced by each of its members from inside.

Our fundamental question is: to what extent is Maya's schizophrenic experience and behaviour intelligible in the light of the praxis and process of her family?

STRUCTURE OF INVESTIGATION

Our picture of this family is based on the following interviews.

Interviews	Occasions
Mother	1
Father	1
Daughter	2
Daughter and mother	29
Daughter and father	2
Mother and father	2
Mother, father, and daughter	8
	45

This represents fifty hours' interviewing, of which forty were tape-recorded.

THE FAMILY SITUATION

Mr. and Mrs. Abbott appear quiet, ordinary people. When Maya was eighteen Mrs. Abbott was described by a psychiatric social worker as 'a most agreeable woman, who appeared to be friendly and easy to live with'. Mr. Abbott had 'a quiet manner but a kindly one'. He seemed 'a very sensible man, but less practical than his wife'. There did not appear to be much that he would not do for his family. He had excellent health, and impressed the interviewer as 'a very stable personality'.

Maya was born when her mother was twenty and her father thirty.

When his daughter was born, Mr. Abbott had been reading of an excavation of a Mayan tomb. 'Just the name for my little girl', he thought.

Mother and father agreed that until sent away from home at eight Maya had been her daddy's girl. She would wake him early in the morning and they would go swimming. She was always hand-in-hand with him. They sat close together at table, and he was the one to say prayers with her last thing at night. They frequently went for long walks together.

Apart from brief visits home, Maya lived away from her parents from eight until the age of fourteen. When she came home then to live permanently with them, they complained she was changed. She was no longer their little girl. She wanted to study. She did not want to go swimming, or to go for long walks with her father any more. She no longer wanted to pray with him. She wanted to read the Bible herself, by herself. She objected to her father expressing his affection for her by sitting close to her at meals. She wanted to sit further away from him. Nor did she want to go to the cinema with her mother. In the house, she wanted to handle things and to do things for herself, such as (mother's example) washing a mirror without first telling her mother.

These changes in Maya, mentioned by her parents retrospectively as the first signs of illness, seem to us to be ordinary expressions of growing up. What is of interest is the discrepancy between her parents' judgement of these developments and ours.

Maya conceived as her main difficulty, indeed her main task in life, the achievement of autonomy.

'You should be able to think for yourself, work things out for yourself. I can't. People can take things in but I can't. I forget half the time. Even what I remember isn't true memory. You should be able to work things out for yourself.'

Her parents appear to have consistently regarded with alarm all expressions of developing autonomy on Maya's part, involving necessarily efforts to separate herself from them and to do things on her own initiative. Her parents' alarm remains unabated in the present. For example, her mother objected to her ironing without

supervision, although for the past year she had been working in a
laundry without mishap. Mr. and Mrs. Abbott regarded their
daughter's use of her own 'mind', independently of them, as
synonymous with 'illness', and as a rejection of them. Her
mother said:

> 'I think I'm so absolutely centred on the one thing—it's well,
> to get her well—I mean as a child, and as a—teenager I could
> always sort out whatever was wrong or—do something about
> it, but it—but this illness has been so completely em—our
> relations have been different—you see Maya is er—instead of
> accepting everything—as if I said to her, er, "Black is black",
> she would have probably believed it, but since she's ill, she's
> never accepted anything any more. She's had to reason it out
> for herself, and if she couldn't reason it out herself, then she
> didn't seem to take *my* word for it—which of course is quite
> different to me.'

'Since her illness', as they put it, she had become more 'difficult'.
She did not 'fit in' as she had done. The hospital had made her
worse in this respect, although Maya felt that it had helped her to
'use her own mind' more than before. Using one's own mind
entails of course experiencing for oneself generally. What to Maya
was 'using my own mind', and 'wanting to do things for myself',
was to her parents 'forwardness' and 'brightness'.

Until eighteen Maya studied hard, and passed all her exams.
She took refuge, as she said, in her books, from what she called
her parents' intrusions. Her parents' attitudes became highly
equivocal, at one and the same time proud and patronizing, hurt
in themselves and anxiously concerned for her. They said she
was very clever, even 'too clever perhaps'. They thought she
worked too hard. She was getting no enjoyment reading all the
time, so she had to be dragged away from her reading. Her
mother said:

> 'We used to go to the pictures in those days and I used to say
> eh—and sometimes she'd say. "I don't think I should go to

the pictures tonight, Mum, I think I should do some home-work". And then I'd say to her, "Oh well, I'm disappointed", or that I'd made up my mind to go or something like that, or, "Well, I'll go on my own", and then she'd say, "All right, I will come". She really had to be forced to go out, most of the time.'

When Maya said that her parents put difficulties in the way of her reading, they amusedly denied this. She insisted that she had wanted to read the Bible; they both laughed at the idea that they made this difficult for her, and her father, still laughing, said, 'What do you want to read the Bible for anyway? You can find that sort of information much better in other books.'

We shall now consider more closely certain recurring attributions made about Maya both by her parents and by psychiatrists.

For ten years she was described uniformly in psychiatric report after report as apathetic, withdrawn, lacking in affect, isolated, hostile, emotionally impoverished. Her parents also saw her in this way. She had been told by them so frequently since she was fourteen that she had no feelings, that one would have thought she would have been fairly inured to this attribution, yet she could still get flushed and angry when she was 'accused' of it. For her part, she felt that she had never been given affection, nor allowed to show affection spontaneously, and that it was exasperation or frustration on this score that was the reason for much of what was called her impulsiveness—for instance, the incident that had occasioned her readmission to hospital eight years earlier, when she was said to have attacked her mother with a knife.

MAYA: Well why did I attack you? Perhaps I was looking for something, something I lacked—affection, maybe it was greed for affection.

MOTHER: You wouldn't have any of that. You always think that's soppy.

MAYA: Well, when did you offer it to me?

MOTHER: Well, for instance if I was to want to kiss you you'd say, 'Don't be soppy'.

MAYA: *But I've never known you let me kiss you.*

Maya made the point that her parents did not think of her, or 'see' her as 'a person', 'as the person that I am'. She felt frightened by this lack of recognition, and hit back at them as a means of self-defence. But this, of course, was quite bewildering to her parents, who could not grasp at any time any sense in this accusation. Maya insisted that her parents had no genuine affection for her because they did not know, and did not want to know, what she felt, and also that *she* was not allowed to express any spontaneous affection for *them*, because this was not part of 'fitting in'.

When Maya said that she had brightened up after having lost her feelings, her mother retorted, 'Well, you were too bright already'. This did not refer to any hypomanic quality about the girl, as there was none.

Another feature of her lack of feeling is illuminated by the issue of being taken seriously or not. As Maya said, her father

' . . . often laughed off things that I told him and I couldn't see what he was laughing at. I thought it was very serious. Even when I was five, when I could understand, I couldn't see what he was laughing at. Both Father and Mother took sides against me.
'I told Father about school and he used to laugh it off. If I told him about my dreams he used to laugh it off and tell me to take no notice. They were important to me at the time—I often got nightmares. He used to laugh them off. He played a lot with me as a child, but that's not the same.'

Her mother complained to us that Maya did not want to understand her: her father felt the same way, and both were hurt that she would not tell them anything about herself.

Their response to this blow was interesting. They came to feel that Maya had exceptional mental powers, so much so that they convinced themselves *that she could read their thoughts*. For instance,

FATHER: If I was downstairs and somebody came in and asked how Maya was, if I immediately went upstairs, Maya would say to me, 'What have you been saying about me?' I said, 'Nothing'. She said, 'Oh yes you have, I heard you'. Now it was so extraordinary that unknown to Maya I experimented myself with her, you see, and then when I'd proved it I thought, 'Well I'll take Mrs. Abbott into my confidence', so I told her, and she said, 'Oh don't be silly, it's impossible'. I said, 'All right, now when we take Maya in the car tonight I'll sit beside her and I'll concentrate on her. I'll say something, and you watch what happens'. When I was sitting down she said, 'Would you mind sitting the other side of the car. I can't fathom Dad's thoughts.' And that was true. Well, following that, one Sunday I said—it was winter—I said, 'Now Maya will sit in the usual chair, and she'll be reading a book. Now you pick up a paper and I'll pick up a paper, and I'll give you the word and er . . .'—Maya was busy reading the paper, and er—I nodded to my wife, then I concentrated on Maya behind the paper. She picked up the paper—her em—magazine or whatever it was and went to the front room. And her mother said, 'Maya where are you going? I haven't put the fire on.' Maya said, 'I can't understand—' no—'I can't get to the depth of Dad's brain. Can't get to the depth of Dad's mind.'

Such experimentation has continued from before her first 'illness' to the present, and came to light only after this investigation had been under way for over a year. In this light, it is only with the greatest difficulty that Maya's ideas of influence can continue to be seen as the effulgence of an individual pathological process, whether conceived as organic or psychic or both.

Clinically, she 'suffered' from 'ideas of influence'. She recurred repeatedly to her feeling that despite herself she influenced others in untoward ways, and that others could and did influence her unduly, again despite her own struggles to counter this.

Now, in general, the nature of the reciprocal influences that persons do and can exert on one another is rather obscure. This is a realm where phantasy tends to generate fact. Certainly it would be easier to discuss Maya's preoccupation with this issue if clearer ideas existed among the sane population on what does and can happen in this respect.

Specifically, it will be very relevant to us to know answers to the following questions.

What influence did her mother and father feel that Maya actually had on them?

What influence did they feel they could or did have, or ought to have had, on her?

What influence did they try to have on her?

What influence did they assume that one person could have on another, especially by action from a distance, and particularly by prayer, telepathy, or thought-control—the media that worried Maya most?

Without answers to such questions, no one could start to evaluate and elucidate Maya's 'delusions' of reciprocal influence. This principle necessarily holds, it seems to us, for every instance of such delusions.

In this case ideas of influence become socially intelligible when we remember that her parents *were* actively trying to influence her, that they believed that she could tell their thoughts, and that they experimented with her and denied to her that they did so. Further, while ascribing these remarkable powers to Maya, they believed, without any sense of contradiction, that she did not even know what she thought or did herself.

Maya's accusations that her mother and father were 'influencing' her in some way were 'laughed off' by them, and it is not surprising, therefore, that at home especially she was irritable, jumpy, and confused. It was only in the course of our investigation, as we have said, that they admitted to her what they had been doing.

MAYA: Well I mean you shouldn't do it—it's not natural.

FATHER: I don't do it—I didn't do it—I thought, 'Well I'm doing the wrong thing, I won't do it'.

MAYA: I mean the way I react would show it's wrong.

FATHER: And there was a case in point a few weeks back—she fancied one of her mother's skirts.

MAYA: I didn't—I tried it on and it fitted.

FATHER: Well they had to go to a dressmaker—the dressmaker was recommended by someone. Mrs. Abbott went for it, and she said, 'How much is that?' The woman said, 'Four shillings' —Mrs. Abbott said, 'Oh no, it must have cost you more than that'. So she said, 'Oh well, your husband did me a good turn a few years back and I've never repaid him'. I don't know what it was. Mrs. Abbott gave more of course. So when Maya came home she said, 'Have you got the skirt, Mum?' She said, 'Yes, and it cost a lot of money too, Maya'—Maya said, 'Oh you can't kid me—they tell me it was four shillings'.

MAYA: No, seven I thought it was.

FATHER: No, it was four you said—exactly—and my wife looked at me and I looked at her—So if you can account for that—I can't.

An idea of reference that she had was that something she could not fathom was going on between her parents, seemingly about her.

Indeed there was. When they were all interviewed together, her mother and father kept exchanging with each other a constant series of nods, winks, gestures, knowing smiles, so obvious to the observer, that he commented on them after twenty minutes of the first such interview. They continued, however, unabated and denied.

The consequence, so it seems to us, of this failure by her parents to acknowledge the validity of similar comments by Maya, was that Maya could not know when she was perceiving or when she was imagining things to be going on between her parents. These open yet unavowed non-verbal exchanges between father and mother were in fact quite public and perfectly obvious. Much of what could be taken to be paranoid about Maya arose because she mistrusted her own mistrust. She could not really believe that what she thought she saw going on was going on. Another consequence was that she could not easily discriminate between actions not usually intended or regarded as communications, e.g. taking off spectacles, blinking, rubbing nose, frowning, and so on, and those that are—another aspect of her paranoia. It was just those actions, however, that were used as signals between her parents, as 'tests' to see if Maya would pick them up, but an essential part of this game the parents played was that, if commented on, the rejoinder would be an amused, 'What do you mean?', 'What wink?', and so on.

In addition to attributing to her various wonderful powers, her parents added further to her mystification by telling her she could not, or did not, think, remember, or do what she did think, remember, and do.

It is illuminating to compare in some detail what she and her mother had to say about the supposed attack on her mother that had precipitated her readmission to hospital (see p. 20 above).

According to her mother, Maya attacked her for no reason. It was the result of her illness coming on again. Maya said she could not remember anything about it. Her mother continually prompted Maya to try to remember.

Maya once said, however, that she could remember the occasion quite clearly. She was dicing some meat. Her mother was standing behind her, telling her how to do things right, and that she was doing things wrong as usual. She felt something was going to snap inside unless she acted. She turned round and brandished the knife at her mother, and then threw it on the floor. She did not know why she felt like that. She was not sorry for what had happened, but she wanted to understand it. She said she had felt quite well at the time: she did not feel that it had to do with her 'illness'. She was responsible for it. She had not been told to act like that by her 'voices'. The voices, she said, were her own thoughts, anyway.

Our construction is that the whole episode might have passed unnoticed in many households as an expression of ordinary exasperation between daughter and mother.

We were not able to find one area of Maya's personality that was not subject to negations of different kinds.

For instance, she thinks she started to imagine 'sexual things' when she came home at the age of fourteen. She would lie in bed wondering whether her parents had sexual intercourse. She began to get sexually excited, and to masturbate. She was very shy, however, and kept away from boys. She felt increasingly irritated at the physical presence of her father. She objected to his shaving in the same room while she had breakfast. She was frightened that her parents knew that she had sexual thoughts about them. She tried to tell them about this, but they told her *she did not have any thoughts of that kind*. She told them she masturbated *and they told her that she did not*. What happened then is of course inferred, but *when she told her parents in the presence of the interviewer that she still masturbated, her parents simply told her that she did not!*

As she recalls, when she was fifteen she began to feel that her father was causing these sexual thoughts, and that both parents were trying to influence her in some queer way. She intensified her studies, burying herself in her books, but she began to hear what she was reading in her head, and she began to hear her own thoughts. She was now struggling hard to think clearly any thoughts of her own. Her thoughts thought themselves audibly in her head: her vocal cords spoke her voice, her mind had a front and a back part. Her movements came from the front part of her mind. They just happened. She was losing any sense of being the agent of her own thoughts and words.[1]

[1] For reasons given in the introduction, we are limiting ourselves very largely to the transactional phenomenology of these family situations. Clearly, here and in every other family, the material we present is full of evidence of the struggle of each of the family members against their own sexuality. Maya without doubt acts on her own sexual experience, in particular by way of splitting, projection, denial, and so on. Although it is beyond the self-imposed limitation of our particular focus in this book to discuss these aspects, the reader should not suppose that we wish to deny or to minimize the person's *action on himself* (what psycho-analysts usually call defence mechanisms), particularly in respect of sexual feelings aroused towards family members, that is, in respect of incest.

Not only did both her parents contradict Maya's memory, feelings, perceptions, motives, intentions, but they made attributions that were themselves curiously self-contradictory, and, while they spoke and acted as though they knew better than Maya what she remembered, what she did, what she imagined, what she wanted, what she felt, whether she was enjoying herself or whether she was tired, this control was often maintained in a way which was further mystifying.

For instance, on one occasion Maya said that she wanted to leave hospital, and that she thought her mother was trying to keep her in hospital, even though there was no need for her to be an in-patient any more. Her mother replied:

'I think Maya is—I think Maya recognizes that—er—whatever she wanted really for her good, I'd do—wouldn't I—Hmm? (no answer)—No reservations in any way—I mean if there are any changes to be made I'd gladly make them—unless it was absolutely impossible.'

Nothing could have been further from what Maya recognized at that moment. But one notes the many mystifying qualifications in the statement. Whatever Maya wanted is qualified most decisively by 'really' and 'for her own good'. Mrs. Abbott, of course, was arbiter (i) of what Maya recognized, (ii) of what Maya 'really' wanted, in contrast to what *she* might *think* she wanted, (iii) of what was for her own good, (iv) of what was a reservation or a change, (v) of what was possible.

Maya sometimes commented fairly lucidly on these mystifications. But this was much more difficult for her to do than for us. Her difficulty was that she could not know when to trust or mistrust her own perceptions and memory or her mother and father.

The close investigation of this family reveals that her parents' statements to her about her, about themselves, about what they felt she felt they felt, and even about what could directly be seen and heard, could not be trusted.

Maya *suspected* this, but her parents regarded just such suspicions as her illness, and they told her so. She often therefore doubted the validity of her own suspicions: sometimes she denied delusionally what they said, sometimes she invented a story to cling to, for instance, that she had been in hospital when she was eight—the occasion of her first separation from them.

It is not so surprising that Maya tried to withdraw into her own world, although feeling at the same time most painfully that she was not an autonomous person. However, she felt that in order to win some measure of separateness from her parents, she required to cultivate what she called 'self-possession'. This had various ramifications.

'If I weren't self-possessed I'd be nowhere, because I'd be mixed up in a medley of other things.'

As we have seen, however, it was just this attempt at autonomy that her parents saw as her 'illness', since it entailed that she did not 'fit in' with them, and was 'difficult', 'forward', 'too bright', 'too proud', and found fault with them.

Maya tried to explain herself in these terms:

'I emphasize people's faults to regain my self-possession.
I can't fit in properly with people: it's not pride.
'Mother is always picking on me. She's always getting at me. She's always trying to teach me how to use my mind. You can't tell a person how to use their mind against their will. It has always been like that with Mother. I resent it.'

But at other times she doubted the validity of this impression. She said:

'She doesn't pick on me, but that's how I look at it. That's how I react to it. I've got to calm myself. I always feel I've got to pick back at her—to stand up and get my own back—get back my self-possession.'

She would feel that her mother and father were forcing their

28

opinions on her, that they were trying to 'obliterate' her mind. But she had been taught to suppose that this was a mad thing to think, that this was what her 'illness' was.

So, she sought temporary refuge in her own world, her private world, her shell. To do this, however, was to be 'negative', in her parents' jargon: 'withdrawn', in psychiatric parlance.

When she was not putting up as belligerent a self-defensive front as she could muster, Maya would admit that she was very unsure of her own faculties. Things were not always real.

'I was never allowed to do anything for myself so I never learned to do things. The world doesn't seem quite real. If you don't do things then things are never quite real.'

Change disturbed her precarious sense of identity.

'I don't know how to deal with the unexpected. That's why I like things neat and tidy. Nothing unexpected can happen then.'

But this neatness and tidiness had to come from herself, not be imposed by her parents' 'correctness' or 'precision'.

'I used to think it a threat when I was younger, when I didn't have the freedom to act otherwise, but I can act otherwise now: but their correctness makes me want to understand why they are so correct, why they do things as they do, and why I am like I am.'

She repeatedly disclaimed any feelings of her own, and any interest in other people's feelings.

'Mother is a person that I lived with. I don't feel any more strongly than that. If something happened to her I should miss her and I should keep on thinking about her, but it wouldn't make any difference to the way I go on. I haven't any deep feelings. I'm just not made that way.'

But she certainly knew what fear was. For instance, when an aunt shouted at her recently.

'I felt just—I've often seen the cat shrink and it felt like that inside me.'

She herself disclaimed being the agent of her own thoughts, largely, it seems, to evade criticism and invalidation.

'I don't think, the voices think.'

They echoed her reading or they made 'criticisms' of people she was terrified to make in her own person.
Just as not she but the voices thought, so not she but her body acted.

'The whole lot is out of my control.'

She had given up trying to 'make out' what her parents or anyone else was up to.

'I can only see one side of the question—the world through my eyes and I can't see it through anyone else's eyes, like I used to.'

This repudiation of any desire to 'put herself into' others was partly a defensive tactic, but it was also an expression of the fact that she was genuinely at a loss.

'I find it hard to hold down a job because I don't know what is going on in other people's minds, and they seem to know what I'm thinking about.
'I don't like being questioned on anything because I don't always know what other people are thinking.
'I can't make out your kind of life. I don't live in your world. I don't know what you think or what you're after, and I don't want to' (addressing her mother).

Her parents could see Maya's attempts at 'self-possession' only as due to 'a selfish nature', 'greed', 'illness', or 'lack of feeling'.
Thus when Maya tried to get into her own shell, to live in her own world, to bury herself in her books (to use her expressions), her mother and father felt this, as we have seen, as a terrible blow.

The only time in our interviews when Mrs. Abbott began to cry was when, having spoken of her own mother's death, she said that Maya did not want to understand her, because she was only interested in her own problems.

Mrs. Abbott persistently reiterated how much she hoped and prayed that Maya would remember anything if it would help the doctors to get to the bottom of her illness. But she felt she had to tell Maya repeatedly that she (Maya) could not 'really' remember anything, because (as she explained to us) Maya was always ready to pretend that she was not really ill.

She frequently questioned Maya about her memory in general, in order (from her point of view) to help her to realize that she was ill, by showing her at different times either that she was amnesic, or that she had got her facts wrong, or that she only imagined she remembered what she thought she remembered because she had heard about it from her mother or father at a later date.

This 'false' but 'imaginary' memory was regarded by Mrs. Abbott with great concern. It also worried and confused Maya.

Mrs. Abbott finally told us (not in Maya's presence) that she prayed that Maya would never remember her 'illness' because she (Mother) thought it would upset her (the daughter) to do so. Indeed, she felt this so strongly, that it would be 'kindest' if Maya never remembered her 'illness', even if it meant she had to remain in hospital!

A curious and revealing moment occurred when she was speaking of how much it meant to her that Maya should get well. Mrs. Abbott had said that for Maya to get 'well' would mean that she would once more be 'one with her'. She usually spoke of her devotion to Maya as laying claim to gratitude from her, but now she spoke differently. She had been saying that maybe Maya was frightened to 'get all right'. She recalled a 'home truth' a friend had given her recently about her relation to Maya.

'She said to me, you know, "Well, you can't live anyone's life for them—you could even be punished for doing it"—And I remember thinking, "What a dreadful thing to think", but afterwards I thought she might be right. It struck me very forcibly. She said to me, "You get your life to live, and that's *your* life—you can't and you mustn't live anybody's life for them". And I thought at the time, "Well what a dreadful thing to think". And then afterwards I thought, "Well, it's probably quite right".'

This insight, however, was fleeting.

In the foregoing we have examined various 'signs' and 'symptoms' that are almost universally regarded in the psychiatric world as 'caused' by a disease, i.e. an organic pathological process, probably largely determined by genetic-constitutional factors, which destroys or impairs the organism's capacity to experience and to act in various ways.

In respect of depersonalization, catatonic and paranoid symptoms, impoverishment of affect, autistic withdrawal and auditory hallucinations, confusion of 'ego boundaries', it seems to us, in this case, more likely that they are the outcome of her inter-experience and interaction with her parents. They seem to be quite in keeping with the social reality in which she lived.

It might be argued as regards our historical reconstructions that her parents might have been reacting in an abnormal way to the presence of an abnormal child. The data hardly support this thesis. Her mother and father reveal plainly, *in the present*, that what they regard most as symptoms of illness are what we regard as developing personalization, realization, autonomy, spontaneity, etc. On their own testimony, everything points to this being the case in the past as well. Her parents felt as stress not so much the loss but the development of her self.

APPENDIX

List of some of the disjunctive attributions and perspectives of mother father, and daughter, most but not all of which have been discussed above. (Condensed from tape-recordings.)

DAUGHTER'S VIEW	VIEW OF MOTHER AND FATHER
She said that:	Parents said that:
Blackness came over her when she was eight.	It did not. Her memory is at fault. She was imagining this. This showed a 'mental lapse'.
She was emotionally disturbed in the years eight to fourteen.	She was not.
She started to masturbate when she was fifteen.	She did not.
She masturbates now.	She does not.
She had sexual thoughts about her mother and father.	She did not
She was worried over her examinations.	She never worried over examinations because she always passed them, and so she had no need to worry. She was too clever and worked too hard. Besides, she could not have worried because they would have known.
Her mother and father tried to stop her reading.	Nonsense: *and* She had to be torn away from her books. She was reading too much.
Her mother and father were trying to influence her in some ways.	Nonsense: *and* Attempts to influence her through prayer, telepathy, thought-control.
She was not sure whether they could read her mind.	They thought they knew her thoughts better than she did.
She was not sure whether she could read their minds.	They felt she had telepathic powers, etc.

DAUGHTER'S VIEW	VIEW OF MOTHER AND FATHER

She could remember the 'attack' on her mother quite clearly but could not explain it.

She was responsible for it.

Her mother was responsible for her being sent away as a result of this episode.

Her parents said they wanted her to get well, but they did not want her to get well.

Getting well was equivalent to: understanding why she attacked her mother; being able to use her own mind with self-confidence.

If your are not allowed to do things yourself things become unreal.

She could not always be sure whether she imagined feelings, or whether she really did have them.

She did not know why she had nightmares.

She could not remember it.

She was not responsible for it. She was ill. It was part of her illness that she said she could remember this, and that she said she was responsible for it.

This was not so. She (mother) did not even know she was going to hospital when the doctor drove them both away in his car.

It was her illness that made her say things like that.

There is nothing for her to understand. Her illness made her do it.

Since she has been ill Maya has been much more difficult—i.e.:

(i) she wanted to do things herself without first asking or telling them.

(ii) she did not take their word for anything. She tried to make up her own mind about everything.

(iii) she tried to remember things even in her childhood. And if she could not remember, she tried to imagine what happened.

She should forget them.

'I don't think dreams are any part of me. They are just things that happen to me.'
(Mother)

FAMILY 2

The Blairs

In contrast to the Abbott family, the Blair family had been recognized as offering an unfavourable environment for their daughter Lucie before this investigation started. However, none of the numerous psychiatrists in whose care she had been for twelve years had ever suggested that the 'schizophrenia' from which she 'suffered' was in any way intelligible. The view held was that Lucie, aged thirty-eight, was 'suffering from chronic schizophrenia', and that her family unfortunately aggravated her condition.

CLINICAL PERSPECTIVE

Lucie had been first admitted to a mental hospital twelve years before our investigation began. For the next ten years she remained an inmate. Thereafter efforts were made to maintain her as an out-patient while she lived with her parents, but these efforts broke down after six months.

The hospital records disclose the usual dismal reports over the years so typical of descriptions of chronic schizophrenia.

Her affect is flattened. She has auditory hallucinations, ideas of reference and influence, varying delusions of persecution. She says she is tormented and torn to pieces: she feels people put unpleasant sexual ideas into her head. She suffers from vague and woolly thoughts. She speculates on religious themes: she is perplexed, puzzled about the meaning of life. When the investigation began she was regarded as no better in all these respects, and was in addition more impulsive. She was said to be suffering from diminished sexual control, and a pregnancy had been terminated and she had been sterilized. She had never married, but had had a baby girl during the war, who was adopted.

We shall give an account of this family in social phenomenological terms, without trying to force our data along the lines of clinical categories. However, our intention remains focused on rendering the 'schizophrenia' of this one person intelligible in the light of the family system, its praxis and process.

STRUCTURE OF INVESTIGATION

Interviews	Occasions
Daughter	5
Mother and daughter	13
Mother, father, and daughter	1
	19

This represents twenty hours' interviewing time, of which nineteen have been tape-recorded.

THE FAMILY SITUATION

I

Inside the Blair house, time has stood still since before the turn of the century. The front garden is overgrown with a profusion of trees, plants, weeds. The inside is stuffy and dark. The living-room and front parlour are cluttered with Victorian and Edwardian bric-à-brac.

Mr. Blair, although now sixty-eight and crippled by rheumatoid arthritis, is still very clearly the master of the house. He married Mrs. Blair forty years ago when she was twenty-four, and they had two daughters, Lucie and Mamie, four years younger, who died shortly after Lucie's admission to hospital.

For a short while after their marriage they stayed with Mrs. Blair's parents. Then they returned to their present house, owned by Mr. Blair's mother. She lived on in the house, with his younger sister, while his wife became virtually their servant. His sister died when Lucie was nineteen, and his mother died when she was twenty-five. The house has been preserved exactly as it was when Mr. Blair was a child.

Mr. Blair is the middle son with an older brother and younger sister. Mrs. Blair described a curiously ambiguous relationship between her husband, his mother, his younger sister, and his brother's wife, in that he was tyrannized by them and tyrannized them in turn. But the whole family seems to have been very odd. Mrs. Blair's account, with Lucie present, of her early married life is extraordinary by any standards. She had been a munitions worker in World War I, but when the war was over she had no money, and her parents could not support her. Mr. Blair's parents were in the same position. They wanted him out of the house,

' . . . because his brother's wife was expecting her first child and they needed the extra room. They wanted him to get married quick so I said, "All right, but I don't want to leave off work until I've got enough money". They said, "Money will be all right". They fooled me into marrying before I'd feathered my own nest. So I had to settle down with my parents. That suited them because they could be blamed for everything that went wrong. He wasn't prepared to be like a husband. Just wanted me to be the nurse to the children. Something beneath him. His trouble is conceit. The whole family is like it.'

In contrast, Mrs. Blair idealizes her own family. According to her, she had a 'wonderfully kind and cheerful father', 'a sage kind of mother', and a 'good' older brother, who, unlike her husband and his sister, was kind to children, and everything in her family was lovely.

However, it emerged that her father's cheerfulness frequently took the form of laughing off anything she said to him; her mother's sagacity included advising her not to try to leave her husband because the difficulties would be too great. Her brother has been in a mental hospital for forty years.

Mrs. Blair has story after story to tell about her husband and his family. Everything is told in such a dull monotone that one can be lulled into not realizing how remarkable is the content of her account.

'The wife of his brother said that I'd said that his mother was a bad lot. They got me there. The old chap, his father, he couldn't walk, he was stuck in his chair. He said to me, "They say you're dementing, Amelia". This sister-in-law said I said all sorts of things I hadn't said. She said she had been up on the landing listening. I didn't see her there. So I said, "I'm not coming round here any more". So I went and told them at home and they said, "It's a pity. He's got a job round there. What are you going to do anyway?" Then the sister-in-law came up to me in the street one day and wanted to make it up. She said we'd always been good pals. So I was obliged not to keep the quarrel going. I hadn't said anything like that about his mother. I'd simply said I wanted to bring the children up away from there. I didn't like her influence. They'd no consideration. My time was nothing to them. They used to keep me standing about with the baby. They were ready to be false witnesses.

'During the war I was knocked down by a car. I was taken into hospital with suspected fractured skull. When Mr. Blair came in he said the medical chart said there was alcohol in the sickness. I was transferred to another hospital and my husband brought my mother and my sister-in-law along. They came in very high-hatted, my husband and Aunt Agnes, the sister-in-law. They gossiped and told Mother I'd been knocked down after having been in a pub. It was only years later that I realized that someone must have forced alcohol down my throat to try and bring me round. Lots of people wouldn't talk to me. A friend of mine said, "Why don't you thrash that out?" I said, "I can't be bothered. If anyone thinks I was drunk I don't care". It just shows you, if you're not wide-awake—my husband said I'm not worldly-wise.

'At that juncture, Lucie was expecting her baby. If I hadn't had this accident I would have been more help. I could have had my way more. As it was this sister-in-law had her for six weeks. Her father wouldn't hear of having her home. I wanted her.'

Her mother's monotone is extremely important, since it is the yardstick whereby her parents judge Lucie to be disturbed when she displays any vivacity or excitement, any raising of pitch or volume.

According to Mrs. Blair, her husband had been subjected to violence by his mother and older brother. Later he adopted an extremely over-protective attitude, first to his sister, then to his wife and daughter, coupled with acts of spite against them and against his mother.

'When the roof was blown off in the war his mother fell down and he kicked her. I told someone that. They said, "It's just nerves". He's had so much illness at home he's always lived under a strain. Now he's gone quite neurotic. You mustn't talk until he wants to be spoken to. He was harsh to Lucie. For no earthly reason he'd fly into a temper. He once gave her a terrific bang and next morning there was a terrific red patch on her back. My mother was away at the time. There were no witnesses. People said I should do something about it.

'He had as much fuss about that girl (Mr. Blair's sister), more than my mother . . . This girl had supervision like two generations before my mother, I should imagine, if there ever was such a thing. I don't know—depends on the novels you read—how much of the population were treated like that— ridiculous—no confidence—always under suspicion. I couldn't understand it because I'd had absolute freedom. I kept up with the times. They were far and away behind the times with their attitude towards women.'

Mrs. Blair said that her husband watched over all Lucie's movements, required her to account for every minute she spent outside the house, told her that if she went out alone she would be kidnapped, raped, or murdered. She tried to bring some friends home when she was in her teens, but her father snubbed them, and ridiculed her. He (and his brother, mother, sister-in-law, and sister) terrorized her by stories of what would happen if she had not the 'security' of her home. He believed it was good for her to be 'toughened' in this way. He would ridicule any feelings she had: he would discourage her from getting any ideas of being able to follow a career: and he would say that she was making a fool of herself, that she was 'simple', etc., if she thought anyone liked her or took her seriously.[1]

Now, whereas this is what Mrs. Blair says to Lucie about Mr. Blair in his absence, she generally does not agree with Lucie *when Lucie says* the same things, even when he is not present, and, in addition, for many years it has been agreed between them that when he is present her mother must side with him.

The chameleon-like changes of Mrs. Blair will become more apparent later.

She told us she feels that she has never been in a position to talk freely about herself and to reveal her real self, even if she knew what her real self was like. All her life she has been discussed 'inside out' by her parents and her relatives. Consequently she has always avoided discussing herself or Lucie with anyone.

She describes her early life in the following way:

'Oh, the decorum and all the rest of the unreality and artificiality, there's no doubt about it, women were so limited in

---

[1] We remind the reader once more that we are fully alive to the inferences to which these facts point, namely, Mr. Blair's struggles with his unconscious incestuous feelings towards Lucie, her mother's jealousy of Lucie and her husband, and Lucie's own sexual attachment to her father.

thought because of over-doing this, but nowadays it's different and they don't find that outlet so—discussing people quite so much. I don't think so. And of course a lot of women have the privilege of going out to work, instead of staring at the walls and waiting for the next bit of criticism about how they live— that's what a woman's life used to be—just waiting for the next piece of criticism—that's how I see it. And as I say I never really go into the subject of what I'm like, because, as I say, I've had such a dose of it, and then of course when I was out of school and at business I used to be discussed a lot—I suppose being red-headed, people often come up to me and speak to me— "You're this", and, "Oh, you know, you're that", and that kind of thing you see—sheer nonsense. You can read articles about that sort of thing, but it doesn't mean anything to me— I don't think they know what they're talking about really. I mean people are different according to who they are with, and you can't label anyone with a certain character, except for matters of honesty, and of course serious-mindedness is definitely that type—there's no blinking at that—it is there.'

And her husband's family:

'The family?—Well I've had the same thing as you Lucie, everything you do is wrong according to them. They sort of sit in judgement. They feel superior to everybody else for some reason. That's what's bothering her. It was concentrated. They say, "Oh you get it in all families"—but this was a science.'

For a long time after her marriage she had a great deal of trouble with her husband's sister, until she died. She thought her sister-in-law was mentally queer. She was always gossiping about people. Like Mr. Blair, she used to frighten children, only she did it by quoting frightening events from the Bible and saying this would happen to them.

'She was peculiar. He (Mr. Blair) had to do everything she wanted. His mother saw to that. She (sister) used to boss and order him around.'

She never married. An invalid with arthritis, she lived with them, and the household revolved around her, even to her having more say in bringing up the children than Mrs. Blair. The children were told by Mr. Blair to look to their aunt, while Mrs. Blair was treated as their nurse. She felt absolutely helpless. She could not even prevent the aunt becoming Lucie's godmother. This sister was put in a position of authority with all her nephews and nieces, that is, with the children of her other brother also. Often she thought of leaving her husband but she had no money, and no one would help her. There were the children to be provided for. There was no hope or help.

Now that her husband is largely an invalid, she is hardly less frightened of him, and certainly has no more liking for him.

'I don't like him. I don't like his attitude towards people, especially women, but I'm explaining why he's like it— because he's seen such a lot of trouble in his life—a lot of helplessness and invalids and had a lot of illness. It's been nothing but illness all our married life, in his family—and talk of illness, and it's made him partly what he is, I suppose. I don't excuse him. I don't excuse him because he does—even when you're trying to help him he baulks you sometimes, if he's feeling funny, he does really. When I help dress him he never stands in the position to make it easy. He knows how to make the collar stud a bit tight. You know, do up the front first and then I twiddle about. He knows I've got a bad thumb and sore fingers. He's like that. I don't like those sort of people, I never shall. Not even if I became a nun, I shouldn't like those sort of people at all. I can't stand it. I don't say, if you've been through a lot and suffered a lot and lost a lot—you can't stand it. You might have to put up with it—or laughed at it when you're young, but you're very silly when you're young, unless you belong to a very strict order, but I didn't, you see.'

We have to be clear here about what is evidence and what is inference. What is clearly evident is that in the present Mrs. Blair repeatedly and articulately expressed the above views about her husband and his family.

They may or may not be true. If they are not true, Mrs. Blair is probably psychotic. If they are, then her husband probably is, or both of them.

II

Lucie's whole account of herself is qualified, first, by uncertainty as to the importance or seriousness of the issues she is expressing, and, second, by doubts as to whether she is describing real happenings or whether everything is her imagination.

'I can't trust what I see. It doesn't get backed up. It doesn't get confirmed in any way—just left to drift, you know. I think that's probably what my trouble is. Anything I might say, it has no backing up. It's all due to imagination, you know. It's just put a stop to, cast away, sort of thing, whether it's because I know some truth about things, and yet I can't defend it— I don't think I've got a real grasp of my situation—What can I do? How can I get on my feet again? I'm not certain about anything. I'm not certain about what people are saying, or if they're saying anything at all. I don't know what really is wrong, if there is anything wrong.'

This offers an occasion for the psychiatrist to 'diagnose' among other things 'thought-disorder'. This thought-disorder is the attempt by Lucie to describe events which are ambiguous and which she is sometimes not able to conceptualize clearly, and for which she often has no adequate vocabulary. She could hardly be expected to conceptualize them since they are not currently conceptualized adequately, either in any scientific language or in the colloquialisms of naïve psychology. One of the objects of this book is in fact to clarify such praxis and process. The structure of the events that she is trying to describe is intrinsically difficult for anyone to perceive and describe adequately, by virtue of their ambiguity, and, further, she is trying to perceive and remember

43

just those things that she feels (in our view probably correctly) that she has been persistently punished for perceiving.

Thus, as described in one psychiatric report, 'she tends to ramble and be diffuse, has difficulty in coming to the point, talks past the point'. She frequently partially retracts her statements or qualifies them in such a way that one is not quite sure what she means.

LUCIE: Well it's something that seems to be so vague—there doesn't seem to be anything in it. I suppose the—I haven't got a clear definition of what I want to do in life, that's the truth of it, and I can't express myself as I'd like to—I seem to be just a blank.

INTERVIEWER: This feeling, you know, as you say, like the truths that people were saying—did they say you were bad, or what is it?

LUCIE: No, there was nothing, it was er—I don't know the word for it now—I used to be able to use words but I seem to have got out of the way of everything—it's no use trying to search for a word that just won't come to you.

However, despite her lack of trust in her own perceptions, she has various things to say about her mother and father, herself, and their close-knit nexus of relatives. For the most part, our investigation confirms Lucie's observations. It is partly for daring to make these observations that her parents have insisted that she should be in a mental hospital.

Let us consider first what mother and daughter have to say about Lucie's father.

LUCIE: When my father first married they wanted him out of the house. He wants me to go through what he went through. And he wanted his mother when she was dying to go through what he went through as a child. She was a bit queer. He's resentful and vindictive against everybody, especially his relatives. First his mother, then his sister, then his brother, now me and his

44

brother-in-law and mother-in-law. Pushing them all away, all out.

She felt she was forbidden to see for herself and think for herself. Any expression of her own was simply ignored, disparaged, ridiculed. Her friends were snubbed. Her mother, she now realized, was in a 'difficult position'. She could not openly take sides with her daughter, because she was in the same boat herself.

But Lucie had not known this at the time. As a child she had tried to turn from her father's pervasive influence to get some backing from her mother.

LUCIE: When I was young I thought my mother was an authority and knew something. I just took it naturally that she was an authority on my father and on people generally. I thought I could base my ideas on what she said. I never realized that she could make a mistake. I should have got my own opinions which would have been a lot better, instead of leaning on other people's opinions all the time. I'm afraid that's what caused my trouble really, leaning on other people and not having an opinion of my own.

But her mother could only give her advice based on what she herself knew. Her daughter was struggling for autonomy, self-confidence, trying to be a person, but Mrs. Blair, if she had ever glimpsed what this meant, had given up years ago.

MOTHER: My time's taken up in trying to make life a bit easier. As for relationships and all that it just doesn't go into my line. Otherwise I'd forget somebody wanted that or somebody wanted the other. There's only a certain amount of time in a lifetime and if you're one of those unlucky persons who's got to accommodate people who can't do things for themselves, well there's not much time for analysis. As for relationships, I don't think of them. It's best not to.

Lucie developed a very close relationship with her sister, and the loss of this sister ten years ago appears to have intensified her despair.

LUCIE: I still believe that quite unconsciously I miss my sister. I lost my sister about ten years ago and I think subconsciously I must be grieving even now in a subconscious way which I'm not really conscious of. I must be feeling terribly lonely and not realizing why. Although as she was married it would take her away from the family circle a little bit. She was, as a matter of fact, living quite a way from us. At the time of her passing I was in hospital you see, and I didn't know much about it. You've really got to realize your loneliness instead of allowing yourself to be stunned by it.

Lucie could not help but see that other people saw her family as odd.

LUCIE: Don't you think when we were very young this sort of trouble was beginning and it showed and other people realized it and said so?

MOTHER: Oh I think there was a lot of ignorance. Don't forget you were born into an age of ignorance.

LUCIE: But other intelligent sort of people noticed there was something quite wrong with the family relationships and said so, even in those early days. Even as a child I can remember you having to listen to strangers, friends, and their comments. I overheard that sort of thing. I thought it was insulting that my mother had to stand up to, well, other people coming out with the truth. I felt rather sore about it, that they should be seeing the truth that things were like that. A nasty atmosphere for children to live in. I thought the situation should be put right in some way. I was angry with the family situation. I realized the atmosphere we were brought up in and all that at an early age. It goes right back.

And she could not entirely deny her own perception of the inconsistencies at home.

46

'They preached to me about God and what we're supposed to do with our lives; but nobody believed it. Only children are supposed to believe it. I believe I've got something special to do with my life. Everyone has. I understood we're all destined to do something in life. Nobody ever explained it to me. I had to arrive at my own conclusions, and they're very vague too. I've never spoken to anyone about it because it's such a search-ing subject that most people would find unattractive. They discover unpleasant things about themselves. You're the first person I've spoken to about this.'

However, it was difficult to make any direct relations with others outside the family. The way she saw them, how she thought they saw her, and how she saw herself, were all equally mediated by her father, backed up by her mother.

'It's father who's been more like that. "Oh you mustn't go out you know. Perhaps somebody will kidnap you", and all that. He's more likely to have that impression on—make that impression on me rather than yourself. You've always been one of those people who like to see people striking out on their own and full of confidence in themselves. I think that is what I lean on my mother for, because she has that—she tries to give me that confidence in myself. But I don't think she's the right person to give it to me really . . . '
'But it is my father's apprehension of me, wondering whether I should be kidnapped or some dreadful thing happen to me. It's my own fault. He's got no confidence in me at all. I'm always going to be led, led away by some crafty, cunning bad man. That sort of thing you see, he's always like that. He's put that into my mind, my subconscious mind—that I can't be trusted, and I'll always be—you know—the big bad wolf will come after me—the world is full of big bad wolves—he's got that impregnated into my brain in some way, into my sub-conscious mind. And occasionally it seems to come to the

surface all the time, you know—that the world is full of big bad wolves.'

Her identity-for-herself had, therefore, the following structure.

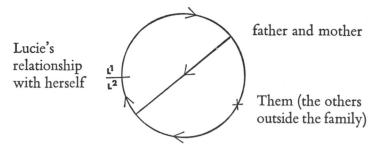

Lucie's relationship with herself L^1 L^2

father and mother

Them (the others outside the family)

There was no way from L^1 to L^2 (if $L^1 \rightarrow L^2$ represents a direct view of herself), except through the circuit $L^1 \rightarrow F$ or $M \rightarrow L^2$: or $L^1 \rightarrow F$ or $M \rightarrow$ Them $\rightarrow L^2$.

That is, she has difficulty in seeing herself except as her father or mother saw her: or as her father or mother told her 'They' saw her.

She has remained unable entirely to break this circuit. When she tries to see herself or 'Them' directly, or to make out how 'They' see her she continues *to hear* what her father has told her and what he continues to tell her in our presence. What she hears is either what her father tells her about herself (that she was a slut, a prostitute), or what he tells her 'They' think about her.

She says of her father and 'Them':

'My father has always been so very critical about my education and everything. I've always been made to feel that I was not very clever and wouldn't get on in the world. He always said that I should be "trodden underfoot". He's nervous of me doing anything. He tells me I'm incapable of doing anything at all and I believe it of course. He doesn't believe in the emancipation of women. He doesn't believe women should support themselves.

'He's always spoken to me as if everybody would treat me

the same as he's treated me. He said, "You'll find that everybody treats you just the same". That's my attitude to life. I've got that in my mind constantly. It's recurring all the time, what he said about me and said to me. "Other people are going to do it"—and of course I'm anticipating them saying all that to me all the time. I don't mean you, Doctor, but people who really wanted to get me down—just for the sport of it. I don't know what it is they've got against me but I think I provide such a lot of people with sport.

'He'd rather keep me poked away somewhere and forget me. That's all, and he'll remember me now and then and send me a few roses, and all that sort of thing—"Poor, everlastingly ill daughter".

'I feel myself that I don't belong to the family. There's some kind of—something to sever it all—my own family, my father —I've been so much away from them you see. I did *try* to start out again in life a couple of years ago and really started to get down to it; but there it is, I got this trouble again. These sort of messages coming into my head, the odd word coming into my head.'

She does, however, reach out towards other people despite this.

'I try to respect people as they should be respected. I usually find one or two people among the patients I can make close friends with. I respect them and they respect me.'

We saw that Mrs. Blair had resolved the difficulties of her position by surrender. Lucie had not entirely done so. In so far as she gave up, she was supposed to suffer from 'affective impoverishment', and when she did not, she was described as 'impulsive'.

' . . . I suppose it's a defiant sort of spirit in me that I must sort of hit back in some way, you know, all the time, to say that my relatives see it the wrong way, you know.

'I'm very sensitive and I'm easily upset over things. Very sensitive—I don't know why, why I should have got like that or perhaps it's natural to my make-up. I can't quite tell really. Because I keep on flying up you see, getting worked up in an effort to try and protect myself, but that's misunderstood very often I think. People think I'm suffering from a temper or something, when all the time I'm trying to shield myself from attacks, you know.'

Her inability to find significant others with authority to confirm or validate her point of view left her, as we saw, mistrusting the fabric of her experience. More than this, it left her disheartened and dispirited.

'I feel I'm being ignored or just forgotten. It's been like that all my life, people just ignore me.'

She says she mistrusts her experience because she is weak-willed, and that she cannot evaluate the words and actions of others, or even be sure that they are saying anything at all. Yet she tends to believe what other people tell her even if she thinks they are wrong. This she calls weakness of will. She feels sometimes that it might be due to lack of confirmation, but she is not sure whether her experiences are not confirmed because they are in fact as incorrect as her mother and father continually tell her. She is very confused, and one of the few certainties she has is that she is weak-willed.

'I would give way if I thought they were nearer the truth, you know, about the importance of things. I'm willing to give way, but I'm not the sort that would really stick out for what I thought was right. I'd be too timid—I'd give way because they'd be stronger, you see I feel myself I'm so very weak-willed—a sort of weak-willed kind of attitude. I feel at work—well I feel I've been dominated over—nobody in particular, everybody around me, everybody I come in contact with who has anything to do with me, any interest in me at all. I wonder if that's what's made me weak-willed—I'm not allowed to express my opinions. It's—it's shunned all the time. I'm not supposed to have an opinion because my opinion is bound to be incorrect you know. Nobody respects my opinion, I don't think. Perhaps, perhaps my opinion isn't what you call reliable, perhaps in every way I'm not reliable, I suppose. I feel I have to accept that I'm not reliable—I feel I've got to accept what everybody says. What everybody else says seems to be right and I'm in the wrong and I wonder why.

' . . . I lost sort of faith in myself, naturally—get no support, no support in anything I want to do. I feel that it's sort of collapsible, sort of in a collapsible state. Can't get any firm backbone at all.'

III

Mr. Blair appears to have made it quite clear what he wanted of Lucie, and he made it clear enough to us, without betraying the slightest impression that his expectations were unusual.

He thought first of all that Lucie should not have refused to continue to play the 'cello when she was sixteen. He played the violin, and when she stopped playing he felt that a bond between them had been severed. Lucie said she refused to play any more when she realized he did not want her to play with anyone other than him. She wanted to become a professional musician. Women nowadays had got ideas about being independent, according to Mr. Blair. His daughter was made to be a gentlewoman. There had always been a place for her at home. With a generous sweep of his arm he said that he did not object to her leaving the house. She could go down to the local shops any time she wished. Going out alone at night was, of course, another matter. He expressed to us that the dangers were of being kidnapped or raped. He definitely disapproved of her entering a cinema alone, and was very doubtful about her visiting a theatre.

During the war Lucie was called up, and became pregnant after three months. Mr. Blair would not have her in the house for one year after she had been pregnant and forbade any mention of the episode, or any mention of her child. He also forbade his wife to see the child.

During this time, however, Lucie did not find any greater freedom. The original situation appeared already to have been sufficiently internalized for her to be unable to use the relative absence of constraints in the external world, outside her family.

Her father believed that the district, a middle-class suburb, was infested by gangs of marauding youths day and night. He felt it was unsafe for a woman to go any distance alone, especially at night.

It was clear that Mr. Blair did not feel his concern about his wife and daughter to be excessive, and it was clear to us what he wanted his daughter to be—a pure, virginal, spinster gentle-woman. His occasional physical and frequent verbal violence towards her were prompted by his view of her as sexually wanton.

The *others* outside the family, the 'Them' who were the concern of Mr. Blair, were all alike for him. None could be trusted. They were all men. By her sexuality his daughter betrayed him. She could not be trusted, she was 'no better than they were', and so on.

Although Mrs. Blair would on occasion refer to all this as hokum, she herself partly shared her husband's view, and, in so far as she did not, she rather focused on different aspects of the phantasy-system, than rejected it. Her view of the world was no less phantastical, but her phantastical 'others' were women. She lived in a world of scandal and gossip. Everyone knew everyone else's business, or wanted to. 'They' were, once more, all alike. It was best to keep oneself to oneself and never to tell anyone 'your business'. Any real friends she had had Mr. Blair had 'snubbed' years ago. Now she just visited her aged mother and her sister, who lived together. She spoke to hardly anyone else.

With this background, Lucie was cut off from both men and women, since she could not discriminate ordinary friendliness from imminent rape, or what her mother called 'familiarity'. She had been brought up to trust no one; never to believe that any remark was an 'innocent' one, that it did not 'mean' more than it seemed to do. Although to some extent she corrected her parents' tendency to ascribe significance to insignificant remarks, she was continually perplexed about what was valid and what was not.

She tried to understand what her life was about, whether it had any significance in any sense, and she found that she was awkward and slow in the company of many people who talked only on the surface. She was never sure whether they talked superficially on purpose, or whether they really did not know what they seemed to be denying. With anyone with whom she could genuinely talk, she was not, however, in any way 'withdrawn', or 'asocial' or 'autistic'.

She shunned occasions when she had to comply with the superficial chatter of others by employing a false self to maintain an empty collusion. Serious discussion, she felt, gave her real self a chance to struggle through to the surface; but people seemed to be nervous of meeting her half-way in this respect. They seemed to have misgivings about her. They wanted her to be talkative and jolly. They seemed to demand it. If she did not comply she felt regarded as antisocial. When she did comply with their sociability she felt weak-willed and ineffective. She longed for a friend with whom she could be silent.

IV

We must now look more closely at Mrs. Blair's position with her husband and daughter.

She is terrified to 'cross' her husband, and Lucie is terrified to 'get out of step' with her mother. But it is extraordinarily difficult for her to keep in step with her mother, even more so, in a way, than with her father.

When we saw Mr. Blair he was plainly living in a very insular world, and if he, his wife, and his daughter were to be believed, he had imposed his view on Mrs. Blair since their marriage, and on Lucie and her sister since birth. This point is not in dispute by any of them, and is the conclusion we are forced to ourselves. This put Mrs. Blair in a situation for which she was unequipped.

Lucie was terrified of being torn to pieces by her father, but equally of losing 'the link' betwen herself and her mother. She felt that if she lost both her father and mother then she could not survive. As a result she tried to 'keep in step' with her mother. This was tricky.

INTERVIEWER: You agreed with me, Miss Blair, when I said that your mother seemed to be defending your father. You had that impression too?

LUCIE: Well I think she's in a naturally difficult position and I find it difficult to think of anything really definite, you know. It's all a bit vague.

Partly because she was sorry for her mother, and partly because she was terrified to sever the relationship with her, she could not bring herself to put together her mother's different attitudes, and her own varying responses to her shifting stances.

Thus, on the one hand she tried to sympathize with her mother:

'Mother mustn't take anything on at all. She mustn't stand by me in any way. It's against father's wishes.'

And yet she could not entirely stifle her reproaches:

'She thinks a lot of herself, but she thinks nothing of me. You're (mother) saying I've got no luck with *my* parents.

'There's nothing been confirmed (by mother), anything at all. It's all been just let drift on. It makes me so uncertain of myself, that—it's a sort of neglect.'

What happens between mother and daughter at this point is very complex and confusing.

Lucie and her mother agree that Mrs. Blair has two stances, according to whether her husband is present or absent. In his absence she takes the initiative in attributing 'the blame' to her husband and his family, but when Lucie sides with her, she often retracts her own statements, even to the point of taking her husband's side against herself.

MOTHER: With all her upbringing she's been at a disadvantage.
There's been a tendency in the family to sort of overrate other
members against her. I don't know why. It seems absurd, but
it's a fact that lots of people have commented on. I think they're
a very unwise lot in some respects—a certain amount of
jealousy, though there was no trouble as a baby, no trouble as
a child. She was rather fond of observing rather than one to
assert herself—very popular with older people. I think there's
a lot of jealousy in the family, and one had to be with the
family a lot because there was an invalid grandfather and we
had to spend our weekends there. That was overdone I think.
She wasn't always dominated. She was happy enough when
she had a sister. I mean that sort of thing (the odd light remark)
didn't matter much. Nobody noticed it, but it was going out
to work I suppose. She didn't have much chance of bringing
friends home for one thing. They were always snubbed a bit.
Mr. Blair would snub anybody and everybody. They were all
no good. He's still doing it. I don't bring any friends home, or
they'd be snubbed.

I was looking out some of her old letters that came when she
left her jobs. 'Miss Blair was highly recommended, but left of
her own accord.' It was always 'left of her own accord'. I think
that was because Mr. Blair was always saying, 'Oh no, that
one's not good enough. You ought to be doing something
better than that.' Criticism all the time you see. That's why
instead of going on to something different she'd just change her
job.

Father is the kind of character that wants you to do things and
at the same time he's nervous of you doing them. He's so
contradictory. He's got a contradictory attitude in his regard
for women. He doesn't like men supporting women, and
at the same time he doesn't like women to support themselves.

Yet she appears to feel that Lucie, even as a child, should have been able to see through her father sufficiently to avoid getting 'worked up', 'angry', or 'excited' about it all.

Lucie is not sure whether after all her whole trouble was not her own fault.

LUCIE: Yes that's right—I feel somebody ought to be reproached but—so I reproach myself.

INTERVIEWER: Somebody ought to be reproached?

LUCIE: Somebody ought to be reproached and if I don't find anybody to reproach I reproach myself.

INTERVIEWER: Who do you think the other person or persons might be?

LUCIE: Well I might think that mother was one to be reproached, but I worry about it. I feel that she'd be too hurt about it, or she'd give me—give me a good hiding.

MOTHER: I think what the situation was there was a lot of unfair criticism and disparagement and well, now you're thinking you ought to recognize the unfairness of it.

LUCIE: At the time—

MOTHER: And that's why you're blaming yourself—

LUCIE: I just let it go on. I just let it pass on—you know—hadn't tackled it in any way—

MOTHER: Not strong enough about it—because it wasn't fair really—I mean a child would see that it was a lot of bunkum.

INTERVIEWER: You say a child would see it was a lot of bunkum?

MOTHER: Well—the present-day child does.

INTERVIEWER: I wonder why Miss Blair didn't see it.

MOTHER: Well I suppose she was brought up to put herself in the back—

LUCIE: Yes I think I put myself in the background. I stifled myself as it were, really stifled myself—snuffed my candle out—a horrible thing really, because if I said anything I was afraid of getting a clout or, or something, you know what I mean?

MOTHER: Oh yes.

It is not clear in this and other passages whether Mrs. Blair is not suggesting that 'the trouble' is in a sense Lucie's fault since she ought to have been able to see through the hokum, and her self-reproaches are thus in a sense justified, in that she did not entirely do so.

Yet Mrs. Blair at times seems to support Lucie by endorsing and amplifying her view that she did not get a chance.

'I think—er—I think that it's a fact—she's quite correct in what she says. There's been everything done to discourage her. A lot of it is through her father who has a natural nervousness. He had the same trouble with his sister. He had to watch over her all the time, like going back into Victorian days.'

But this support is curiously ambiguous. She tells her that she should not 'waste time' on such considerations, that she should think of 'something more interesting.'

'Well I don't know about people casting doubt on everything she did. She is a bit inclined to listen to the odd girl's remarks. I do think Lucie took too much notice of the odd woman's light remark, perhaps, but I think that there's always been this, with her father at home pointing out these things. He had the same thing from his mother. If he had anything to do with anyone she didn't like, he'd pay for it. It was just the code of the family.'

Often she 'supports' Lucie by a form of reassurance that entails an imperviousness to Lucie's repeated statements about herself as weak-willed, indecisive, wavering, continually in doubt about the reliability of her own perceptions of persons, etc. Mrs. Blair states that she sees her as stable, honest, and accurate.

MOTHER: I always think Lucie's got enough stability and honesty and accuracy in her nature and seriousness not to have to take too much notice of the light side—if you're not that sort of character that mixes with a lot of light—rather light-thinking and light talk. If you're naturally serious and more studious and like the deeper subjects of life—there's plenty of them and I think Lucie's like that, and if you're that type why should you worry yourself about or take seriously a remark that isn't worth emotional consideration. I mean to say, I don't see really—why be angry about—but why you should ever take too much notice of light talk, except sometimes you get people who take a superficial interest in things.

When her mother speaks like this Lucie is out of the frying-pan into the fire. Her mother's world is as closed as her father's. These two worlds overlap, and both contradict and reinforce each other. She has a barely tenable position in either her father's or mother's world. Short of fleshing out a world of her own, which is forbidden her, she has only her mother's bizarre sense of reality to oppose to her father's. Gossip, nosiness, familiarity, sexual suggestions, cheekiness—what in clinical terms would be regarded as a typically paranoid world, is Mrs. Blair's as much as her husband's. The main difference between Mr. and Mrs. Blair appears to be that she does not wish to control and possess Lucie quite so much as does her husband. Interpreting each analytically, one could impute jealousy to each. Mr. Blair cannot bear Lucie to have relations outside the family. Mrs. Blair does not wish Lucie to be at home, because she cannot bear to see the close bond between Lucie and her husband.

'One meets it all the time,' says Mrs. Blair, 'but one has to be tough—don't be put out by it, forget it. One has to keep cheerful and busy to put up a stand against it.' Mrs. Blair depicts her life as a continual battle against many forces, her husband being only one of them.

While often endorsing Lucie's persecutory phantasies, she is especially capricious about what to us are Lucie's sanest moments.

She confirms Lucie in her persecuted position, but tells her that she is mad or bad to be angry about it. She should forget it, but she should not 'be taken in'. She offers Lucie her own solution. Mrs. Blair sees herself as the subject of a forty-year long persecution by her husband, but she has been unable to leave because 'They' and the world outside are just as persecutory, if not more so. The only solution is to accept one's helplessness in the persecuted position. There is nothing to be done. There is no help or hope, either for herself or for Lucie. All Lucie can do is to realize this and stop fighting a losing battle against impossible odds.

Lucie's efforts either to fight her persecutors, or not to see herself as persecuted, are regarded by both Mr. and Mrs. Blair at best as signs of foolishness, but more usually as tokens of madness and badness.

v

Neither of Lucie's parents had emerged from their relations with their parents as persons in their own right. Both had been hopelessly immersed all their lives in phantasy unrecognized as such. Although Lucie made many statements that indicated she partially realized the state of affairs, Mr. and Mrs. Blair spoke without the slightest recognition that the modality of their experience and actions was phantasy.

If a perception is not confirmed by another person, we all have a tendency to doubt it. We may say, 'I wonder if it was my imagination.'

Our thesis on this family is that what Lucie has to say and her way of saying it are perfectly intelligible when seen in the context of her situation.

We must recognize of course that this situation as internalized by her undergoes further refraction in the process of internalization and re-projection: she sees the world at large in terms of her original family experience. That is, her experience of the world continues to resemble the social realities that were mediated to her by her family.

Within this situation, what can she do? At the very beginning of our investigation Lucie asks this question:

LUCIE: . . . there doesn't seem to be any solution to it—it doesn't leave you any kind of er—hopeful move at all—you can't make any kind of hopeful move, can you? Seems hopeless. It's just like a game of chess, you're absolutely cornered, you know. MOTHER: Yes, well, the thing is if you want to—if—if—if there's a chance of anybody helping you—it's not much good trying to get people who are already in a tight corner themselves, is it, that's the point . . .

The Churches

CLINICAL PERSPECTIVE

Claire, aged thirty-six, had been hospitalized for five of the past six years when we began our investigation of her family. She was a paranoid schizophrenic, treated by insulin and many electro-shocks. She was deluded and hallucinated, showing thought-disorder and impoverished affect.

Everyone, parents and psychiatrists, seem to have been agreed that for at least five years before our investigation began, that is, at least since the 'onset' of her 'illness', Claire lacked normal feelings of affection for her parents and others. She was said, in the typical manner used to describe such people, to lack warmth, to be distant, to be difficult. She was given to outbursts of violence, when she smashed teacups; she had threatened to hit her father if he kept on trying to kiss her when she told him to stop. She was described as 'impulsive'.

One of her delusions was that she had an atom bomb inside her. She was usually listless: she appeared to be 'empty' (*autisme pauvre*): occasionally her emptiness seemed highly charged with violent energy seeking apparently random discharge. She was subject to ideas of reference and persecution and her outbursts were sometimes directed towards the person or persons (usually unknown) who were tormenting her (calling her a prostitute, cutting her up into little pieces, torturing her without mercy).

STRUCTURE OF INVESTIGATION

Claire's family consists of her mother, her father, and a brother seven years younger. A sister was born when Claire was three and died seven months later. We have not been able to form a picture of this family from every angle because no one in the family wished her brother, Michael, to be interviewed. He had had a schizophrenic breakdown when he was sixteen, but is said to be quite well now. Many things point to this not being the case. However, we have first-hand data on father, mother, and Claire.

Interviews	Occasions
Daughter (Claire)	3
Mother	3
Father	2
Mother and father	1
Mother and daughter	15
	—
	24

This represents twenty-four hours of interviewing time of which fourteen were tape-recorded.

THE FAMILY SITUATION

In this presentation of Claire's family, we shall concentrate on her so-called 'impoverishment' of affect and on her apparent detachment from what she says (incongruity of thought or affect) and explore these mainly in terms of her relationship with her mother. Taking this issue as our conducting thread, we shall inevitably find ourselves involved in many other aspects of her madness.

We shall now have to begin once more at the beginning, and explore afresh, without presuppositions, whether these schizophrenic signs and symptoms are intelligible in terms of the praxis and process of her family nexus.

Now, although the issue for parents and psychiatrists had been

Claire's 'lack of affection', we discovered at the start of our investigation that this was not the main issue for Claire. What Claire was more concerned about was her parents' lack of real affection for her. Everyone seemed more or less aware that this was what *she* was trying to talk about, but this concern of Claire's was somehow thought about, if it was at all, as another expression of *her* lack of genuine feeling and of a general demanding, greedy, querulous attitude, and lack of insight.

Claire said of her mother and father that they were not her real parents, that they were not a husband and wife, or a mother and father, but simply a pair of business partners. This was taken to be a delusion.

What Claire herself had to say was:

'I have a self that hasn't grown up. Sometimes when it gets the upper hand I get afraid . . . '

She said she thought that her

'mother never wanted me to grow up. I think that to a certain extent the way she behaved towards me prevented me from maturing.'

Her mother, she maintained, never let her live her own life. 'She didn't like me to have my own ideas about things.' Without being obviously angry, her mother, she said, prevented her from being her real self, and using her own mind. She (Claire) grew up afraid to express her own feelings or ideas but 'followed her way instead of my own'. But she could not say specifically in what ways her mother made her feel afraid. If she was at all pressed on this, she would become more vague, plead loss of memory, or talk about people in general, but of no one in particular.

'She is more of a managing-director than a mother. She was more interested in business than in being a mother and she brought the business-woman's attitude into the home. She failed me mentally.'

63

Claire's view was that she had had affection for her parents as a child but had lost it for them very early because she said they did not have any real affection for her, and did not really want her to have any, though they wanted to pretend that they were an affectionate family.

Until the present investigation started, mother, father, and daughter had never discussed such 'accusations' together. Her parents both dismissed such statements as her 'illness'. Besides, as her mother said, 'We've never been a chatty family'.

Claire had made little effort to force discussion on these issues, because she felt it was hopeless, although when given only a little validation of her point of view by the interviewer, she stated her position quite clearly. Both her parents, she said, had simply ignored her, while giving her all manner of material things. Of her mother: 'She ignores *me*, the real me. I can't get through to her.'

However, her mother and father's united view was that they had always been a happy and affectionate family but that they both had had to devote themselves very hard to business, and that her mother had undermined her health for some years as a result. Moreover, it had all been done for the children's sake. Claire, they said, had always been an affectionate child, and although she had got some strange ideas into her head when she was about fifteen, she had never 'fussed', but had been quiet, contented, happy, and affectionate until her 'illness' came on out of the blue.

This shared family myth was radically discrepant with the stories both parents told about their family life, as we shall see. We did not have the impression, however, that they were lying, or that they even realized that such a discrepancy existed. Mrs. Church, for instance, had no small number of complaints to make about her husband when seen alone. But the view she thought she held of her husband was that, though times had been difficult, they had both done their best, and had nothing to reproach themselves about.

The incongruence between what Mrs. Church said she said, and what she did say, that is, between metastatement and statement, as well as other incongruences between tone of address and content, was quite confusing even to the interviewer. One could listen to the paralinguistic 'music' of her statement, and have to pinch oneself to realize that she was in the course of describing how, during all those happy years, she had lain in bed most of the time as a result of her constant exhaustion through 'overwork'. She had done, in fact, very little work until her children were in their teens. A child had been born when Claire was three, which had died after seven months. Mrs. Church (who at all other times without exception maintained that Claire's 'illness' had been due to air-raids) remarked, when speaking of the death of this baby, that if this child had not died perhaps Claire would not have become ill. She could not explain why, except to say that there might not have been any sorrow in the family.

Michael was born when Mrs. Church was (from our view-point) profoundly depressed. Michael had been 'ill from birth'. He had had pneumonia, and was reported to have become a confirmed asthmatic by the time he was two years of age. He seems to have spent an extraordinary percentage of his early years in one bed or other, either his sister's or his mother's. It appeared to be the practice to 'cure' his asthma by one or other of them taking him into bed, or getting into bed with him.

Michael apparently became obviously hallucinated and deluded when he was sixteen and after several months' stay in a mental hospital has lived with the family since.

When Michael became psychotic, the family business was clearly failing. At this point Claire, then twenty-three, had made a move that her parents said greatly disturbed them and Michael. She refused to kiss her mother and father, and refused to let them kiss her. She also said she was fed up having to 'nurse' Michael: that is, to spend so much time in his bed, or bedroom, or to have him in her bed to stop him having asthma.

In the following we shall try to reconstruct tentatively the early period of the life of her mother and herself.

Claire's mother has always been under the impression that she knows Claire's feelings very well, because they are so *very* alike. She pointed out that both had mothers who were 'business-women'. Neither saw much of their mothers. But both had mothers who 'did everything for them'. Both were *'only'*, that is, they had no sisters living; both had younger sisters who died in early infancy; both had younger brothers, who needed to be looked after by them.

The similarity between mother and daughter's family constellations as seen by mother led her to think she knew what the daughter's 'feelings' were better than Claire knew herself.

In precise descriptive terms,[1] she attributed to her daughter memories, experiences, and actions that were disjunctive with Claire's self-attributions, while being impervious both to Claire's own feelings and actions and to her attributions about her self.

MOTHER: I used to think at times you were sensitive about certain things, about different things. I sometimes think you see I was very like you—an only daughter, and when you haven't any sisters to mix with, I do think one is inclined to be a little sensitive in those directions.

DAUGHTER: I don't think with me—

MOTHER: No?

DAUGHTER: —it was a case of not having any sisters—it was the case of having a brother very much younger than myself.

MOTHER: Of course I had two brothers, but I didn't have very much to do with my eldest brother, but my younger brother—I was in a very similar position again.

DAUGHTER: Of course the more you mix in your own home, the more people you're among in your own home, the easier it is to mix in the outside world.

MOTHER: Maybe. I should think that's very true. I have noticed myself now, and Auntie Cissie and Auntie Elsie, the three of us,

---

[1] A psycho-analytic construction would be that Mrs. Church saw Claire through a film of projective identifications.

we've all been *only*, and we've all had very similar ways, and we often used to say, 'Oh, we're really three odd ones out, we're only daughters', and we often used to feel a little bit out at times—used to see other girls go off with perhaps sisters, and we didn't have one you see. Well we did have one but unfortunately lost her. But you mixed well with them socially didn't you?

DAUGHTER: No.

MOTHER: No? Oh what about the tennis club, with Betty and that little crowd?

When Mrs. Church occasionally did seem to recognize that Claire was different from her image of her, she was puzzled or worried. Claire's own feelings (from *our* point of view) seemed in part to coincide with disavowed feelings of Mrs Church, in part, to be clear perceptions of mother by daughter that her mother could not bear; in part, they were feelings that her mother did not realize existed, because she had never felt them herself and could not imagine them; and finally, in part, actual feelings apparently induced in Claire by repeated attributions by her mother that she had them.

Mrs. Church could maintain only with difficulty her impression that they were 'very alike'. They were certainly in somewhat similar positions in their family constellations, but there the resemblance all but ended, as far as we could see. In order to see a similarity that approximated to identification, Mrs. Church had both to deny her own perceptions, and to try to induce Claire to deny her experience and so to moderate her behaviour, her words, gestures, movements that she would not jar too discordantly with the identity that her mother delineated for her.

Mrs. Church's attempts to fit Claire's whole existence into her own schema is illustrated in the following.

MOTHER: . . . and you definitely showed signs of not liking Mrs. Frome, and you also said you couldn't stand her and she got on your nerves. Well from that time onwards I did notice you were rather on edge about different things. It seemed very difficult to ask you things sometimes, as though you'd had a hard day at work, or something had annoyed you. Well you took another cruise, and before you took that cruise I remember you saying several times, 'Oh I must have a holiday, I feel I need it badly'. You were rather agitated, but of course we didn't pay a lot of attention because I knew you were working hard you see, and during this cruise you were ill, you remember?

DAUGHTER: Mmm.

MOTHER: Also while you were on this cruise, there was a disturbance on the boat. Do you remember that?

DAUGHTER: What do you mean by a disturbance on the boat?

MOTHER: Well I wondered if it worried you. A man broke into a girl's cabin.

DAUGHTER: I don't remember.

MOTHER: And there was a dreadful struggle and he tried to take advantage of the girl I believe, and at the time I did think you were rather disturbed.

DAUGHTER: Don't remember that.

MOTHER: I spoke to one or two friends and they said, 'Oh don't pay any attention, Claire's old enough to look after herself, she'd understand'. But we did think you were rather disturbed after that cruise. You never seemed to be the same somehow. You seemed as though, you know, you were edgy all the time. Whether it was that illness you had on the cruise, whether it was the disturbance on the cruise or what I never found out you see, because once or twice I did try to open the subject and you seemed to put it off. And anyhow this illness you had on the cruise, you had to visit Dr. Nolan when you got back. I don't know what he said to you. I wanted to come with you but you wouldn't let me go. You said, 'No, I'm old enough to go alone'. So I don't know what it was all about really, but the ship's doctor told me you should have had an X-ray, and Dr. Nolan didn't think it necessary. I think it was something to do with your internal problems. Anyhow, you seemed to

68

get over it, and that was that. Well I often wondered if you worried about that illness.

DAUGHTER: No.

MOTHER: No? Now while we were staying at the Boyd Hotel— we stayed there for quite a long time, I forget how long—two or three years I believe—and during that period I was getting fed up with hotel life. I wanted to rent a house. Dad and I went to buy a house, but each time you said, 'I don't want to leave the hotel.' 'I don't want to live in a house, I want to stay in the hotel.' But you never gave us an explanation why. I've often wondered why.

DAUGHTER: Well because I liked hotel life. I liked the freedom of it.

MOTHER: Yes well . . .

DAUGHTER: I liked meeting all those different people.

MOTHER: Well, Claire, you see now, that goes to show that before your accident you were willing to meet people, and you did meet people, and you went about a lot. You had a good time and all at once, since your accident, you just don't want to.

DAUGHTER: Since my accident, or since my illness?

MOTHER: No since your accident,[1] Claire, definitely. To us it appears since your accident.

DAUGHTER: Well it doesn't to me. It only appeared to me within the last . . . Since I've been back in England.

Claire has been saying that her parents gave her many material things but they did not want to know her. Her mothers hears this as an accusation that she has neglected Claire materially and starts to give instances to show that she was not 'neglected'.

(1) MOTHER: You see as far as Dad and I are concerned, we did everything that we thought was for the best, and I'm *very* surprised to think that you can blame us for your illness.

(2) DAUGHTER: Well you mention the word 'neglect'.[2] I am not

---

[1] Claire had broken her collar-bone about a year before her breakdown.
[2] This was earlier in the exchange.

inferring at all that I have been neglected from the material point of view, and I know that I have had everything, and in fact probably much more than many other people have had on the material side.

(3) MOTHER: Yes.

(4) DAUGHTER: But it's the mental side that I'm thinking of. A child wants attention, and to feel that it's wanted when it's young, but you see, for example, I went to school and during my school-term there were often events at school to which the other parents came.

(5) MOTHER: Yes I know.

(6) DAUGHTER: But you—

(7) MOTHER: I couldn't go.

(8) DAUGHTER: Couldn't go.

(9) MOTHER: Occasionally I couldn't go.

(10) DAUGHTER: More often than not you couldn't.

(11) MOTHER: That's true.

(12) DAUGHTER: No I hardly remember an occasion.

(13) MOTHER: Quite true.

(14) DAUGHTER: And that's one of the things I felt very much.

(15) MOTHER: Well it's a great pity that you couldn't express yourself more when you were younger and tell me, and then I would probably have tried my utmost to correct it.

(16) DAUGHTER: Well you see I didn't tell you, I didn't tell you anything did I?

(17) MOTHER: Well you didn't fuss, you didn't say, 'Mummy I want this', and 'Mummy I want that', I know that. I always thought you were a very good little girl.

(18) DAUGHTER: Well you see, I always, and I suppose I still am to a certain extent, a very happy person—appear to be a very happy person on the surface, but underneath there always has been a terrible lot boiling up inside me, and there is still, though I don't always know what it is.

(19) MOTHER: It's a pity I suppose that sometimes you didn't express yourself and let me—I can think of occasions where

I have thought sometimes that you should have expressed yourself more. But I have spoken to our family doctor about it years and years ago—I can remember it perfectly well, and he made allowance for the fact of your age and that you were studying at the time. He said, 'Don't worry about her. If she wants anything it's here, and she'll ask for it.' Well naturally I took notice of him. I can see now I probably should have said, 'Claire is there anything wrong?' And you would probably have gone into a corner and howled your eyes out. Well, and I should have had to put up with it you see. But you always struck me as a very happy and contented child. You had everything you could wish for, as far as I knew.

(20) DAUGHTER: I had all the material things, yes.

(21) MOTHER: Yes, so it's a pity as I say that you didn't express yourself more, which I did sometimes wish you would have done.

(22) DAUGHTER: Well I never have been able to express my feelings very easily—express what I feel or what I think.

(23) MOTHER: Yes, yes. Now I'll continue with instances, Claire, which no doubt you'll remember. Now when you had your half-term holiday or holiday at school and I hadn't time to spare, I used to try and pick the time to spare and take you up to town. We used to go out to tea and have a look at the shops.

(24) DAUGHTER: I don't remember that.

(25) MOTHER: I've often come back and said to Dad, 'You know Claire doesn't seem a *bit* interested in the shops.' I used to take you to the big stores, and where other little girls might say, 'Oh Mummy, look at this!' 'Oh Mummy, look at that!' 'Isn't that pretty?' 'Isn't that lovely?' I even pointed things out to you and I'd say, 'Oh Claire, isn't that a beautiful frock?'—'Mmm, I suppose it's all right for some people—It might suit some people.' I was *always* very fond of clothes, and *being* a dressmaker, I was naturally interested. I used to think that you were ... But you didn't seem in the *least* bit

interested and I mentioned it to the doctor once or twice. 'Oh,' he said, 'When she gets older she'll soon be dress-conscious.' Well you are dress-conscious to a certain extent and you like nice clothes, but you don't put yourself out, and you don't express yourself to that effect.

(26) DAUGHTER: Well I believe I'm—

(27) MOTHER: And that's why I feel in lots of things you were like that.

(28) DAUGHTER: Well I believe I was rather a difficult adolescent anyway, in many respects. I know I didn't worry about my appearance at all. I was a real tomboy.

(29) MOTHER: At one time, yes.

Claire has not blamed her mother for her illness (1). She has denied being ill. She is trying to talk about 'neglect'—neglect in the sense of having been given no confirmation as a real person.

Her mother expresses regret that Claire did not express herself more (15, 19, 21).

But in the exchange her mother shows no desire for Claire to express herself now, as she is trying to do. Claire's efforts to do so (4, 6, 8, 12, 16, 18, 22, 26) are either interrupted, or received by a pseudo-agreement which is subsequently withdrawn, or passed by tangentially.

One notes here the imperviousness of the mother to the daughter as a person separate and different from herself. She cannot understand that her daughter does not seem to like what she likes. There must be something wrong with her. This is coupled with a concealed shift of meanings in the terms 'expressing oneself' and 'fussing'. 'Expressing oneself' is given approval, but 'fussing' is not. The mother complains that the daughter did not express herself more. On the other hand, since she did not 'fuss', she always thought she was a good little girl. But if she expresses herself now, this is fussing.

That is, a statement of the daughter, according to mother, is 'expressing oneself' if it expresses a 'self' conjunctive with the one attributed to Claire by her mother ('other little girls might say . . . '). However, when Claire expresses herself clearly enough but is saying something different from her mother's notion of what her daughter should feel, this is taken to be something for the doctor. The category of something-wrong-needing-'cure'-not-punishment—doctor rather than police—is evoked persistently. And when she (the daughter) may be beginning to express her 'real' self the mother hastens to seal off the opening (23, 25). Her mother, by switching the issue from that of *her* possible neglect of Claire to that of Claire's failure to express herself, and by confusing 'expressing oneself' with asking for things and 'fussing', muddles her daughter up, and Claire finds herself discussing whether or not she was a 'difficult' adolescent. Mrs. Church appears to grasp the issue of 'expressing oneself' only in terms of asking for things, being difficult, and fussing.

What Mrs. Church says she says is bewilderingly incongruent with what she says. She repeatedly maintains, for instance, that she forgets things and lets bygones be bygones, advising Claire to do the same. But she 'forgets' things in a peculiar way. She recounts them at length and qualifies her account by saying that she forgets them. After one such story from twenty years back, she said, 'I think of *those* things, Claire—I mean I forget it and let it pass.'

Unless one has a vantage-point outside this relationship, it must be very difficult to know where one is. She says, 'I am doing X'. She then does Y; then she says she has been doing X, and expects Claire not to perceive that she has done Y.

The present situation seems similar to that existing before Claire's breakdown, in that it appears that the mother and father did not simply tell her to be afraid of crowds, to fear men, etc., they told her she *was* and *is* afraid of crowds and men.[1] Claire was

---

[1] Is the pre-psychotic child in some sense hypnotized by the parents, or is hypnosis an experimentally induced model psychosis, or, perhaps more precisely, an experimentally induced model pre-psychotic relationship? Experimental hypnosis certainly simulates some aspects of the pre-psychotic child–parent relationship that occurs *in vivo*, as it were. This relationship, however, is too complicated to be simply designated a hypnotic one without qualifications.

not told she was bad to feel X; or forbidden to feel X; or openly threatened or punished for feeling X. She was simply told that she felt Y. What happens to the person who is the recipient of attributions of this kind from the earliest years?

A constantly repeated sequence is that Claire makes a statement, and her mother invalidates it by saying:

(i) she does not really mean what she says, or
(ii) she is saying this because she is ill, or
(iii) she cannot remember or know what she feels or felt, or
(iv) she is not justified in saying this.

Then Mrs. Church follows with a statement that unintentionally validates what Claire has said but in which she contradicts herself, adding to this a final metastatement in which this contradiction is itself denied and the disparity between all she has said and what Claire said is reinstated.

An example of this is when

1. Claire says her mother is trying to 'discourage' her from coming out of hospital.
2. (i)   Her mother invalidates this by saying she wants to see her out of hospital, and
    (ii) then proceeds to 'discourage' her from leaving, sealing this off by implying that
    (iii) she has just been *encouraging* her to come home.

She then goes on:

MOTHER: Unfortunately we are very small where we are at the moment. I mean we've always been used to a large place. I like space as well, but there you are. When it has to be as we are today you see, we've just got to put up with it. And I don't think your father and I will ever be able to afford a large place like we've had in the past. As I told you once before, as you get older, and as we've been placed, you can't afford these luxuries any more.

DAUGHTER: Well I don't have to live with you though, do I?

74

MOTHER: No. The point is, Claire, you see even if you lived in a hostel you'd be mixing with more than half a dozen people.

DAUGHTER: I know.

MOTHER: You see, and you'll have to have a very small room if you have a room to yourself.

DAUGHTER: Well there's a hope that by the time I leave hospital that I'll have overcome that difficulty.

MOTHER: Hope so, hope so.

It is the compounding of many manoeuvres simultaneously that provides the full quality of the mystification in these interviews.

Here the issue is again the feasibility of Claire staying at home.

MOTHER: You're more settled down now than you were when you first went in?

DAUGHTER: Oh yes.

MOTHER: Yes, that's beginning to be a difficult problem because it limits you in what you can do for activities doesn't it? And also in your family's activities come to that, because you see if you come home I don't like to ask anybody while you're at home, because I feel you want to be quiet.

DAUGHTER: Oh I don't mind having people home.

MOTHER: So you see.

DAUGHTER: I'd welcome it in fact.

MOTHER: You would?

DAUGHTER: Oh yes, I'd be glad to see somebody different.

MOTHER: But you see on one or two occasions when Auntie Cissie and Auntie Elsie popped in, you set the table to sit down and have a meal, and then you got up and said, 'Oh I can't sit with a crowd of people', and you went up to your room.

DAUGHTER: Well I don't know how I'd react to it now.

MOTHER: Well there you are Claire you see, and it embarrasses other people, that's the trouble, I mean I can stand up to it, and your father can, but you see naturally other people feel they're in the way, that's the point.

DAUGHTER: It just has to be accepted. If they feel they're in the way it's just too bad.

MOTHER: Well it is in a sense, but the point is you can't go on *living* like that. One's life has got to be a mixed and varied sort of business hasn't it?

Friends are another issue. The nice friends that her mother says Claire used to like, Claire says she did not like, and does not want to see. Her mother feels that this would be another difficulty that her daughter would have to overcome before she could return home.

DAUGHTER: No, I don't feel like seeing them.

MOTHER: No.

DAUGHTER: I prefer making new friends.

MOTHER: You do?—Even Lucy Green?

DAUGHTER: Oh I shouldn't mind seeing her.

MOTHER: Of course she's very excitable, you know that, don't you?

DAUGHTER: Yes, but at the same time, she's somebody who I've spent a lot of time with.

MOTHER: Yes.

DAUGHTER: And who knows me very well.

MOTHER: Yes. Would you like her to come over one Saturday perhaps, when you're at home?

DAUGHTER: She could do.

MOTHER: Of course the only point is that I don't know how many children she has now. I think—

DAUGHTER: Two.

MOTHER: She has two or three. Well of course if she has to bring the children, the children might be too much for you. Of course they're girls, but they're terrible tomboys.

DAUGHTER: Yes I'm sure they are.

MOTHER: I haven't seen them for about two years now, so what they're like today I wouldn't know. (Five seconds' pause.)

Well is there anything else *you* want to ask Claire, or talk about?

DAUGHTER: My mind's almost completely blank this afternoon.

MOTHER: Is it? . . . Still have your cold?

DAUGHTER: Still a bit, yes. (Ten seconds' pause.)

We must remember that the parents are struggling desperately within the limitations set them in turn by their parents.

Her mother rebelled against her own mother, once. Her only holiday was two weeks in the year. Just before she was due to go on this holiday, *alone* for the first time in her life (when Claire was nineteen), her own mother 'offered' to take Claire abroad during this fortnight. Since Claire was helping in her parents' business this meant that Mrs. Church would have to stay behind. Mrs. Church's mother said that she should, of course, do this, which involved cancelling her bookings at the last minute and losing money into the bargain. She objected.

MOTHER: Er, of course you know your Grandma, what she could create, and she said I was selfish. I said, 'No, I'm not, if *you* knew what I give up for my children, for my family, and for the business, you wouldn't say that I was selfish. Just for once', I said, 'I've rebelled. I've always said yes, yes, yes to everything. For once I've rebelled and of course it doesn't suit you.' And of course we ended up by you going and me cancelling my holiday so that was that.

At times it looked as if Claire and her mother might ally themselves against Mr. Church, but this never quite happened because her perceptions of him were just what Mrs. Church had to suppress in herself.

The following shows Claire struggling to affirm the validity of her experiences.

DAUGHTER: Well I think I must have been extremely sensitive.

MOTHER: You must have been.

77

DAUGHTER: Over all these things, because they do still come back at times.

MOTHER: Well try not to think of them.

DAUGHTER: I *don't* think of them. I just don't think of them.

MOTHER: No.

DAUGHTER: But the point is they come back to me.

MOTHER: Yes.

DAUGHTER: Even though I don't think—

MOTHER: Well they come back to me. Well you know you mentioned that holiday occasion. It's very strange because lying in bed one night about a fortnight ago I remembered it as though it was yesterday, and I thought, 'Now I wonder if that little incident upset Claire'. I did think that because when you wrote that little letter to me a short while ago I thought, 'Well I wonder if that is one of the incidents that upset Claire. She's still impressed by it!'

DAUGHTER: Well the thing is that when these things come back to me I rebel.

MOTHER: Mmm.

DAUGHTER: My whole self is in action against that particularly and I feel helpless to control it.

MOTHER: Well I suppose it's up to the doctors to see what they can do about that feeling.

DAUGHTER: You see when I turned against my father about four months ago—

MOTHER: End of August.

DAUGHTER: Well I was already very worked up and when he walked in that day he said something to me which I didn't like, I forget what it was now, and immediately, before I knew what I was doing, I had lost control of myself and I started to throw things about the place, and I got hold of him and nearly turned him out of the hospital. Well I just couldn't control it. Why I did it I don't know.

MOTHER: Then afterwards you felt sorry for it and you cried, didn't you?

DAUGHTER: Well I don't know whether I was sorry for it. I don't think I am in a way. I'm not sorry for it from my own point of view, and I was from my father's point of view of course, but I just accept it as something that *I* alone can do nothing about.

MOTHER: Well that's a problem, isn't it?

DAUGHTER: And I feel that I'm still going to be like that. There's still something there which is making me—

MOTHER: Making you aggressive?

DAUGHTER: Making me feel like that. I suppose one would call it aggression.

MOTHER: Claire, the sun isn't too much in your eyes?

The incident is clearly of immediate and direct importance for Mrs. Church, but she denies this by making out that she is remembering it primarily for its importance to Claire, while at the same time minimizing its significance ('that little incident').

The validity of rebellion, which Mrs. Church was reaching for in herself, is invalidated by *her* when Claire begins to endorse her mother's own rebellion and to express any rebellion herself ('Well I suppose it's up to the doctors to see what they can do about that feeling').

That is to say, Mrs. Church seeks endorsement from her daughter: when she gets it, she invalidates it. This is one form of betrayal. It is complete at the sudden *non sequitur*: 'Claire, the sun isn't too much in your eyes?'

Again, Mrs. Church invalidates Claire when she discusses her father with her in the same terms as Mrs. Church used in discussing him with us in her daughter's absence. For instance, Claire said:

'I don't feel aggressive because he changed his business, but I do feel aggressive because he was a failure.'

Her mother, however, could not allow herself to confirm unambiguously this feeling of the daughter's although she has admitted to us to feeling this way herself.

79

MOTHER: Yes well you can't entirely blame him for that.

DAUGHTER: Well I think in some ways I do.

MOTHER: You see he was working under—he was in great difficulties at the time—lots of things that you knew *nothing* about—his age for one thing.

DAUGHTER: Well I think I feel that he had let you down.

MOTHER: No I shouldn't say he let me down Claire, oh no.

DAUGHTER: Well that's how—

MOTHER: Well that's *your* opinion. I can't alter that, but I shouldn't say—He didn't let us down.

Claire is mystified in another way when Mrs. Church says that they have always got on well together. Claire feels that if this seems to be so it is because her mother has always so 'domineered' her that she found it best to submit rather than argue. Her mother's response then is to say, *in effect*, that this is partly true, but she ends up by stating, with an air of finality, that it is not the case. Claire is at loss for a reply to this, and her mother then asks her if there is anything else she can think of. Claire says that she finds it difficult to put her thoughts into words and her mother then tells her that she (Claire) is not one for making a fuss. A 'fuss' here clearly means saying what her mother does not want to hear. She next asks Claire if she can now put into words what she wants to say. Claire replies that she has forgotten, and her mother ends this exchange by putting her seal on this loss of memory.

MOTHER: I think we've got on very well together. I don't think we've had any real disturbance ever over the years.

DAUGHTER: The only thing is that you are a domineering character.

MOTHER: Well being a business-woman, Claire, that comes with it you see, I've always been—

DAUGHTER: I like to submit rather than to argue against your decision.

MOTHER: Yes I suppose so at times. When you *are* an organizer in business you sort of carry it a bit into the home as well, but,

I don't know what you think, but we seem to have got on very well throughout the years.

DAUGHTER: Oh yes, but as I say with you a domineering character.

MOTHER: We've always worked in with one another, and there have been times when I've asked your opinion and you'd tell me—aired your views, same as I would air my own views, but in an understanding fashion, we've been able to overcome these things. (Thirty-five seconds' pause.) Is there anything else you can think of?

DAUGHTER: What I am thinking of I'm trying to put into words, and I'm finding it very difficult.

MOTHER: I suppose it's something that you can't put into words. (Twenty-five seconds' pause.) I know one point Claire, you never like to be . . . you never like a lot of fuss do you?

DAUGHTER: Depends on what you mean by 'fuss'.

MOTHER: Well to put it in the crude way, I know any time you weren't well, which was very rare, and if I asked more than once or twice, 'Oh Claire, how are you feeling—better?' You know—'Oh I'm all right, don't keep worrying me—I'm all right, don't keep worrying.' I will say very often you appeared as though you didn't want anybody to fuss around you too much. (Forty-five seconds' pause.) Well, have you managed to put into words what you want to say?

DAUGHTER: Well I've forgotten what it was now. (Fifty seconds' pause.)

MOTHER: Of course it's very strange, when you're away from the place you think of all sorts of things, when it comes to the point you forget.

We wish to emphasize here not so much the mother's evident *intra*-personal defences but that she has to defend herself from the evocation in her of her own feelings by acting on Claire to muddle *her* up, to render *her* speechless, to obliterate *her* memory —in short, by inducing a disorganization *in her daughter's* personality. That Mrs. Church's actions serve this function does not of course mean that they necessarily have this intention.

To return to the issue of affection. In our view Mrs. Church could not bear to admit this but had to believe that Claire and she had given affection to each other. What she found particularly upsetting was not the emotional impoverishment of their relationship but that Claire should wish to ventilate this issue.

When in the supportive context of our interviews Claire managed to keep on 'fussing' for a little longer than usual before starting to lose her memory and falling silent (clinically showing amnesia and mutism), she claimed that whereas her mother kissed her and expected to be kissed in return, her mother never gave nor wanted to receive really spontaneous affection. Moreover, according to Claire, her mother had never 'really' wanted her to be 'really' affectionate towards *anyone*. Her mother, she said, tried to 'kill' her (Claire's) affection for her (her mother), her girl-friends, and for men. Claire said that she now had no affection for her mother. She did not hate her nor was she bitter. She simply felt indifferent.

Claire's term for what we refer to as disconfirmation, invalidation, or lack of endorsement was 'discouragement'. She said that she had been discouraged from feeling or showing genuine affection. This probably refers particularly to the period after the death of her infant sister when Claire was three. She said also that her mother had no affection for Michael, or for her husband, and that everyone had to pretend they were different from what they were.

It is remarkable that while Mrs. Church usually effectively stopped Claire from remembering specific incidents that supported this view, the evidence we have for its validity came from Mrs. Church herself.

Her negation of warmth in herself and in her daughter was registered strongly by over twelve psychiatrists and social· scientists who have studied these interviews. We wish to insist particularly on the *impact* on Claire of the denial of this denial, and the denial of the denial of the denial.

Mystification entails a constant shifting of meaning and of position. It is evidently very important for her mother and father to believe that Claire was affectionate before her 'illness'. However this is never taken up in terms of what are usually said to be 'feelings', but only in terms of conduct. Thus, they put forward the argument that Claire was affectionate because she kissed her parents goodnight. Claire's statement that she did this only out of fear and duty is ignored. Her parents also are concerned that Claire should *say* she is not affectionate, particularly in front of us, because it will give us wrong ideas.

Mrs. Church had, as we have seen, failed to achieve autonomy from her own family. Some of the circumstances contributing to this are known to us—the death of a younger sister when she was three, the death of her father when she was eight, an ailing younger brother whom she had to nurse, a mother who confused and exploited her, marriage to a man who married her, as he said, 'because she was good to her mother'—the loss of her second daughter, and so on. Mrs. Church herself had been subject to her own four hundred blows, leaving her, as one report of her put it, an empty shell. Understandably, and indeed necessarily, Mrs. Church tended to destroy not only her own inner world but Claire's,[1] since she was so largely living in and through Claire.

Claire was, therefore, caught in her mother's failure both to achieve autonomy from her own mother and to work through the various losses in her life. Two *new* persons, Claire and Michael, were both partially killed, in this mourning of the mother for her old lost objects.

The 'shell' Mrs. Church retained was constructed from institutionalized attitudes and conduct she imported into her relations with her husband, Michael, and Claire. However, both parents could not entirely avoid being spontaneous with their own children. They themselves needed affection as much as they could

---

[1] 'There seems to be no agent more effective than another person in bringing a world for oneself alive, or, by a glance, a gesture, or a remark, shrivelling up the reality in which one is lodged.' (p. 41) Goffman, E. (1961). *Encounters. Two Studies in the Sociology of Interaction.* Indianapolis: Bobbs-Merrill.

not give it. Mr. Church once remarked, 'We did all we knew to get their affection (Michael's and Claire's) but I doubt if we gave them very much'. Affection when expressed frightened them, however, and they stifled its further appearance. Along with the institutionalization of family life, everyone outside the family became seen in the same way, interchangeable, menacing, watching and to be watched, not to be trusted. The genuine affection that Mr. and Mrs. Church so longed for and feared thus receded more and more as their world came to preclude the possibility of any spontaneous, unguarded, trusting expression of self with others, without contracting rights or obligations. We do not know whether they 'knew', as we are accustomed to say 'on some level', what real affection was; there is evidence that they did fleetingly. But in practice, however, 'affection' was only stereotyped role-playing and 'affection', 'attention', 'neglect' and so on were not issues for discussion ('We were never a chatty family.'). This was 'fuss'.

When Claire called her not a mother but a managing director, as she did frequently, Mrs. Church would deny this and then, apparently unaware of what she was doing, she would give examples of just what she denied. In the following, Claire has said that her mother tends to 'minimize' her feelings. In a tone and manner that suggests that she is giving a report to a board meeting, Mrs. Church says:

MOTHER: Oh I don't know. I know it is a serious matter, certainly but I haven't noticed that I try to (laughs) minimize anything— haven't noticed it at all. You (interviewer) notice all these points.

DAUGHTER: I realize that.

MOTHER: Maybe. Perhaps I haven't noticed it. I think that may come from the fact that I know I always do try and—I always have done—tried to make people feel at ease, and you see during my life I've had a lot to do with all kinds of staff you see, and I tried if I possibly could to appear pleasant to them. Any little thing that happened I'd always try to, you know, look as though 'Okay. That's all right'—to make them feel more comfortable in their job you see, so perhaps I suppose perhaps through doing that I might do it in other directions unconsciously, I don't know. I remember years ago when my husband and I were in business we had a lot of young staff, and young people as you know are very sensitive in their jobs, and when the boss walks through they look at you as if to say, 'Here comes the Terror!' (laughs). And I used always to try and make them feel comfortable in their jobs—used to try to make up a happy party, sort of thing. So perhaps that is one reason. (Ten seconds' pause.) Is there anything else, Claire, you could say?

In this context sexual feelings were tolerated only if they functioned institutionally. Sexual feelings that Claire kept entirely to herself were condemned in the strongest terms as much as sexual behaviour. This condemnation appeared to stem from her mother's enclosure in a form of relatedness in which each person feels himself duty-bound to fulfil the role that the institution requires of him. To do so is no less than one's duty, to do less is to be selfish.

Spontaneity, especially sexual spontaneity, is the very heart of subversion to institutional mores, to pre-set role taking and assigning. Spontaneous affection, sexuality, anger, would have shattered Mr. and Mrs. Church's shells to bits.

MOTHER: . . . and one day I wanted to kiss you and you flew at me—created—'Don't kiss me! Don't kiss me!' And of course I spoke—you were under Dr. Reading at that time—and I spoke to Dr. Reading about it and he must have mentioned it to you. Well anyhow he told your father, 'Tell your wife not to kiss Claire'. I often wonder why it was you sort of went off like that. Ever since that incident we don't kiss you when we see you or kiss you goodbye.

DAUGHTER: Kissing is a sign of affection. (Note that the issue for Claire is her *mother's* affection for her.)

MOTHER: Well it is yes.

DAUGHTER: Well I don't think I feel—

MOTHER: You don't feel affectionate, is that it? (She adroitly shifts the issue to the daughter's affection for her.) No? Oh, it seems strange though, doesn't it—your mother and father?

DAUGHTER: I don't think it does really.

MOTHER: Especially when one hasn't seen one for, say, a few days or a week and when you leave you usually kiss one goodbye. Of course I know a lot of people don't do it these days, but I didn't know if it was one of these strange modern ideas you've cultivated.

DAUGHTER: No, I think it's just lack of feeling of affection, that's all.

MOTHER: And why the lack of a feeling of affection?

DAUGHTER: Well I never have had much affection for you.

MOTHER: You haven't? Can you give any reason?—And yet you did when you were quite tiny Claire. I remember when you were a little girl, I remember when you were a year old, it comes back to me now. I was in bed, I was ill for three months. I was in bed and you used to love to sit on my bed and hug me. As a matter of fact sometimes I know I was in such pain I almost couldn't bear it, and you loved—you were just a year old when you began to walk. You'd climb on to the bed, and right up to the time you went to school I remember, every afternoon your father used to rest, because he got up at three in the morning in those days, and he used to go up and rest on his bed and you used to go up with him and rest and play about with him. And then sometimes in the afternoon when my legs weren't too good I used to rest, put my legs up on a chair, and you used to climb up and hug and fuss with me all the time, and when I was about the house, up to the time you went to school, you'd be following me everywhere. And I remember after that illness I went to the seaside for six months for a rest, to cure my bad leg—and I just—you just wouldn't let me out of your sight. 'I want my Mummy, I want my Mummy!'

86

You kept on for a long time. I remember one weekend my mother offered to take you home for the weekend. She said, 'Let me take Claire home with me. She'll stay with me, that'll break it.' And mother took you home that weekend. It must have been a horrid weekend, but I had to promise I'd come on Sunday and fetch you. 'Don't you leave me too long!'— Well that's all a sign of affection isn't it?—all a sign of affection.

In this passage Mrs. Church implies that it is almost incomprehensible that her daughter is not now affectionate. She asks Claire, 'Can you give any reason?' Characteristically she then herself proceeds to supply part of the answer. She could not bear Claire's hugging, so she gave the little girl to her own mother to break her of it. Between them they seem to have succeeded. But having offered an answer, she denies that she has done so, for although her story can hardly be construed other than that at her instigation her own mother helped to break Claire's tie to her, she does not explicitly admit that this is the story she has told, for less than a minute later this exchange occurs:

INTERVIEWER: The possibility that your daughter may not have a great deal of affection for you, Mrs. Church, seems to make you rather uneasy.

MOTHER: Pardon?

INTERVIEWER: You are uneasy that your daughter says she has not much affection for you.

MOTHER: Well I wouldn't say it would make me uneasy. I just accept it naturally, but I wonder when she says that she never had any affection. I wonder when she started on this, because she was certainly affectionate enough when she was a child. Of course I know youngsters grow up and don't like to be hugged and kissed and all that. (She once more turns the issue round: in her own story, she could not bear her daughter's signs of affection, and so tried to 'break' her of them. Now it is Claire who inexplicably does not want to be hugged and kissed.) Well naturally you drop that out when they grow up,

87

because it's not accepted, and also the same if one offers advice, it's not accepted, so after the second time, if it isn't accepted, well just drop it, at least I do. But we've never made any fuss about it. We've just let the children carry on their own sweet way, whatever way they wanted to go, provided it was the right one. We never really interfered an awful lot with their activities.

INTERVIEWER: Provided it was the right way...

MOTHER: Provided it was the right way. Yes I don't think we ever had ... Claire's been a good girl really compared with what I hear from different parents, today especially. And the same with my son Michael. I mean they've both been good children. We never had a lot of ... any cause for anxiety I don't think.

INTERVIEWER: You wouldn't have allowed Miss Church to go any way which you would have regarded as the wrong way?

MOTHER: Oh definitely not, definitely not. You see we are a church-going people, and well, say for instance, Claire stopped going to church, I'd want to know why you see, definitely (ten seconds' pause). And her friends as far as I could see were acceptable. There was no cause for alarm in that respect (1 minute 20 seconds' pause). Anything else Claire?

Although the paralinguistic qualifiers cannot be reproduced here the frequency of disqualifying words and phrases is evident. We just let the children carry on their own sweet way, *provided it was the right one*, we never *really* interfered *an awful lot* ... Claire's been a good girl *really* compared with what I hear from different parents ... 'Good' here appears to mean that she has never dared to say what she thought, or felt, to have ordinary girl friends, or boy friends.

Almost totally lacking in spontaneity, Mr. and Mrs. Church were particularly fearful of gossip and scandal. Another aspect of this was their fear of what they called 'a crowd'. We must look more closely at what this word denoted for them.

One aspect of a crowd is that it is a collection of people not bound together by strong personal rights or obligations. It is without organizational or institutional safeguards. Mrs. Church was terrified of 'crowds'—especially those small 'crowds' (in ordinary language, a party) where sexual and other possibilities arise—small parties where people drink, let their hair down, and are a little more spontaneous than usual for a short while.

Her mother repeatedly tells Claire that she (Claire) does not like 'crowds', particularly crowds in the house. One notes also that 'crowds' is used in a special family way by both mother and daughter in the following passage:

DAUGHTER: You see Michael was ill a lot which meant that I was with him a lot, and I feel that having been with him so much and away from other children I didn't mix with other children as perhaps I might have done otherwise—that that sometimes had something to do with my mixing with crowds of people now. I find it very difficult to mix, not among a group, but with a crowd, but I don't—

MOTHER: But have you always felt like that Claire?

DAUGHTER: Well I think that if you think back you will remember that I have never mixed well with a crowd. I've always been on the outside of a crowd.

MOTHER: Well—

DAUGHTER: I would never, even when I was working, when I was grown up and I was working, I never mixed, really mixed easily, with a crowd of people.

MOTHER: Well in that sense Claire, you take after your mother and your father because I don't mix with crowds.

DAUGHTER: No you don't mix easily.

MOTHER: And your father doesn't. We have our little sets, but that's sufficient. We're quite contented. We're not the type of people that want to go with crowds, and your grandparents were just the same—never went with crowds. We went to our church, and we mixed with the people at our church, and intermarried with our church people, and most of our friends have been on the same footing. You see we've never been the type to go about in crowds.

DAUGHTER: Well you could never . . .

MOTHER: We've had dinners and big socials, but that's only been occasionally. But we've never been people for asking crowds of people *home* and all that sort of thing.

DAUGHTER: You really haven't had much social life yourself.

MOTHER: No, we've had very little social life.

DAUGHTER: And consequently I've not really been encouraged tremendously to mix with many people.

MOTHER: I suppose you could say that.

DAUGHTER: Well I think that is true. Nevertheless, I don't mean that I'm a bad mixer, and that I can't mix with all different types . . .

MOTHER: No, as I say you're very like we are, you see.

Again:

MOTHER: Well Claire has always been, well rather quiet—not exactly quiet, I'm wrong in saying that, she didn't seem . . . never wanted to discuss very much with you you see. Now I remember the time that one of her friends—you know, Gillian when she was in the R.A.F. during the war, and I'm afraid she got mixed up with a crowd and got herself into trouble, and I remember Claire coming home and telling me. So I found out that girl was rather fond of whisky—just cultivated that habit during the war you see—the Forces. So Claire went to a party at her house some time after that, and I remember saying to Claire, 'Now listen, Claire, when you go to these parties, you're not used to drinking. Have a sherry and don't let *anybody* mix you a drink and do be very careful with the menfolk.' And she said, 'Oh you don't have to worry about me Mummy, I'm all right. I can look after myself.' I said, 'Listen, Claire, all girls say that, but there is sometimes a time when you can't look after yourself—a time when a man gives you too much to

90

drink'—A few cases do happen as you know. So, anyhow, after that (laughs) if I used to say something to Claire, if she was going to a party, she was quite . . . I suppose twenty-three, twenty-four at the time, I used to say, 'Now, Claire, watch the drink'. She didn't like me saying that I noticed—I thought, 'Well I've told her three times now'.

Mrs. Church, as we see, was very concerned about dangers that might befall Claire at the hands of other people, in particular at social gatherings, especially sexual dangers.

But the 'Claire' who was the object of Mrs. Church's concern was much more an object of her phantasy than a real person in her own right in a real world. Actual real dangers in the real world seemed hardly to concern Mrs. Church at all. For instance, Claire as a little girl was allowed to work in the top storey of a house, at the height of air-raids in one of the heaviest bombed areas, after having narrowly missed being killed when running to a shelter in an early air-raid.

MOTHER: . . . and after that you see we had these doodlebugs and rockets and things and you were very scared after that, both you and Michael. As a matter of fact I was myself (laughs) . . . Do you remember anything of the war and what went on?

DAUGHTER: Very little.

MOTHER: Do you remember how you used to go up into your room and sit up there and do your studying, while the raids were on right on top of the house? And you wouldn't come down. I mentioned that to Dr. Reading and he couldn't understand it. He said, 'Didn't you think it was rather odd for your daughter to do that?' I said, 'No—that I thought you were very brave'. You used to go right to the top of the house. Was it three-storey or four-storey, our house then?—Anyhow you used to study until about two in the morning with the air-raids going on I remember—never bothered. And then you gave your Grandma courage and she went to bed, she wouldn't go in the shelter any more. She said, 'If Claire can be at the top of the house I can go to bed' (laughs). You don't remember? Well the raids couldn't have disturbed you very much then, otherwise I don't think you'd have stopped up there.

Mrs. Church's theory of Claire's 'illness' is that it is the 'after-effects' of these air-raids.

Once more we have set ourselves a limited aim and in our view we have now achieved it. More evidence could be presented, many more aspects of this family could be discussed, but we have, we believe, adduced sufficient evidence that two particular symptoms that are usually taken to be primary symptoms of an organic schizophrenic *process*—impoverishment of affect and incongruity of thought and affect—are here intelligible as social *praxis*.

APPENDIX

If one puts some of her mother's attributions about Claire, past and present, alongside Claire's self-attributions, one gets the following table.

Each person's point of view is given in condensed form, which, however, remains faithful to their own expressions.

None of her mother's attributions in this list appears to express recognition of Claire as a real separate person. Projective identification is used, as are the other attributions we make about Mrs. Church's attributions, purely descriptively.

MOTHER'S VIEW		CLAIRE'S VIEW
We are very alike.	Projective identification.	We are not alike.
You were always very affectionate.	Denial.	I used to be—but I stopped being so.
I did everything for you.		You never gave me affection. You were more of a business-woman than a mother.
You were always frightened of crowds. Wearing glasses made you 'sensitive'.	Projective identification.	Not as much as you were. This had something to do with it. But I was 'sensitive' because I thought I looked ridiculous to the other children because I was never allowed to play with them; and they laughed at me because I had to wheel my brother around instead of playing with them.
You were unhappy like I was because we took you from school (just before G.C.E., when she was expecting to go to University) and made you work in the business.	Minimization, imperviousness.	It was the biggest disappointment in my whole life.

MOTHER'S VIEW		CLAIRE'S VIEW
You were upset about going to Canada.	Projective identification.	I was delighted at a change.
You did not like living in hotels there.	Projective identification.	I never enjoyed myself more.
You were always sensitive, and so did not like meeting people in hotels in Canada.	Projective identification.	I met 'people' there for the first time. I enjoyed doing so: I was rather timid however.
You were terrified of 'crowds'.	Projective identification.	I did become frightened (for some reason) in a room of about six people.
The air-raids made you ill.	Projective identification.	My 'illness' has nothing to do with the air-raids.
You were a perfectly good little girl before your 'illness'.	Denial and imperviousness.	This was because I was frightened of you.
We always used to get on perfectly well.	Denial and imperviousness.	I simply complied with you.

FAMILY 4

The Danzigs

CLINICAL PERSPECTIVE

From the clinical psychiatric viewpoint, Sarah Danzig began to develop an illness of insidious onset at the age of seventeen. She began to lie in bed all day, getting up only at night and staying up thinking or brooding or reading the Bible. Gradually she lost interest in everyday affairs and became increasingly preoccupied with religious issues. Her attendance at commercial college became intermittent, and she failed to complete her studies. During the next four years Sarah failed to make the grade at whatever job or course of study she undertook.

When she was twenty-one her illness took a sudden turn for the worse. She began to express bizarre ideas, for instance that she heard voices over the telephone and saw people on television talking about her. Soon afterwards she started to rage against members of her family. After one outburst against her mother she fled the house and stayed out all night. On her return she was taken to an observation ward where she remained for two weeks. Thereafter, she was listless, apathetic, quiet, withdrawn, and lacking in concentration. Although from time to time she made bizarre statements, for example that she had been raped, on the whole she was able to live quietly at home, and even return to work, this time in her father's office. She continued like this for fifteen months, and then relapsed. Once more she

95

persistently expressed bizarre ideas. She complained that people at the office were talking about her, were in a plot against her, and did not wish her to work with them. She insisted they intercepted and tore up her letters. She also insisted that her letters were being intercepted at home. She complained to her father that his staff were incompetent, and quarrelled with him and his secretary over keeping the books. Eventually she refused to go to work, and took to lying in her bed all day, getting up only at night to brood or to sit reading the Bible. She spoke hardly at all except to make occasional statements about religion or to accuse her family of discussing her, or to complain that the telephone operators were listening in to her calls. She became irritable and aggressive, particularly towards her father, and it was following an outburst against him that she was again brought into hospital.

STRUCTURE OF INVESTIGATION

The family consisted of mother (aged fifty), father (fifty-six), Sarah (aged twenty-three), John (twenty-one), Ruth (fifteen). At her parents' request, Ruth was not included in the investigation.

Interviews	Occasions
Daughter	13
Father	1
Mother	1
Mother and father	4
Mother and daughter	1
Father and daughter	1
Son	3
Son and daughter	3
Mother, father and daughter	8
Mother, father, daughter and son	4
	—
	39

This represents 32 hours of interviewing time, of which 18 hours were tape-recorded.

THE FAMILY SITUATION

In this case the necessity for a variety of 'sightings' of the family in action is revealed particularly clearly.

We shall first describe certain aspects of the family interviews, with particular reference to what makes intelligible various delusions and psychotic manifestations relating to Sarah's behaviour in hospital. She said that

1. The Ward Sister was withholding letters from her and failing to pass on telephone messages from her mother. She knew the letters from her mother were being withheld because her mother was writing to her every other day. She knew that her mother was writing to her every other day because she was her mother's child and her mother loved her.

2. The hospital was maliciously detaining her, while her parents wanted her home at once.

3. She was afraid of being abandoned in hospital and never getting home again. She did not say who would abandon her, but the heart of her fear was that she would be cut off from her mother.

4. She said that her mother had only agreed to her coming into hospital because she had not wanted her to leave home. Her mother did not want to lose her children. She said that she did not blame her mother, and emphasized that she and her mother loved each other.

5. She was angry with her father and was afraid of him. She saw him as the prime agent in her detention in hospital. She said that he was a liar, and would tell lies about her.

Throughout these interviews Sarah, for the most part, passively complied with her parents and her brother.

In the first family session the issue of her fear of being abandoned was raised. Her parents and brother reassured her that they had telephoned every day, and had left messages for her. This was not in fact so. They told her that she was ill, that they only

97

wanted her to stay in hospital for her own good, not because they wanted to abandon her. They loved her and wanted her back home. Sarah made no attempt to argue.

John was soon to remark that she was unusually amiable and acquiescent, whereas 'normally she was highly resistant to suggestion'. The significance of this remark emerged more fully when he warned us in private against being fooled by her. She was just pretending to agree with them. It was an act to get out of hospital. With her, however, he was sympathetic and loving, giving *her* no hint that he thought she was trying to fool him.

It seemed therefore that a mistrustful perception of the hospital was necessary for her if she was to maintain her trust in her family, since greater perceptual and cognitive dissonance would have been experienced by Sarah had she distrusted her family rather than the hospital.

When her family was asked in what way they felt she was ill, they replied that she was lazy, stubborn, sluttish, terribly impudent to her father, rebellious, obscene, etc. They seemed to be describing wickedness, not sickness. At least this is how Sarah felt it. She remarked timidly that she had changed her mind about going home.

One of the main features of her illness in the view of her parents was an unreasoned, senseless, persistent hostility to her father, but when she was seen alone, her mother, without any apparent awareness of being inconsistent, also described Sarah's hostility as a meaningful response to various things her father did. Indeed, she said he acted in the same way towards her (mother) and John, making them angry too. In fact it emerged that they were constantly quarrelling. It thus became clear that Sarah's anger against her father, which her family now could not tolerate, was hardly more intense than the enmity her mother and John had directed against him for years. But they objected to Sarah acting similarly. Sarah was finally singled out by her mother, father, and brother as the one person who was *really* expected to comply with her father's wishes. This was not put to her in so many

98

words, but each of the others privately realized that she was put in a special position although without their being fully aware of its consequences for her. They argued that if Sarah could not get on with her father she must be ill.

But it was not her father who was the promoter of the idea that Sarah 'had to go'. Although he and Sarah fought and screamed at each other more than her mother and John could tolerate, they also got on together in a much more affectionate and intimate way than her mother or John liked to admit.

When interviewed alone, her mother said plainly that if Sarah did not give up her hostility to her father she should remain permanently in hospital. When she was with Sarah, however, she conveyed to her again without any sense of inconsistency that it was not she, but her husband and John, who wanted her put away. She told Sarah plainly that John was fed up with her, that he could not stand her at home, and that he was not going to be bothered with her. This was true, but it contrasted with John's frequent reassurances to Sarah to the contrary. John admitted that Sarah was only saying to his father what he had said to her about him. But, like his mother, he thought that Sarah must be ill if she said such things, since it was not her place.

When he was alone with the interviewer, Mr. Danzig said that his wife had wanted to get rid of Sarah for some time, had wanted to 'sacrifice' her, but he had refused to agree. He regarded himself as Sarah's ally, but the support he accorded her was more imaginary than real since he did not support her either when his wife and son were attacking her or when he was alone with her.

He did, however, remonstrate with them in Sarah's absence, even to threatening to leave home himself if they did not leave her alone.[1] It is ironical that Mrs. Danzig insisted that it was for her husband's sake that Sarah had to be 'treated' in hospital for her 'illness'.

Thus, Sarah's construction that her father and the hospital, not

---

[1] His motives for leaving home were more mixed than this and he had never been clear about them (see p. 109).

her mother and John, wished to keep her locked up was as reasonable as it was unreasonable—in fact, with the evidence available to her it was possibly the most likely construction.

Sarah was continually mystified in this respect. For instance, when the interviewer introduced the issue of whether Sarah got on everyone's nerves, and not only her father's, Mrs. Danzig took this as a criticism of Sarah and told her how 'ungrateful' she was for upsetting her father. Sarah tried feebly to defend herself, and then pleaded that she was tired. Her mother sympathized, and then went on to describe Sarah in her usual terms as selfish, ungrateful, inconsiderate, and so on. It was always difficult to get past such attributions to specific items of behaviour. When Sarah listlessly fell in with her, her mother took it as evidence that she was right. She then advised Sarah to follow our advice and to stay in hospital, in the interests of her health. We had not given any such advice.

Another mystifying feature of this family is the marked conspiratorial tone and manner they adopt with each other and with us in Sarah's absence. They have then a solidarity otherwise lacking. It is impressive how their conflicts are then forgotten.

On one occasion, when Sarah left the room, her mother, father, and brother began a furtive whispered exchange about her. As Sarah re-entered she said uncertainly that she had the impression that they were talking about her. They denied this and looked at us significantly, as though to say: 'See how suspicious she is.'

After these glimpses of this family in action in the present and recent past, we shall now try to reconstruct some crucial historical facts.

Sarah left school at sixteen to go to secretarial college for fifteen months, then to art school for two years. Recently she had been working in her father's office. She had had a previous 'breakdown' eighteen months ago.

According to her mother and father, until the age of twelve she had been a most lovable child. She had always tended to lack self-confidence, however, and to be concerned about how she appeared to others, continually relying on her parents and her brother to tell her how people saw her. Nevertheless according to them, she had been very popular, and had had a number of friends. She had had a sharp wit, a good sense of humour and she was artistic. She liked paintings, good music, good books, and had an exceptional talent for writing and drawing, showing promise in these respects at school. She had insight into other people's characters and did not like cheap talk. They did not, however, wish her to be an artist.

After fifteen months at secretarial college she stopped attending. She lay in bed until late in the morning, and stayed awake all night thinking or reading. She began to lose her friends one by one. At this time she began to read the Bible and tried to interpret for herself what she read.

Father, mother, John, and Sarah all agree on the following features of Sarah's behaviour *before* admission to hospital.

1. She had been saying for some months that telephone operators (or someone) had been listening in to her calls.
2. She believed that people in her father's office had been talking about her and did not want her to work there.
3. She believed that someone at the office intercepted and destroyed her letters, and that some of the staff were incompetent.
4. She believed that her parents and brother were talking about her.
5. She believed that they were keeping letters from her.
6. She was irritable and aggressive towards members of her family especially her father, towards whom she did not have the right attitude for a daughter. In particular she called him a liar, and said she no longer believed in him or trusted him.
7. She was very shy and self-conscious.
8. She did not mix with other people, but was quiet, withdrawn, miserable, and discontented.

9. She lay in bed all day and sat up into the small hours of the morning.
10. She lacked concentration and had been thinking too much.
11. She had been reading the Bible a great deal.

Twelve months earlier Sarah had gone to work in her father's office. She soon began to feel that she was being discussed disparagingly. In her turn she complained to her father that certain employees were incompetent. Finally, she refused to go any more. About this time (it is not clear when it began), she discovered that her salary had been over-stated in the books and told her father. He tried to explain it to her, but she failed to understand either his explanation or that of his son and secretary. 'She wore us all out' (Mother). She insisted that the clerk responsible was incompetent, and when they did not agree accused them of being against her, and began to act provocatively at home, e.g. by smoking in front of her father on the Sabbath, putting lemonade into his tea, and so on. These acts were regarded with a mixture of anger, guilt, shame, and concern by her parents and brother, who eventually resolved their dilemma by treating them as signs of illness.

Her parents regarded Sarah's madness as a calamity visited on the family.

MOTHER: Well I did sort of think all this business of going, you know, thinking unusual things, saying people are not—to me these sort of things—they always happen to other people, they never happen to us. You know the sort of thing, you think it always happens to other people—you know people flooded out, you know, I feel sorry, but you do sort of think 'Oh I'll never be flooded out where I'm living now'—you see? I'm only giving you an example. It's never occurred to me that I'll ever get flooded out where I live now—that's how I look at it.

And:

FATHER: We didn't realize what was happening.

MOTHER: We didn't, as I told you, we thought these things only happened to other people's children. You read in the paper a little girl is murdered, or kidnapped, you feel very sorry for the people, but you don't associate it with your own child. As I say, everything terrible happens to other people.

FATHER: When it happens to you—

MOTHER: And then it happens with you unfortunately, then other people say 'Oh how terrible', then it becomes a tragedy. It *never* occurred to me that she'd ever go sort of mentally like this, to turn out in this sort of way.

What was the calamity comparable to these floods, murder, and kidnap, that had befallen this family? The more we probed, the more elusive it became, but what was obvious was her parents' shame and fear of scandal. In particular, they were worried about Sarah's social *naïveté* and lack of discretion. They regarded her as a 'breaker of the family front'. When she first went to work in her father's office he had urged her to keep quiet about her breakdown. Unfortunately it leaked out and his staff began to gossip behind her back, although to her face they were kind and forbearing. She was also resented for being the boss's daughter. Sarah felt their hostility without being able to get her feeling confirmed by anyone.

She also discovered certain actual mistakes that had been made and told her father. She was resented more than ever now, but she could not be attacked directly. Instead, she was exposed to more innuendoes that no one would confirm explicitly. She became more and more isolated and unhappy. At this time some of her correspondence was mislaid 'accidentally' by another employee. She perceived the 'unconscious' motive of the other, and tried to challenge her. The other girl insinuated something about her sanity, and in an agitated state she went to her father to complain. Her father, anxious to avoid any open recognition among his employees that his daughter had been a mental case, pooh-poohed her complaints, casting doubt on the validity of her suspicions—'You are unwell. No one dislikes you. No one is talking about you. It's imagination', and so on. Without confirmation from her father she became more agitated, and started calling him a liar, accusing him of being in collusion with the others. She refused to return to the office.

In addition, while working with him, she had discovered that her father, while generally a meticulously honest man, engaged in certain petty dishonesties. We of course have no difficulty in reconciling this paradox, since it is quite characteristic of the compulsive-obsessive person, but Sarah could not understand this and became very confused, especially as her father now had to defend himself desperately, not against his own dissociated impulses, but against her. This involved him, unwittingly, in order to preserve her trust in him, in destroying her trust in herself, and as far as he could he enlisted his secretary, wife, and son to this end.

They said in effect: 'You are imagining that there is a flaw in your father' *and*, 'You are mad or bad if you imagine such a thing', *and*, 'You are mad or bad if you do not believe us when we tell you that you are mad or bad to trust your own perceptions and memory'.

Much of what they called her illness consisted in attempts to discuss forbidden issues, comments on their attempts to keep her in the dark, or to muddle her, and angry responses to such mystifications and mystification over mystifications. She had been put in the position of having to try to sort out secrecy and muddle, in the face of being muddled up over the validity of trying to do so. With some justification, therefore, Sarah began to feel that they were in collusion against her.

We have to explain why this girl is so naïve in the first place. It may be argued that with such a naïve girl the family would want to keep her in ignorance of their secrets, that their mystification of her was a consequence of her *naïveté*. This was partly so. But our evidence shows that her *naïveté* had itself been preceded by a prior mystification. The family was thus caught in a vicious

spiral. The more they mystified her the more she remained
naïve and the more she remained naïve the more they felt they
had to protect themselves by mystifying her.

Mr. Danzig lived a scrupulously correct family life, and needed
to be seen as a man of stern and perfect rectitude, and as the head
of the family. His wife complied with him in this, but at the
same time encouraged John to 'see through' him, but not in
public. John helped to maintain his father's public image, but his
co-operation at home was intermittent, and he was often supported
in these lapses by his mother. Mr. Danzig knew of the mother-son
alliance, and mother and son knew he knew, and he knew they
knew he knew. There was thus complete understanding among
the three of them in this respect.

With Sarah, however, it was different. Mother and son often
criticized Mr. Danzig in front of her, but she was not supposed to
do so. They thus presented her with a very difficult task. Mr.
Danzig's view of his marriage (and, incidentally, something of
his style of thinking in general) can be seen in the following
passage.

'It may well be that my wife in her moments of forgetfulness
speaks to me sharply in the presence of the children. In other
words she doesn't show for me the respect that a wife should
in the presence of children. And I've told her more than often,
"If you've anything to say to me, say it not in front of the
children".

'We differ a lot on that (keeping the house clean—e.g. the
children's bedrooms). One of the excuses is, "I haven't got the
time, patience", or, "Have no help".—All right, I try to
alleviate her worries. I chime in sometimes. I help her. Then she
comes back—I have no right to interfere. I get erratic. I say,
"No, I like—I'm only interfering when I see something which
I don't like".

'I want a certain clean way and it can arise from an attitude—
perhaps she may think—indifference on my wife's part. She

feels—er—she can't go out very well. I can accept this. She feels she doesn't go out very well. I object to her—I want her to dress very nicely, very neatly and cleanly and smartly. I want to go out watching her. She doesn't care. She's indifferent to this. I don't like that. I say "Whatever position arises between me and you privately or otherwise, publicly, come out clean. Go out occasionally. It's not nice for the children. It gives an example to the children if you go out occasionally." 'It may well be perhaps, shall I say—I may even go a bit further than this. It may well be and I've often thought about it, it may well be that *I* may not have been her ideal in marriage— I'm going to admit to you that *she* may not be *my* ideal in marriage . . .

' . . . She was an only child. She was quite an intelligent person, well-read, musical. I thought, "We might blend. Possible, possible. I may be a possible to her." You get near enough the possibilities, near the next best. Maybe she felt the same thing. I did have ideas in my mind but—my wife wasn't bad looking. And so I came to the point. We met and it seemed possible. We didn't dislike one another, not to say—I'm not going to say I was ravingly in love with my wife, and I don't think my wife was with me; but maybe I wasn't experienced enough to understand certain things. Oh I wasn't a bargain—I wasn't a bargain—I was a young man. I hadn't the remotest idea of running around with other people—with other women—picking them up at dance-halls or a ball, when I was single, and I thought, "Well this is a nice set-up—I might be able to work this round"—so we both felt the same thing. We were both of the same mind.'

It was not surprising that Sarah maintained an idealized picture of her father, dissociated from her dissonant perceptions, until she was over twenty-one. She had had squabbles with her father before, about unannounced intrusions into her bedroom when she was undressed, unsolicited insistence on tidying up her bedroom, listening in on her telephone calls, intercepting her letters, and so on, but in none of these was she sure that her father was in the wrong. All such behaviour was either denied by him or rationalized as out of love for her. If she found this love annoying, she felt that she was at fault.

As her idealization of her father broke down, she clung all the more desperately to her idealization of her mother, which her mother helped her to maintain. Her mother's behaviour over the issue of Sarah's lying late in bed illustrates this. Both her parents continually reproached her for not getting up early. They shouted at her to mend her ways, saying that now she was grown up, and should not behave like a baby. Their actions, however, were markedly at variance with this, for her father insisted, for instance, on his right to enter her bedroom whenever he wanted, which her mother did not oppose, and she, while complaining bitterly of the inconvenience, continued to cook her meals whenever she chose to get up. When we asked why she did not lay down fixed times for her daughter's meals, and refuse to let her routine be disorganized, she replied that if she did that she would feel guilty and a bad mother. Sarah's father replied indignantly that if that happened he would carry food up to his daughter himself, and Sarah felt that her mother would be mean if she did not give her her meals whenever she felt like eating.

The more her parents did things for her, the more they wanted her gratitude and the more ungrateful she became. Searching for gratitude they did even more for her. Thus, while expecting her to grow up they treated her as a child, and she, while wanting to be considered as an adult, behaved more and more as a baby. Her parents then reproached her for being spoiled by them, and she reproached them for not treating her as an adult.

When Sarah said she was afraid of her father her parents not only could not understand this, they refused to believe it. After all he had never abused her or shouted at her or hit her. Apart from insisting that she obey certain religious rules such as not smoking on the Sabbath, he had made no demands on her. In their opinion the trouble was that he had not been firm enough and had over-indulged her. Nor could Sarah gain any support from John. His position was very equivocal. He was, as noted above, privately supported by his mother against his father, and he obtained her open support when he defied him to his face. He was also encouraged by both parents to see Sarah as the favoured and indulged child. For a short time in his teens he had supported his sister, but had broken with her. He then engaged in an alliance with his mother. We have evidence that she was jealous of the closeness between him and his sister. To what extent was she responsible for stimulating John's jealousy of his father's 'indulgence' of Sarah as an aid to bringing him to her side? To what extent did she stimulate his defiance of his father, and win him by supporting him in it? What is the evidence that Sarah was indulged more than he?

According to them all Mr. Danzig was 'firmer' with John than with Sarah and Ruth, because John was a boy. But John reproached his father for not being firm enough with him. He said that his father should have hit him to make him work better at school. He was not afraid of his father as a child, and he thought he should have been. All children should be afraid of their fathers. He thought his father had bad children, although there have been worse boys than himself. He tried to comply, but did not always succeed. He did not think his father's demands unreasonable, but . . .

Mr. Danzig felt he had over-indulged his son. He should have 'bullied' him more. He had spoiled both John and Sarah.

'I was patient with him and very happy to say that although I spoilt him—I spoilt Sarah, I spoilt John . . . '

We may say that John *believes* Sarah was indulged more than himself. His reasons for so believing, as they emerge, are obscure.

This family therefore functioned largely through a series of alliances—mother and father; mother and son; mother, father, and son. Sarah was left out. She received, as she said, no 'backing' from anyone in the family, and this seems to have been the case. These alliances offered protection against impossible ideals. Sarah, with no ally, was expected to conform with no let-up to the rules that the others all managed to break. For instance, John was not supposed to have a sexual life, but he had one, with his mother's collusion. Mrs. Danzig broke Sabbath rules, with John's connivance, unbeknown to her husband, and so on. Mr. Danzig was secretly sexually dissatisfied and had often thought of leaving his wife in recent years. Even though regarded as ill, indulged, and spoiled, Sarah alone was expected to govern her thoughts and actions according to Mr. Danzig's obsessive-compulsive interpretation of a rigorous orthodoxy. Her social *naïveté* has thus to be set within the context of her parents' demand for *total* compliance from her alone.

Nor could she compare her parents' praxis with that of other people, since her contacts with the extra-familial world were effectively cut off. Although her parents were concerned because she had no friends, they were even more worried in case she was seduced if she did mix socially.

FATHER: Well one of the reasons why I personally was interested in her social life is not because I was prying into her private affairs; I was mainly interested in watching that she shouldn't be impressed by funny stories, by all sorts of—all and sundry— I realized she was a very sensitive young lady, very highly impressionable, and that she should not be impressed, to get wrong impressions. Because there are so many young men around with glib tongues and fancy themselves and able to get hold of a girl like Sarah and tell her all sorts of funny stories, and can lead to a lot of complications—that was the main reason why I was interested in her social standing and social life. But I wasn't interested to pry into her private affairs.

They did not forbid her to go out with boys, in fact they told her she should, but they watched her every move so closely that she felt she had no privacy at all, and when she objected, if they did not deny what they were doing, they reproached her for being ungrateful for their concern. She thus became muddled over whether or not it was right to want to go out with boys, or even to have any private life in the first place. Her father tried to investigate her boy-friends without her knowledge in various ways. As John explained.

JOHN: But I don't want you to get the impression that Dad hangs over like an eagle and tries to control Sarah's social life. Before she was ill he was always very careful about his intrusions into her private life, because he knew that if he did make an obviously nosey approach she would *flare* up, so therefore we tried to—very very carefully about her social life—the questions, if there were any, were always put by Mum, put in a sleeky way, sometimes or—(protest from Father about the word 'sneaky')—I didn't say 'sneaky' I said 'sleeky'—a silky sort of a way (Mother tries to calm Father, explaining John's statement to him). By sheer—by continuous nagging on Mummy's part —'give a name'—whether it was the right name or not, she gave a name—that satisfied her.

And while denying that he minded her going out to places where she would meet boys:

FATHER: But I understand, I fully understand a young lady and a young man enjoying themselves—they enjoy flirting or neck-ing what they call it, and young men, I understand that—I'm human—I was once young myself—I'm still young but—

her father implicitly forbade her to enter these places by uttering vague, ominous warnings about their dangers.

FATHER: I didn't say coffee bars generally—there can be certain coffee bars which are very dangerous to visit as well. I'm not particularizing *any* coffee bar, *any* restaurant, *any* dance-hall, or *any* place of amusement—I'm making a general statement how much I am concerned about *both* of you.

Although John could to a large extent see what was going on he failed to back Sarah in this matter, as in others. As we have seen, *he* defied his father's prohibitions and demands\ with his mother's help, but when similar demands were made of Sarah he sided with his father against her.

JOHN: From my point of view when it comes to *Sarah* it's not intrusion—when it comes to me it *is* intrusion.

In the face of this alliance Sarah gave up attempting to meet anyone outside her family.

Sarah at one point had become virtually catatonic, that is, she would not speak or respond to their approaches, or only compliantly. While she was in hospital this quietness and compliance were very noticeable. As we have noted, her family took this as a trick to deceive the doctor and get him to agree to her leaving. Her dilemma at this point appeared to be that if she talked about what she thought, she would have to remain in hospital, and if she remained silent her family would see this as deception, and would demand of the doctor that she be detained and 'treated' until she had the 'right' ideas. If she tried to impose the 'right' ideas on herself, then in a sense she would be killing herself. But even this would not save her from mental hospital, and from being cut off from her family, because then she would be 'dead', 'a shadow of herself', 'personalityless', to use her brother's description, and so would still need 'treatment'.

Sarah, they said, was obsessed with religion. For the past few years she had been continually reading the Bible, quoting from it, and trying to understand it. They did not believe she understood anything about it, however. According to them, it did not really mean much to her. She merely repeated it parrot-fashion. They suggested her interest in it was possibly due to guilt. It was 'a form of atonement by forced hardship', according to John.

There was deep confusion in this family about the nature of religion.

Mrs. Danzig's parents came from Eastern Europe. They were

Orthodox Jews, her father because he believed in Orthodoxy, her mother because she wanted to please him. Mrs. Danzig was an only child. She respected her father, and never did anything in front of him that she thought would upset him. Her parents had been strict with her, but not as strict as her husband's parents had been with him. Her father had been a diplomatic man and knew when to turn a blind eye towards minor infringements of Orthodox regulations.

For example, on the Sabbath it was forbidden to carry money, but in the summer, on the Sabbath, she used to go to town. Her father, as she left the house, tactfully refrained from asking where she was going, or how she was going to get there without carrying money for fares and meals and so forth. She in her turn acted tactfully towards him, and at home she abode strictly by the ritual regulations. Her father never left the house on the Sabbath except to go to Synagogue, while her mother stayed home.

According to Mrs. Danzig, her husband was very Orthodox. His father had been a Hebrew scholar. She did not object to his Orthodoxy. She knew about it when she married, and was happy to keep a kosher house 'because that's the way it should be'. It was the way her mother had done it.

'I do agree to a certain extent that if you're Jewish you keep to the Jewish religion. You *go* to Synagogue on Saturday, there's no harm in going to the Synagogue on Saturday, that's all right. I mean you can't run away from the fact that you're what you are.'

It is true that she disagreed with many of the Orthodox regulations, because they were inconvenient, but she complied with them to please her husband, as her mother had complied to please her father. For example, she now never went out on the Sabbath, and she never struck a light in front of her husband. Although, unlike her mother, she would do certain things such as striking a light if her husband was not present to see it, she would not upset him by doing it in front of him. It was her duty as a wife to comply in these matters, and show respect for her husband. If he wanted her to appear as an Orthodox Jewess, then she was prepared to appear in this way to him. And besides it was not worth having a row about. There were, however, certain areas that had nothing to do with a man: for example, the kitchen, where she tolerated no interference.

Mr. and Mrs. Danzig, although strictly religious, were, in their opinion, also fairly 'modern', for instance, in the matter of sex. Particularly was this so with Mrs. Danzig. She liked her daughter to go out with boys. It was the right thing to do. She did not even object to her daughter going out with a boy on the Sabbath, though Sarah herself regularly remained at home on that day trying to comply with her father and with ritual law.

'If she wants to go out with a fellow on a Saturday, I don't think it's such a terrible thing. She's not doing anything immoral. She's not doing anything very bad by going out with a girl or a fellow asks her to go out on a Saturday.'

In fact, Mrs. Danzig used to urge Sarah to go out and meet boys. It was good for her. It would help her to get over her self-consciousness.

'I often used to tell her, I said, "I think you ought to go out and meet boys and meet girls. You should go out more and get dates and get to know people and go somewhere else. You meet them if you already know somebody. If you've seen them before you can approach them. You feel you've seen them once before, you know them and it doesn't make you so shy."'

Of course the relationship must be of the right kind. In other words, it was not only all right to go out with the opposite sex, it was a social obligation for all normal girls; but naturally nothing sexual must enter into the relationship.

'Well I would have liked her to go out with boys. I think it's very normal for young girls to go out with the opposite sex, and I think it's the right thing that she should go out with the opposite sex, in the right way of course, to go out socially, yes.'

Her parents, however, secretly investigated the boys she went out with, and regarded it as their right to listen in on her telephone calls—without, of course, admitting to her that they did so.

Sarah had got into the habit of reading at night and sleeping in the morning. This was repeatedly referred to as 'laziness' by all members of the family. In fact, she slept rather less than they did, and they were trying to get her to take sleeping tablets to sleep more, and tranquillizers to 'think' less. For it was not only the fact that Sarah lay in bed that upset them, it was also the fact that she was thinking so much. As Mrs. Danzig said,

'Sitting up all night thinking and not telling anyone what she thought. Not that we particularly want to know what Sarah's thinking or doing, although it's only natural that a mother should be curious.'

Sarah's 'thinking' worried them all a great deal. Mrs. Danzig knew that 'thinking', especially a lot of 'thinking', was liable to make you have peculiar thoughts, because it 'turns the brain'.

' . . . sitting up all night in a blue nightdress in the kitchen—just the lights on, nobody making a sound. She's thinking and thinking—goodness knows what the heck she's thinking about. It's enough to twist anybody's mind.'

According to mother, father, and John, Sarah's breakdown was due to lying in bed 'thinking' instead of getting up and occupying herself and meeting people. No matter how her mother shouted at her she would not stop 'thinking', and to their greater alarm she thought inwardly, not out loud. She even pretended to put some beauty preparation on her legs as a pretext for staying up in her room and thinking. Mrs. Danzig reproached herself. She should have called in a psychiatrist sooner. They know how to handle such people.

'They could have knocked some sense into her. I should have called in a doctor, at that time, and said, "Look—she's upstairs, you talk to her". If she refused to listen to him—he's a medical man, he might give me another suggestion. It didn't *dawn* on me at the time that it was a psychiatric case, or whatever you call her.'

Her father tells us that he came into a room and he saw Sarah just standing looking out of the window. He asked her what she was thinking, and she said, 'I don't need to tell you'.

Sarah and her brother argued in front of us about 'thinking'. Sarah claimed that John 'thinks' also.

JOHN: Yes, but not like you do.

SARAH: Well, just yesterday I came into your bedroom and you were lying on your bed—thinking.

JOHN: No I wasn't.

SARAH: Yes you were.

JOHN: I was listening to the radio.

Reading the Bible was also a very doubtful activity, especially for a girl. Religion was one thing, but reading the Bible was another. The Bible was possibly all right to glance through, and perhaps, even, a religious person *should* do that; but to want to sit down and read it and make a fuss if it was missing from its usual place . . .

MOTHER: Well she couldn't find the Bible, raised havoc out of the bookcases—'Where is it?—That one's got it—this one's got it'—I said, 'Who wants to read your Bible?' I said, 'Is it normal for a girl to sit up all night and read the Bible all night?' I also think it's nice to read. I read. I might read a magazine or a book, but I've never read the Bible. I've never heard of it. If I saw another girl read the Bible, I would come home and say, 'That girl's got a kink somewhere'—Yes, know about it, look at it for five minutes—just a glance through; but you never make a study of the Bible. I could never sit down and read the Bible for two to three solid hours. I don't think she reads it. I think she just glances at the pages.

INTERVIEWER: I'm a little surprised at this, I had the impression that this is what your husband would like.

MOTHER: What, to read the Bible all night?—Oh no, Oh no, Oh no. He likes to get down to things. He thinks every girl should know, you know have natural accomplishments. I used to teach her music. She didn't want to practise—all right, we'll drop that. And now with television, they don't want to. And she used to play—all right, don't learn. He likes her to go out with boys. He likes her to mix, to go to socials, you know, like debates. She used to like to go to debates, they used to have special film shows, you know, interest—show it to a group of people—Oh he likes her to have an interest in all these sort of *normal* things. We used to go very often, the four of us, not Ruth, she was too young—go out at night to the cinema or to a theatre—the four of us, and we'd go out and have dinner. Oh he's not—I tell you—he's been brought up—his father was very religious, he was an officer of the Synagogue and a great Hebrew Talmudist . . .

Sarah's thinking and reading of the Bible evoked a mixture of alarm, concern, dismay, and disparagement. Her brother scorned her, her mother told her she was lazy, her father rebuked her. Yet they all felt that they were judged in some way by her. But it was not difficult for them not to take seriously the stumbling efforts of a girl to come to terms with her experience.

The fact that she read the Bible in an effort to throw light on her present experience was completely incomprehensible to this family. Accustomed to meet with ridicule and admonitions not to be lazy, selfish, or ungrateful, and so on, she either kept silent or gave out a short statement from time to time that only caused her family to lament the more the calamity that had befallen them.

Sarah had taken seriously what she had been taught, so that when she discovered the double standards of her family she was bewildered. She could not bring herself to accept her brother's openly avowed double standards, which were her father's also, but unavowed by him. Indeed, she *was not allowed to do so*. Her mother and father both felt that this was necessary for John, but they insisted that she adopt their point of view without reservation. But it was impossible to do this without adopting their particular stratagems, and this they forbade her to do.

We have presented above only a small fragment of our data on this family. In the rest of our data the mystifications around this girl are in no way attenuated. Once more, we have given, we hope, *enough* to establish the social intelligibility of the events in this family that have prompted the diagnosis of schizophrenia 'in' one of its members.

The Edens

CLINICAL PERSPECTIVE

When Ruby, aged seventeen, was admitted to hospital she was in an inaccessible catatonic stupor. At first she refused to eat, but gradually she was coaxed to do so. After a few days she began to talk.

She rambled in a vague and woolly way, often contradicting herself so that we could get no consistent story from her of her relationship with her family or with others. One moment she would say her mother loved her and the next that she was trying to poison her. She would say that her family disliked her and wanted to get rid of her and abandon her in hospital and then she would say that they were good and kind to her.

In clinical psychiatric terms there was shallowness of affect and incongruity of thought and affect. For example, sometimes when she spoke of her recent pregnancy and miscarriage she laughed while at other times she discussed it indifferently.

She complained of bangings in her head, and of voices outside her head calling her 'slut', 'dirty', 'prostitute'. She thought that 'people' disliked her and were talking disparagingly about her. She said she was the Virgin Mary and Cliff Richard's wife. She feared crowds and 'people'. When she was in a crowd she felt the ground would open up under her feet. At night 'people' were lying on top of her having sexual intercourse with her: she had

given birth to a rat after she was admitted to hospital: she believed
she saw herself on television.

It was clear that the fabric of this girl's 'sense of reality', of what
is the case and what is not the case, was in shreds.

The question is: Has what is usually called her 'sense of reality'
been torn in shreds by the others?

Is the way this girl acts, and are the things she says, intelligible
in terms of social praxis: or are they purely and simply the
unintelligible effluxion of pathological process?

This girl was confused particularly as to who she was—she
oscillated between the Virgin Mary and Cliff Richard's wife, and
she was confused as to whether or not her family and 'people'
generally loved her and in what sense—whether they liked the
person she was, or desired her sexually while despising her.

How socially intelligible are these areas of confusion and her
mode of communication?

STRUCTURE OF INVESTIGATION

Interviews	Occasions
Daughter (Ruby)	8
Mother	2
Aunt	1
Uncle	1
Mother, daughter	3
Aunt, daughter	1
Mother, aunt, daughter	2
Mother, uncle	1
Mother, uncle, cousin	1
Mother, uncle, aunt, cousin	1
Mother, aunt	1
	—
	22

This represents eighteen hours of interviewing time, of which eight are tape-recorded.

THE FAMILY SITUATION

In order to spare the reader the initial confusion of the investigators, not to say of this girl, we shall tabulate her family nexus.

Biological status	Titles Ruby was taught to use
Father	Uncle
Mother	Mummy
Aunt (mother's sister)	Mother
Uncle (mother's sister's husband)	Daddy—later Uncle
Cousin	Brother

For the sake of clarity the names of her biological relatives will be printed in roman type and the names by which she called them, and/or by which they referred to themselves, in italics.

Her mother and she lived with her mother's married sister, this sister's husband (*daddy* or uncle), and their son (her cousin). Her father (*uncle*) who was married, with another family elsewhere, visited them occasionally.

Her family violently disagreed about whether Ruby had grown up knowing who she was. Her mother (*mummy*) and her aunt (*mother*) strongly maintained that she had no inkling of the real state of affairs, but her cousin (*brother*) insisted that she must have known for years. They (mother, aunt, and uncle) argued also that no one in the district knew of this, but they admitted finally that, of course, everyone knew she was an illegitimate child, but no one would hold it against her. The most intricate splits and denials in her perception of herself and others were simultaneously expected of this girl and practised by the others.

She fell pregnant six months before admission to hospital and had a miscarriage at four months.

Like all these families, this one was haunted by the spectres of scandal and gossip, with what people were saying or thinking, and so on. Ruby's pregnancy intensified all this. Ruby thought people were talking about her, and her family knew that in fact they were, but when she told them about this they tried to reassure her by telling her not to be silly, not to imagine things, of course no one was talking about her.

This was just one of the many mystifications surrounding this girl.

Here are a few of the others.

In her distracted paranoid state she said that she thought her mother, aunt, uncle, and cousin disliked her, picked on her, mocked her, and despised her. As she got 'well' again, she felt very remorseful about having thought such terrible things, and said that her family had been 'really good' to her, and that she had a 'lovely family'.

They in fact gave her every reason to feel guilty for seeing them in this way, expressing dismay and horror that she should think that they did not love her.

They told us, however, with vehemence and intensity, that she was a slut and no better than a prostitute. They tried to make her feel bad or mad for perceiving their real feelings.

She guiltily suspected that they did not want her at home and accused them, in sudden outbursts, of wanting to get rid of her. They asked her how she could think such things. Yet they were extremely reluctant to have her at home. They tried to make her think they wanted her at home, and to make her feel mad or bad if she perceived that they did not want her home, when in fact they did not want her home.

Extraordinarily confused attitudes were brought into play when she became pregnant.

As soon as they could after hearing about it from Ruby, *mummy* and *mother* got her on the sitting-room divan, and while trying to pump hot soapy water into her uterus, told her with tears, reproaches, pityingly and vindictively at once, what a fool she was, what a slut she was, what a terrible mess she was in (just like her *mummy*), what a swine the boy was (just like her father), what a disgrace, history was repeating itself, how could one expect anything else . . .

This was the first time her true parentage had ever been explicitly made known to her.

Subsequently, Ruby's feeling that 'people' were talking about her disparagingly began to develop in earnest. As we have noted, she was told this was nonsense. They told us that everyone was 'very kind' to her 'considering'. Her cousin was the most honest. 'Yes, most people are kind to her, just as if she were coloured.'

The whole family was choked with its sense of shame and scandal. While emphasizing this to Ruby again and again, they told her that she was only imagining things when she thought that people were talking about her. Their lives began to revolve round her. They fussed over her and, at the same time, accused her of being spoiled and pampered. When she tried to reject their pampering they told her that she was ungrateful and that she needed them, she was still a child, and so on.

Ruby was made to feel both that she was mad and bad for thinking that her uncle did not love her, and that he wanted to get rid of her. She was repeatedly told by her mother and aunt how he would do anything for her. Her uncle certainly had intense feelings for her.

Her uncle was first of all represented by her mother and aunt to us as a very good uncle who loved Ruby and who was like a father to her. They assured us that he was willing to do anything he could to throw light on Ruby's problem.[1]

According to the testimony of her uncle, mother, and aunt, this girl had repeatedly been told by him that if she did not 'mend her ways' she would have to get out of the house. We know that on two occasions she was actually told by him to go,

---

[1] However, at no time was it possible to see him for a pre-arranged interview. Six mutually convenient appointments were made during the period of the investigation and every one was broken, and broken either without any notice at all, or at no more than twenty-four hours' notice. He was seen only once by us and that was when we called at his house without notice.

and she did. But when she said to him that he had told her to get out, he denied it to her though not to us! It was only when his wife and son would not back up his stories to us, although apparently they did in his stories to Ruby, that he admitted that he lost his temper with her, that he called her names when he was angry, but that he did not really mean it.

Her uncle told us tremblingly how she had pawed him, run her hands over his trousers, and how he was sickened by it. His wife said coolly that he did not give the impression of having been sickened at the time.

Ruby had apparently no idea that her uncle did not like being cuddled and petted. She thought he liked it—she did it to please him.

Not just in one area, but in all aspects of her life, in respect of her clothes, her speech, her work, her friends—this girl was subject to multiple mystifications.

The following summary of a home visit reveals some of them.

The family lives in a small working-class street where everyone knows everyone else.

First, mother was seen alone: she reported that things were all right, Ruby was very well and so on. There was no trouble.

Her uncle was then seen alone. He let out a flood of invective.

UNCLE: That girl—what I've done for her—her ingratitude. I've a good mind to turn her out. What is she doing? She's always swearing—the foul language is terrible.
INTERVIEWER: What does she say?
UNCLE: 'Bollocks' (mouthed)—because I tell her to stop stroking me. The language—I've no idea where she gets it from. She won't leave me in peace—she's always stroking me, just like that, pawing me. She knows it gets on my nerves, but she does it deliberately. I won't pamper her like her mother and aunt. She's got them running round her in circles. They give her everything, tea in bed, everything. She's been spoiled. She's been given everything. She thinks she can get away with

everything. If I pampered her she'd stop pawing me but I don't.

INTERVIEWER: Her mother says everything is all right.

UNCLE: Her mother says everything is all right?—I'll be frank, you can't take any notice of what she or her aunt say. She's always been spoiled and disobedient, contrary. Even when she was being toilet trained, for months they tried to sit her on the pot, but as soon as they let her off she'd go and do it somewhere else. I'll give you another example: when she was small I used to take her and my son out together. We'd get on a bus and I'd say, 'Come and sit here beside your dad', but not her. She'd go and sit on the other side, just to be awkward. Another thing she'd get away with was examinations. She'd never sit an examination, instead she'd go to bed the day before. She'd say she was ill and she'd vomit, to get out of the examination.

INTERVIEWER: What about her pregnancy?

UNCLE: The pregnancy? That was a shock to me. I nearly went grey overnight. It was the last thing I expected of her. I always said that she'd scratch out any man's eyes who tried that sort of thing on her. I used to take her photo to work—she used to be very pretty, she looks terrible now. I used to be proud of her looks. I'd take her photo to work and show it, and my mates would say: 'That's a fine bit of stuff there', and I'd say, 'Just watch it, she'd scratch out the eyes of any man that tried that sort of thing'. It was a terrible business. There's no excuse for it.

Mother and uncle were then seen together. We reported to mother what uncle had just said. She pitched into him.

MOTHER: It's not true she's spoiled. You're the one that's spoiled, you and Alistair. We're always doing things for you, Peggie and me. You're pampered more than she is.

Moreover, she accused him of being more nervy and tense than Ruby was. Uncle was quite taken aback by this and at a loss for words.

UNCLE: Mmmm . . . Me tense?—Not me, I've got nerves of steel. Yes, a bit edgy, maybe that's it—edgy (trembling all over).

We asked her mother about the issue of Ruby's stroking her uncle, an issue that so incensed him.

MOTHER: Stroking? Yes, she's always stroking her uncle. Very irritating but she doesn't mean any harm. She's always doing it to her dad. He was playful.
UNCLE: Yes, she used to stroke him and slap his leg. I've seen her slap his legs till they were red and he just sat there and laughed. He seemed to enjoy it. It irritates me. I'm not the playful type, not even with my son.
MOTHER: Oh but you play sometimes with me and Peggie. She's a good girl Ruby.

Uncle then brought up another issue.

UNCLE: Another thing that's very annoying, the way she knocks on the door. She doesn't just knock like an ordinary person. She bangs on it like that. Not like Alistair—he knocks.
MOTHER: Oh Alistair can bang too.

When the fighting over Ruby between her mother and uncle began to give way, another facet of their relationship was revealed as they began to develop an alliance.

MOTHER: Of course you know about my trouble. I had a bad time.
UNCLE: Yes, she's the one that's had the hard time, not Ruby.
MOTHER: Yes, my father wouldn't have anything to do with me, but I came here to stay with Peggie and Jim.
UNCLE: Yes, we stood by her.
MOTHER: I've a room here with my own furniture.

In this mood of alliance, mother accepts uncle's way of playing Alistair off against Ruby.

UNCLE: Alistair is the studious type. He's just passed another examination. He likes to sit down with a book—not Ruby.

MOTHER: No. She was never very good at school. She always says, 'I wish I was as clever as Alistair'. She used to get into a terrible state before examinations. She'd be ill. I went once to the headmaster and he said his daughter was the very same, but he said she (his daughter) had got to sit the examination even if she has to be dragged across the threshold. When Ruby was fifteen she was ill, terrified of the examination. She drank scent. You didn't know that did you?

UNCLE: No.

MOTHER: She says: 'I drank scent. What'll happen?' So I says, 'Don't worry, Ruby, come and wash your mouth out'. She was so frightened that time that she ran into the street. She had her jumper tied round her neck, and her knickers on and a coat over it. She ran into the street and then—she had no idea where she was going. A man brought her back.

We brought the conversation back to whether (as uncle had said) or not (as mother said) there had been 'trouble' with Ruby before we had arrived.

MOTHER: Trouble with Ruby tonight? No.

UNCLE: Oh you weren't there at the time. She was starting with Alistair while we were trying to watch the TV. He doesn't mind it so much as me, but it makes him annoyed. Sometimes he does it back and they have a game.

We were then joined by her cousin.

Her uncle (his father) immediately asked for corroboration from Alistair, on his view that Ruby stroked him against his wishes, and was spoiled.

COUSIN: She starts on you, stroking you when you want to do something else.

UNCLE: Yes, and she's always asking questions.

COUSIN: Yes, she expects to know all sorts of things about the characters in the play—his name, his occupation, his religion, and so on. The stroking, it gets on my nerves, it's not entirely her fault, but she knows it gets on my nerves and she shouldn't do it.

UNCLE: Yes that's right.

COUSIN: She's pampered, spoiled. She's given too much her own way.

UNCLE: What did I say?

At this point, with an apparently firm alliance between uncle and cousin in full swing, and mother looking decidedly crushed, we were joined by Ruby's aunt (uncle's wife, mother's sister, cousin's mother, alias *mother*).

Alistair began to become more expansive, and to get somewhat out of hand. He started to develop criticisms of the ways Ruby was handled by his mother and aunt, which in a curious way, they agreed with.

COUSIN: She should be left to do things for herself. She's indecisive. She's not allowed to make a decision. It's put on her plate for her. If she's not allowed to make a decision in small things she won't learn to make them in big things.

AUNT: Yes, she won't make any decision. Do you remember when she left that job? I thought she should do this, and you thought she should do that?

MOTHER: Yes, I thought she should do that, but you were right, Peggie.

AUNT: Yes, so I told her but she wouldn't do it. I couldn't get her across the doorstep.

UNCLE: That's right. She expects others to do it for her.

COUSIN: She won't sit any examinations. She gets ill before examinations. She won't take a decision.

AUNT: Yes after the examination she's able to do the things all right. Do you remember her dancing? Mrs. Smith said, 'Isn't that funny, she wouldn't do the examination, and yet she's doing it lovely now'. That time she couldn't write for the exam, but afterwards she wrote and wrote all things that she should have written.

UNCLE: No, I couldn't have expressed myself properly. She doesn't put it on being ill before the examination. She works herself up to a pitch so she's ill. Oh I wouldn't say she did it deliberately.

We asked Alistair whether he thought Ruby was made a 'favourite'.

COUSIN: Favouritism? I think she felt I was being favoured. Well I'll be frank. I think it's fair to say I was the apple of my grand-mother's eye and I think Ruby felt it.

UNCLE: I treated them equal, no difference.

AUNT: What one got the other got.

MOTHER: Yes.

We asked how he felt about her pregnancy.

COUSIN: Pregnancy? I've got nothing against her for that. It could happen to anybody, nice people, respectable people, one of my friends. No, it wasn't being pregnant, it was her attitude—casual, couldn't care less—that shocked me.

UNCLE: Yes.

MOTHER: It was a shock. I'd just had a letter from her father and I said, 'Ruby, I've got a shock for you', and she said 'I've got one for you, I'm in trouble'—Oh it was terrible.

AUNT: Yes I was there. I said, 'Don't joke, Ruby, it's serious, how can you say that at a time like this?' And she said, 'I'm not joking'. What a shock. We rushed her off to the doctor to make sure.

UNCLE: Yes I took her. We had to know.

MOTHER: Yes.

COUSIN: I wasn't surprised. My cousin Edith was at that party and a couple of days after she said to me, 'You should have seen Ruby'. I hushed her up because there was someone else there at the time. I didn't tell anyone because I didn't know if it was true. Edith's a trouble-maker. But as I say it could happen to anyone, but it was her attitude.

The chap wasn't up to much. He was as much to blame. He came round and said he would marry her but he asked us not to tell his father. I believe he knocked her around too.

MOTHER: Yes, she used to show me the bruises.

UNCLE: He was a bad one.

MOTHER: But she said she liked him for all that.

AUNT: It's often like that. They treat them badly, and they're still liked.

UNCLE: Yes.

We asked about the neighbours—one of the most important issues to clarify—since much of Ruby's 'illness' was her supposed delusions of reference that 'the whole district' knew about her, talked about her, and pretended to her they did not.

MOTHER: Neighbours, no. Nobody said anything.

AUNT: Yes the neighbours are so helpful. They're so sweet. Mrs. Smith says, 'No need to leave Ruby alone, I'll always look after her for you'. We talked over about a job for Ruby. We're a close community here, everyone helps everyone else. They are so kind to her. They're all interested in her welfare. No one has said a word to her about it or going into hospital, not a word, there's no gossip. I don't know why Ruby should think the neighbours are talking about her.

UNCLE: No.

MOTHER: No.

AUNT: Ruby once asked if I thought the neighbours talked about her, if they knew she was in hospital, and I said, 'Of course not'. Ruby is the one who can't keep things to herself. She'll tell everyone her business, but she will do it.

MOTHER: Yes.

UNCLE: Yes.

AUNT: Remember that time she was going on a visit to Auntie Joan. She went to the hairdresser and told the hairdresser, and the next I heard from Mrs. Williams—'I heard Ruby's gone to her Auntie Joan'—No she won't keep anything to herself. But the neighbours don't gossip. They're so sweet. Whenever she comes home on leave from the hospital, they greet her, 'Hello Ruby, home again?'—Nobody's ever been unkind to her.

COUSIN: They don't talk in front of her. They're sweet to her, but they talk about her all right in private. It's like a coloured person coming to stay here. Nobody will say a word against her to her face, but they'll have plenty to say when she's not there. They talk about her all right.

Firmly within this situation of contradictory attributions, inconsistencies, multiple disagreements, some avowed, some not, not able as we are to see it from outside as a whole, Ruby could not tell what was the case and what was not the case, she could not have a consistent perspective on her relation to herself, or to others, or on theirs to each other, or to her.

FAMILY 6

The Fields

CLINICAL PERSPECTIVE

June Field, aged fifteen, was admitted to hospital in a catatonic stupor. She was said to have shown no mental symptoms until six months earlier when her personality had begun to change. She had become rude and aggressive at home and had given up her old interests. She no longer played games or went to church or mixed with people, not even going out with her best friend. Three days before admission she had begun to sleep badly and had become increasingly agitated, complaining that voices threatened her, telling her that she had destroyed the world. In hospital she lay rigidly in bed refusing food and remaining mute. When asked about herself she simply looked suspiciously at the questioner. The most pressing nursing problem was her refusal to eat, and it was arranged that her mother should come to feed her. This worked well, and within a week she was feeding herself and had begun to talk. From the clinical point of view she showed such features as withdrawal from external reality, rigidity of posture and movement, thought-disorder (vagueness, thought-blocking), affective flattening, incongruity of thought and affect, and bizarre delusions, e.g. that she was being poisoned, that she was liable to be tortured, that her parents were dead, that she had destroyed the world, that she had harmed people who had died for her.

Her family consisted of her father, mother, June (fifteen), her sister Sylvia (aged nineteen), and a grandfather who was too old to be interviewed.

Interviews	Occasions
Daughter	14
Mother	11
Father	1
Sister	1
Daughter, mother	4
Daughter, father	1
Daughter, sister	1
Father, mother, daughter	3
Mother, sister	1
	37

This represents twenty-eight hours' interviewing time, of which sixteen hours were tape-recorded.

Our data on this case cover the following phases in June's life

Phase	Evidence
1. From birth until the summer before admission when her mother first felt that June was becoming ill.	Anamnesis by mother, father, sister, June, headmistress.
2. From the summer until June was admitted to hospital six months later clearly in a psychotic state.	Family Headmistress Two General Practitioners

Phase	Evidence
3. Four weeks when June was in the middle of her breakdown.	
	Period
4. Three to four months. Phase of recovery, during which she went through a hypomanic period.	of
	Investigation
5. The present. Period of complete clinical recovery.	

THE FAMILY SITUATION

Phase I

The factual parts of the following are unanimously corroborated by mother, father, June, and Sylvia. Her parents see the first fourteen years of June's life in the same way. This is not, however, the case in phase II when her mother saw June as becoming ill and her father did not. Sylvia, who makes no attempt to conceal her dislike of June, remembers nothing of the events of June's first ten years.

INTERVIEWER: Could you give us some sort of picture of what the circumstances of June's childhood have been, what your family has been.

MOTHER: Yes, I will. Well June was born—she was a lovely baby, she weighed nearly 12 lb. And when she was nearly two we discovered she had congenital dislocation of the hip. She went to hospital under Mr. Green and she was put into a butterfly plaster for two years, it was altered accordingly, every three months I used to take her, and then after two years Mr. Green had her walking—em splint you know, I forget the name of it now—however that doesn't matter. Her left foot was—her left side is the affected side, was the affected side, and she had a piece of steel on her shoe, and the iron for the right leg made accordingly and she walked with that for two years because of her weight. However she was very happy, she very quickly learnt to walk in this iron. As I say, she's always been a wonderfully happy child, and she's given us a great deal of pleasure. And then she went to school but of course she couldn't sit with the other children at school because she was rather a big child and also she couldn't get her legs under the table (slight laugh) with this iron you see, and she wore that until she was six. Then Mr. Green said she could come out of it and just learn to walk gradually which she did. I used to take her about of course. She's *always* been with me, I took her with me, I never left her. And she learned—she had a tricycle after she came out of irons, I asked Mr. Green if that would help her, you know, because this left leg was rather wasted, but you see it's not wasted at all now, she rides a cycle, she rides to school, she can swim, play games. And we live quite happily together, all of us. I have another daughter, Sylvia, who is nineteen, we have Grandad who is ninety-three, that's my husband's father—he's a jolly old man and a very fine old man. Then there's my husband who is rather quiet and retiring, and myself. And I'm at home all day. June always comes home to her dinner, has it with Grandad and myself. My husband and Sylvia come in the evening, home to dinner from work.

INTERVIEWER: This would mean of course that June is—partly because of this congenital hip—that is, that her childhood would be a very different affair from Sylvia's, wouldn't it?

MOTHER: Oh very different doctor, because, well, she didn't walk, you see. You see I pushed June around for four years. You see when she first had the iron Mr. Green said, 'Well June will learn to walk now'. Well each morning at nine o'clock I used to take her near to the park, I'd push her in a push-chair and then take her to the railing, hold one of her hands you see and she would gradually learn to walk. She learned to walk very quickly, very quickly alone. It was exactly five weeks when she had mastered them and could really go on her own. And then she walked a little way, not too far because she would say she had enough. Well as soon as June said she had enough I'd put her back in the push-chair. I didn't want to tax her naturally.

INTERVIEWER: So this would mean I expect that she would have, of course, a much closer bond with you—

MOTHER: Oh yes, she was *always* with me, always. Well naturally I wouldn't leave her because of her irons in case she fell or anything. She did fall as a matter of fact, she knocked her front teeth out. But she played with the other children too you see—there was Billy, my nephew, and of course there was Sylvia, I know Sylvia was older but we all used to take June out because I always took her everywhere with me, always. Naturally I would. I didn't ever leave her. You see when June was in plaster I didn't put her on the ground because the plaster would have been very quickly worn out (smiling). I put her on the bed, you see, like that (demonstrates)—and then I had—she had a good leather straps on because she's always been a very strong child and I had a dog-lead there and a dog-lead there, then June could move freely up and down and across, not very far, but always up and down. And she jumped on this bed *so* hard that (laughing) in a matter of two years all the springs had gone. She wasn't there all the time because as I say I always took her out with me. And then we used to put her in the garden and I put her on the ground in the garden under the trees if it was summer time, on the rug you see, and I tied her to the tree which meant that June could get all round the tree but not on the concrete. Because the plaster's—well they're not so terribly strong, you know what friction is on concrete, they very quickly go through. And you see there was this bar between, it was a butterfly plaster and each time it extended more. And once she got it off, of course June used to get hold of this plaster you see, this bar, and really almost rock herself on it, she could do, quite easily. And early one morning she got it out, I had to take her back to hospital to have another

one put in. As I say, she was always a very boisterous child, she's always been such a happy little girl—haven't you June?
JUNE: Mmm.
MOTHER: Yes you have dear.

Mrs. Field's story was told in a cheerful brisk manner. As much is revealed in the manner of telling as in the remarkable content. One notes the absence of Mr. Field as an effective figure in Mrs. Field's world. The first person she consulted when she suspected something wrong with June's leg was her sister. Her husband was only told after June had already been taken to hospital. This is characteristic. It is noteworthy too that Mrs. Field denies not only her own unhappiness, but June's misery. This also is characteristic.

In all the discussions about June's childhood Mrs. Field never varies her attributions about her—she was a lovely baby, a very happy child, boisterous and affectionate (the latter attribution does not happen to be made in the two extracts quoted above, but is made frequently elsewhere).

Not only does Mrs. Field never express one word to the effect that June might have been a painful sight at times to her mother, as well as 'lovely'; unhappy, wretched, miserable perhaps, as well as very happy; quiet as well as boisterous; and not necessarily always affectionate, but her repertoire of positive attributions never varies. This picture of June up to the age of fourteen is held with certitude and with rigidity, and is surely an extraordinarily constricted view of any human being. It is impervious to direct confrontations from June to the contrary. Powerful pressure is put on June to accept this picture as her own, and attacks are made on her life if she dissents. It is timeless. As Mrs. Field says repeatedly: 'That isn't my June. I can't understand June now. She was always a very happy child. She was always a very boisterous child.'[1]

---

[1] It is a curious feature of psychiatric theory that a person who holds such a view in such a manner about his own person would be regarded as hypomanic, but if the person holds it about another person and attempts to fit the other into that mould Procrustean-fashion, there is no term in general currency to describe him or her. We have clinical terms for disturbed, but not for *disturbing* persons.

Throughout the investigation, Mrs. Field had only two views of June, with one brief exception (see p. 145, when she saw her as 'evil'). June was either 'my June' (happy, affectionate, boisterous), or she was ill.

This brings us to phase II.

Phase II

In the summer before the winter of her admission, June was separated from her mother for the first time since admission to hospital for six weeks at the age of two, for her hip condition. This was when she went to a girls' camp run by the Church. Alone of all the girls' mothers, Mrs. Field accompanied June to the camp. During the month she was away, she made a number of discoveries about herself and others and unhappily fell out with her best friend. She became aware of herself sexually with much greater force than before.

In her mother's view, when she came back from camp she was 'not my June. I did not know her'.

The following is a list of June's qualities before and after her separation from her mother, as described by Mrs. Field.

Before	After
a lovely girl	looked hideous
	put on terrible make-up
	had got fat
a very happy girl	was unhappy
boisterous	withdrawn
always told me everything	wouldn't tell me her thoughts
would sit in room at night with mother, father, and grandad	went to her own room
used to love to play cards with mother, father, and grandad	preferred to read, or played, but without spirit

Before	After
worked too hard at school	worked less hard—didn't work hard enough
was always obedient	became truculent and insolent (e.g. called mother a liar on one occasion)
was well-mannered	gobbled her food wouldn't wait at table until everyone was finished
believed in God	said she didn't believe in God; said she has lost faith in human nature
was good	looked at times evil

Her mother was very alarmed at these changes and between August and December had consulted two doctors and her head-mistress about her. None of these other people saw anything abnormal in June, nor did her sister or her father. However, Mrs. Field could not leave her alone.

It is important to realize that Mrs. Field's picture of June was, of course, never true. June's whole life was totally unknown to her mother. She felt shy, self-conscious, unsure of herself, but was big for her age and active in swimming and other sports that she had undertaken to master her prolonged childhood crippled condition (she was not finally out of calipers until she was ten years old). Although active, she was not independent for, as she told us, she had largely complied with her mother, and had seldom dared to contradict her. She did however begin to go out with boys when she was thirteen while pretending to be at Church Club.

When she came back from camp, she began for the first time to give some expression to how she really felt about herself, her mother, her school work, God, other people, and so on, by ordinary standards, to a very subdued extent indeed.

This change was actively welcomed by her schoolteachers, was regarded with a certain amount of ordinary sisterly cattiness by Sylvia, and seemed part of the upset of having a daughter to her father. Only her mother saw it as an expression of *illness*, and felt confirmed in this opinion when June began to become more withdrawn at home over the Christmas vacation and thereafter.

The view held by her mother as to the events leading to June's state of almost complete immobile passivity can be put as follows: June was becoming ill from August onwards. She underwent insidious changes in her personality, becoming rude, aggressive, truculent, and insolent at home, while at school she became withdrawn and self-conscious. According to this view, a mother knows her own daughter best, and she may detect the beginnings of schizophrenia before others (father, sister, teachers, doctors).

Phase III
The phase in which June was clinically catatonic and in which her mother nursed her like an infant lasted three weeks, and was the most harmonious phase directly observed by us in their relationship.

Conflict only began when June, from our point of view, began to recover.

Phase IV
In the period of recovery, almost every advance made by June (in the viewpoint of nursing staff, psychiatric social worker, occupational therapists, and ourselves) was opposed vehemently by her mother, who consistently regarded as steps back what to us and to June were steps forward.

Here are a few examples.

June began to take some initiative. Her mother expressed great alarm at any such show either on the grounds that June was irresponsible, or that it was not like June to do anything without asking. It was not that there was anything wrong in what June did, it was that she did not ask permission first.

INTERVIEWER: What do you perceive as being wrong with June this weekend?

MOTHER: Well on Saturday for instance, June wanted to go to the Youth Club—well she went down to the Youth Club and that was all right, I didn't mind her going. Well I went in to attend to Grandad, and then I saw June coming down the road with two boys from up the road, she had no coat on— June has a shocking cold in her head this weekend and you know how cold it was on Saturday—and so I went and called after her of course and asked her where she was going and she was going with Eric to the—to a dance at the Church Hall. Well I knew *nothing* about it at all.

JUNE: (voice raised) Well *I* didn't until I went and called round.

MOTHER: Yes I know, but I would expect you June to *come and say* where you were going.

JUNE: Well I'd have been back at the same time as I'd come back from the ordinary Youth Club, so I didn't see any reason for—

MOTHER: You wouldn't have come back at all.

JUNE: (indignant) I *would* have done!

MOTHER: June you would *not*. You couldn't possibly come back from the dance in the time that you usually come back.

JUNE: Well I don't know. I was home at nine o'clock from the other place.

MOTHER: And in any case you had no money to go to the dance or anything—

JUNE: Well Eric would have lent me some, it would have been all right.

FATHER: There you are you see—

MOTHER: There you are you see, how do you know that Eric even wanted to take you there?

JUNE: Well—

MOTHER: You went to his house, June went to his house—hunt him out—

JUNE: Well he was going to come any rate because he always comes on Saturdays.

MOTHER: Yes, but he didn't go to the Youth Club, he went up to the Church Hall.

JUNE: (angrily) Yes I *know*—you don't have to tell me that a thousand times.

MOTHER: What's where I feel—you see I wouldn't have known where June was.

JUNE: Well I'd have come home at the same time as I would have come home from the Youth Club so I didn't see the need to tell her.

MOTHER: And in any case June—when you feel tired you know yourself, you just drop off to sleep—don't you?

JUNE: Mmm.

MOTHER: You just go. Well I couldn't have you going, falling asleep—

JUNE: (simultaneously, inaudible) . . . well I wouldn't go falling asleep at the dance would I? What are you talking about?

MOTHER: Well I don't know what you'd have done, I only know that you fall asleep at home, you just go dead asleep—look at last weekend—you slept all Friday afternoon, all Saturday afternoon and all night, Sunday afternoon, and on Monday you were perfectly all right. You see *I* don't know whether you're going to drop off to sleep.

JUNE: Well I wouldn't have done at the dance. I felt perfectly all right—

FATHER: Yes but—

MOTHER: And in any case on Saturday you *wanted* to go to bed didn't you and I said, 'Oh let's go for a walk first and then you can go to bed', and then you decided to go to the Youth Club. Well that's perfectly all right, I don't mind June going providing I *know* where she is.

Mother saw June at the hospital gate with a young male patient called Robin.

MOTHER: Well—for instance tonight June at the gate with Robin, well that's all right, arm in arm—not arm in arm—June takes Robin's arm, Robin doesn't take hers (laughs heartily)—and he was just as anxious for June to come with us.

JUNE: He half dragged me there, didn't he?

MOTHER: Yes, well he could see that it was right that you should come. I think it's very nice of him to take care of you—like that.

JUNE: He can take care of himself and I can take care of myself.

MOTHER: Can you!

Characteristically, it is difficult to pin Mrs. Field down when she raises issues more by implication than directly.

The interviewers commented on her concern about Robin.

INTERVIEWER: I think Mrs. Field feels that June is at the moment inclined to be a bit forward with boys and that boys might take advantage of her, I think this is very much—

JUNE: No I don't think they would, I don't think Robin would.

INTERVIEWER: No, this is what your parents feel and June feels that—

JUNE: Well it is because Robin's never been unfair to me in any way. He's always been nice to me and I've always been nice to him; but I don't see what they've got to moan about. I think it's quite—

MOTHER: We're not *moaning* June, we are *concerned*.

JUNE: Well I don't see why you *are* concerned because, I mean, it seems stupid to me, I mean I'm all right and Robin's all right with me.

FATHER: Yes but you see June, if you were with boys of your own age—

JUNE: Well he's nineteen, that's all right.

FATHER: —but that's older than you isn't it?

JUNE: Yes, well why can't I go out with boys older than me? I don't want to go out with boys of my own age.

FATHER: Well I used to when I was a boy.

JUNE: Well I *know* but it's different these days.

INTERVIEWER: You're afraid that Robin will take advantage of June?

MOTHER: Oh no I'm not, no, because I've seen Robin and talked to him and really he seems a very nice boy.

JUNE: He is.

MOTHER: A very nice boy indeed. No it isn't that, Robin isn't the only one. I mean for June just to go off to town with another man—Jack or whoever—Tom, Dick, or Harry or whoever he is, I don't know who he is (pause)—How do I know that he can be responsible for her?

A little later her mother complained about another boy because he was too young for June, and was not responsible enough.

Another example her mother gave that alarmed her was how June ate a threepenny bar of chocolate after breakfast, once more without asking.

MOTHER: And then in the morning you see I sent June to get Grandad some razor blades. Well I gave her two shillings, the shop is only round the corner, just on the corner there, and um, June had had a good breakfast, she'd had two pieces of bacon and an egg and bread and butter and marmalade and her coffee and then after breakfast I asked her to go and get the razor blades and she was quite willing to get them—and she did. *But* she had to spend some of that money on a bar of chocolate and scoff it, you see. Well previous—the week before I had said to June, 'Now June when you take—when I give you money to get a thing, I only want that article, I don't want you to go and get yourself a bar of chocolate without *asking*'. And of course she came in the house and she (slight laugh) shot upstairs to her money box and got out the threepence she'd spent on the bar

of chocolate you see and put the change back in my hand—
there you are! But that isn't June at all.

Mother and father occasionally approach some moment of
truth, but it is never consolidated. In the following passage they
recognize transiently that they have cast June into a rigid role she
is trying to burst out of, and that they are fighting a losing battle.

FATHER: Sylvia's not affectionate—
MOTHER: She doesn't show it.
FATHER: She hasn't shown any affection for years—now June is—
MOTHER: Oh she's the most loving child—and you could really
love June couldn't you.
FATHER: —but not from Sylvia—we've never expected it from
Sylvia.
INTERVIEWER: No, Sylvia's more reserved isn't she?
MOTHER: She's more refined than June really.
INTERVIEWER: Why do you think she doesn't show any affection?
FATHER: (smiling) Well she never wants to be kissed or anything
like that, Sylvia.
MOTHER: (smiling) No. Not Sylvia. Well June doesn't now.
FATHER: Not now.
MOTHER: Oh, she said to me, 'I'm not going to kiss you' (laughing).
But June has been a very affectionate child.
FATHER: Oh yes.
MOTHER: (sadly) But there, of course, she's not a child any longer.

June was allowed no pocket money by her parents, but was told
that they would give her money if she explained why she wanted
it. Not surprisingly, she preferred to borrow small sums from
others. The smallest amount in her possession had to be accounted
for.

This control was taken to extraordinary lengths. Once June
helped herself to sixpence from her father's money-box to buy
ice-cream, without asking him. He told her mother that if June
was stealing she was lost to him. Another time she had found a

shilling in a cinema and her parents insisted that she should hand it in at the desk. June said that this was ridiculous and taking honesty too far as she herself would not expect to get a shilling back if she lost it. But her parents kept on about it all the next day and late that evening her father came into her bedroom once again to admonish her.

The above examples can be multiplied many times over. They epitomize the intense reactions of her parents to June's emergent, but brittle, autonomy. Mrs. Field's term for this growing independence was 'an explosion'.

Phase V

So far June has held her own. Her mother continues to express herself in extremely ambivalent terms over evidences of June's greater independence. She tells her she looks hideous when wearing ordinary make-up, she actively ridicules her expectancy that any boy is interested in her, she treats any expressions of irritation or exasperation on June's part as symptoms of the 'illness', or construes them as tokens of 'evil'.

June, however, appears to be coping. She can see that her mother is opposed to her independence—she regards her mother as a 'terrible exaggerator', she keeps certain secrets tactfully from her, she feels entitled to her own privacy, she is much less often mystified into expressing gratitude by fitting her mother's preconceptions, she realizes that her mother does not understand her, and she is not too frightened at perceiving this. She has a certain understanding of why her mother and father are as they are, and why they need to see her in the way they do. She has to keep a tight control on herself however because if she shouts, screams, cries, swears, eats too little, or eats too much, eats too fast, or eats too slowly, reads too much, sleeps too much or too little, her mother tells her that she is ill. It takes a lot of courage on June's part to take the risk of not being what her parents call 'well'.

FAMILY 7

The Golds

CLINICAL PERSPECTIVE

At the time our investigation began Ruth was twenty-eight. Since the age of twenty she has been hospitalized six times and has spent most of these years as an in-patient. During the first eighteen months of her patient career the diagnosis fluctuated between hysteria and schizophrenia but it finally firmed into schizophrenia, and this has since been the unanimous diagnosis of different psychiatrists of differing orientations in different hospitals.

Her symptoms over the years had varied somewhat, but she had been persistently described as paranoid, subject to feelings of unreality, and subject to schizophrenic thought-disorder. On some occasions she was said to have been suicidal and depressed on others both suicidal and over-excited, silly and giggly.

As frequently happens with someone who comes to be regarded as a 'long-standing schizophrenic', whether in and out of hospital or chronically hospitalized, reports tend to become more stereotyped and succinct as time goes on.

STRUCTURE OF INVESTIGATION

Ruth lived with her parents when not in hospital, and had a brother of thirty-two, who had left home when she was fourteen.

Her father said he agreed with everything his wife had to say and refused to be interviewed except in the presence of his wife.

Interviews	Occasions
Ruth	6
Mother	2
Brother	1
Ruth and mother	1
Mother and father	2
Mother, father, and Ruth	1
	13

This represents sixteen hours of interviewing time, of which thirteen hours were tape-recorded.

THE FAMILY SITUATION

Mr. and Mrs. Gold share the same point of view on the course of Ruth's life. Their account appeared to be simple and uncomplicated, at first. As the picture unfolds, however, we shall see that the 'identity' Ruth has for them has the simplicity of a Procrustean bed. One might speak here of a *Procrustean identity*.

According to them her 'breakdown' occurred suddenly and unaccountably. Until that moment Ruth had been a normal happy child and had never been a trouble.

INTERVIEWER: Did she ever play the game with you when she was very young of throwing things over the side of the cot or the pram and you'd pick them up?

MOTHER: No, can't remember that—can't remember her doing anything like that, no.

INTERVIEWER: And her toilet training, when she was dry—out of nappies—when was she out of nappies?

MOTHER: I suppose at the age of two. She was very good in *all* ways, she wasn't difficult. And when she had childish ailments

they were always very mild. I remember when she and my son
—they both had tonsilitis together and *she* recovered very
quickly.

Father entirely concurs:

INTERVIEWER: Your wife has described her relationship with Ruth
in the early days as very close. How would you describe *your*
relationship with her?

FATHER: Well, not so close as my wife. Naturally a girl and her
mother—but I was always caring for what was happening—

MOTHER: A very considerate child always.

FATHER: She was, yes.

MOTHER: A very respectful child and never a moment's anxiety
with her.

And again:

FATHER: She was a·*very* good child.

INTERVIEWER: It was all pretty uneventful?

FATHER: Uneventful, exactly.

MOTHER: Yes.

And:

INTERVIEWER: You said that Ruth was a very easily brought up
child.

MOTHER: A very easy child to bring up. A very thoughtful child,
very considerate, never had a minute's anxiety with her. She
had tantrums occasionally as a child—um—if she was upset
you know, she'd come in and cry and run up to bed, lie on the
bed for a minute or two and scream and cry and come down
and it was all over.

INTERVIEWER: Would you say she was an affectionate child?

MOTHER: Very. Very.

INTERVIEWER: Was she close to you, or to your husband?

MOTHER: Very close to me, *very* close to me.

INTERVIEWER: More to you than your husband would you say?

MOTHER: I think so, yes, yes.

Thus as a child she is described in the above passages as very good, not difficult, very considerate, very respectful, causing no anxiety, easy to bring up, very thoughtful, if she had tantrums they were over in a minute or two, very affectionate and very close to her mother.

She 'conformed' completely, they say approvingly.

Then when she was twenty she inexplicably became depressed, and complained of feeling 'unreal'. Her behaviour became 'uncontrollable', and since then she has been 'ill' again and again, although between 'attacks' she can still be her old self. That is, very good, not difficult, very considerate and so on.

Let us examine more closely what her parents mean by her illness.

To her mother and father, and also her brother, the principal signs of Ruth's 'illness' are her abuse and resentment at her parents, and uncontrollable behaviour.

MOTHER: She's very abusive at times and not—she doesn't resent us nearly so much now as she did earlier in her illness.

INTERVIEWER: When was that?

MOTHER: Well you know she's been ill for many years now and she used to say it's our fault, we want her put away in hospital and it's because of us that she's ill and she used to hit out occasionally, you know, but she doesn't blame us so much for it now.

INTERVIEWER: How do you account for this blaming it on you? How do you account for this?

MOTHER: Well I just—I don't account for it at all, I just, I realize that she's ill and disturbed and doesn't know what she's saying.

INTERVIEWER: Do you know what she means when she—

MOTHER: Because she has hit out at us, you know, and the minute after she's done it she apologizes—'Oh I'm sorry, Mummy, I didn't mean it, I didn't mean it'.

We shall return to this when we consider the situation from Ruth's point of view. We may note at present that in eight years the assumption that her 'abuse and resentment' of her parents and her uncontrollable behaviour were due to illness has been made not only by her family, but by the psychiatrists who had 'treated' her for this 'condition', and had never been called in question, as far as we could gather, by anyone.

When she was 'ill', she also dressed 'strangely' and tried to 'ape' her brother who is a writer.

INTERVIEWER: Would you say Ruth conformed all right?
MOTHER: Yes, yes.
INTERVIEWER: There was no difficulty there?
MOTHER: Not at all. It's only during her illness, you know, when she becomes ill. She dresses strangely, tries to ape the writers.

Her brother realized, as he put it, that his parents were very 'limited people'. He had 'made a break for it'. They had accommodated themselves to some extent to his 'artistic' pursuits, but they could not see any validity whatever in Ruth's propensities in that direction. Their attitude to things 'artistic'—literary, visual, or musical—is exemplified in the following passage.

MOTHER: I was taught to play the piano—*forced* to practise, which I hated, and studied it for many many years, used to go to concerts with my music teacher and *loathed* it all the time.
FATHER: Well I think a person who can play an instrument—it's like a man who learns a trade—whereas an artist is very abstract.
MOTHER: It's precarious, I mean, art today.
FATHER: It's so *precarious*.

And as for painting,

FATHER: I suppose you've noticed me looking at that picture, but I wouldn't care two hoots for the finest picture in the world. But my son has, you know, if you live with someone who comes occasionally to you and—you get the gist of what they're talking about and that's why I'm a little bit interested.

So when Ruth is 'ill' she dresses 'strangely' and 'apes' her brother.

INTERVIEWER: What is there about what she says and does that makes you think of her or see her as being ill?

MOTHER: I know in a moment when she's having an attack—when it starts.

INTERVIEWER: Yes, can you tell me what it is you see her saying or doing, or what it is about her behaviour?

MOTHER: Well it's just odd—it isn't right. She doesn't dress properly either. She puts on the weirdest clothes she can find when she's got an attack.

INTERVIEWER: But is she doing—say she brought home one of these young men—is she dressed like that, is she looking odd at that time?

MOTHER: Yes. It's happened in the past when she's had an attack. It hasn't happened for a long time.

INTERVIEWER: What kind of dress—could you describe it?

MOTHER: Yes, well she used to find coloured stockings and put on all sorts of peculiar things that she wouldn't normally wear. It isn't her.

Ruth exhibited other 'uncontrollable' behaviour, as we shall see, but it is not possible to develop our account further without beginning to note certain specific contradictory and highly significant attributions that her mother and father make directly to Ruth.

Her mother tells us that before Ruth became 'ill' she used to have many friends and go to socials and clubs, but now—

INTERVIEWER: Is she not having any social life at all?

MOTHER: Not really. She mixes with older people, she has one girl-friend—they go out—she goes out very occasionally with this one girl-friend.

INTERVIEWER: But she doesn't mix on the whole with young people?

MOTHER: No—but I would like her to lead a normal active life, also to mix more than she does now. She seems to have lost all her friends since she's been ill; she has no social life at all; she used to read a lot—she doesn't read at all these days; she's not able to concentrate. I'd like her to mix with young people more.

Her absence of social life, her withdrawal, appears to be an unwitting invention of her parents that never seems to have been called into question.

RUTH: Well the places I like to go to my parents don't like me to go to.
MOTHER: Such as?
RUTH: Eddie's Club.
MOTHER: ⎫
FATHER: ⎬ Oh, goodness. You don't really—
RUTH: I do.
INTERVIEWER: What is 'Eddie's'?
MOTHER: It's a drinking club. She doesn't really drink. It's just that she likes to meet different types.
INTERVIEWER: She sounds as though the people that she does want to go out with are people she feels you disapprove of.
MOTHER: Possibly.
FATHER: Yes.
MOTHER: Possibly.

Her parents' attitude to the life Ruth actually leads involves both the negation of its existence and the perception of mad or bad behaviour on Ruth's part. Thus, she is said to drink excessively, while, simultaneously, she is said not to drink at all.

MOTHER: Well, first of all most of these people in these places are very undesirable, from my point of view, and for a young girl to sit and drink all evening—
FATHER: Well she doesn't drink a lot.
MOTHER: No, but when she's not well she's confused, and she

152

doesn't know what she's doing, so she probably does have more drink than she really would—

INTERVIEWER: I'm sorry—I thought you said before that she doesn't drink very much.

MOTHER:
FATHER: } She doesn't.

MOTHER: But when she goes to these places and she's at all unwell and doesn't realize what's happening she does have more to drink perhaps than she normally would.

INTERVIEWER: How much do you drink?

RUTH: I don't drink such a lot—one or two drinks.

INTERVIEWER: Has she ever come home drunk?

MOTHER:
FATHER: } No.

Her parents repeatedly say that Ruth does not realize what is happening or what she is doing. We are unable to find any evidence to support these attributions.

Ruth, however, according to her mother,

MOTHER: —doesn't like being reminded of all this. We try not to talk about these things you know. She wants to forget it all.

INTERVIEWER: Do you perceive yourself as being ill on these occasions?

RUTH: No.

MOTHER: No, she doesn't realize she's ill when it's happening.

RUTH: I don't think I'm ill at all.

INTERVIEWER: What do you perceive is happening? How would you describe yourself on these occasions—what are you doing?

RUTH: Well I just—I think my parents make a fuss about—I just like to dress you know, sort of, if I'm going to these places I like to dress sort of in the type of style they dress.

INTERVIEWER: Can you say why you like to dress in that way?

RUTH: Well it appeals to me aesthetically.

INTERVIEWER: You feel that that type of dress is really more artistic perhaps than something more conventional?

RUTH: Yes. I also know girls who wear coloured stockings—I still do today.

INTERVIEWER: You could see where this would be a source of tension in the house if—

MOTHER: No, there isn't any tension. There isn't any tension because as soon as the attack passes and she becomes well she's as she used to be. But she still likes to see these arty people you know. If she sees anybody in the street she says, 'Oh look, that's nice, he's nice, she's nice', you know, if they are artistically dressed in any way.

FATHER: It's—to conformist reasoning—these chaps who dress oddly and these girls—they're odd.

MOTHER: They appeal to her.

FATHER: They're odd.

Then, she brings people home.

MOTHER: She's brought people home—when she's been ill she's brought people home that she normally wouldn't tolerate, you know, these beatniks.

FATHER: There have been writers and God knows what.

MOTHER: People have come home and requested to be put up for the night.

INTERVIEWER: You don't approve of writers?

MOTHER: Oh, it isn't writers—no, no—of course we approve.

FATHER: I approve.

One notes again how contradictory is her mother and father's attitude—oscillating between implicit expressions of disapproval and explicit avowals of approval.

INTERVIEWER: I'm a little bit confused here and I'm just trying to sort something out. You are saying that when she brings these people home she is ill?

MOTHER: It hasn't happened for a long time.

FATHER: Don't think she brings them home every night—on occasions—very very occasionally.

MOTHER: Only when she's unwell.

FATHER: It's not her habit to do this.

Mr. and Mrs. Gold, despite these contradictory attitudes about what Ruth *does*, have a fairly simple and consistent view of who she *really* is. This essentialism is a feature of all these families. When she is her 'real' self, that is, when she is 'well', she is not to be seriously interested in writers or art, not to wear coloured stockings, not to listen to jazz in a jazz club, not to bring friends home, not to stay out late. It is only from time to time that Ruth tries to assert herself over against this parental eternal essence, and when she does she wears clothes to her liking, and insists vehemently on going where and with whom she wishes. Then her mother 'knows' an 'attack' is coming on. She is told she is being difficult, inconsiderate, disrespectful, thoughtless, because she is causing her parents such anxiety—but they do not blame or hold her responsible for all this, because they know she is odd and ill. Thus mystified and put in an intolerable position, she becomes excited and desperate, makes 'wild' accusations that her parents do not want her to live, and runs out of the house in a dishevelled state.

In the light of the current conflict whose very existence is negated by her parents, we are in a better position to examine the 'mad' account that Ruth gives of why she is having such a struggle to live.

She goes back to the fact that she was called after her mother's younger sister, who committed suicide at the age of nineteen after an unhappy love affair. Ruth's illness became manifest at the age of twenty, and followed a love affair that kept closely to the sequence of the affair that had led to the first Ruth's suicide.

Whatever part her mother may have played in fact or fantasy in the outcome of her sister's love affair, she played a most curious role in her daughter's affair.

The story is as follows.

Her mother's sister Ruth committed suicide by drowning.

INTERVIEWER: Why did your sister do that?

MOTHER: Well it was an unhappy love affair too. She was engaged and had broken off her engagement.

INTERVIEWER: I see. It's almost like history repeating itself in a way.

MOTHER: Yes, she was very young when she became friendly with this boy. He was about ten years older than she was and she was about sixteen when she met him and he came home—my father insisted on that—he said, 'Of course you're much too young', but eventually they persisted and he allowed them to become engaged when she was about eighteen, and he was very possessive at first with her, and he made a lot of money very quickly and I think it went to his head a bit and he used to play around a little you know—started to play golf—I'm going back forty years—and neglected her somewhat, and of course she resented this—she broke her engagement off two or three times and each time he came running back full of apologies, but on this particular occasion she'd broken her engagement and he hadn't come back for a week. She cried a lot and I think she really did it more to frighten everybody, you know, I don't think she intended—well she didn't know what the outcome would be—she left a note that she'd covered her clothing and taken off her beads and ear-rings and that, and from the note it didn't seem as if she really intended to kill herself. She wanted to frighten him—she thought that perhaps frightening him would bring him back, I believe at the time, but of course she was terribly young, she was only nineteen and he was a man of twenty-nine.

Ruth's (daughter's) love affair followed a somewhat similar course, in that it was ended, so it appeared, by Ruth, and the boy showed his indifference by not pleading with her to continue.

INTERVIEWER: Do you know what she means when she accuses you? Do you know what she's referring to?

MOTHER: 'It's because of you I'm ill', and—I had a sister who committed suicide at the age of nineteen and Ruth is named for her, and she often brings that up—'Why did you call me after your sister? I'm like her aren't I?' She talks a lot about my sister. She didn't even know her.

INTERVIEWER: Ruth was born after your sister died?

MOTHER: Oh yes. My sister's been dead now for thirty-three years.

INTERVIEWER: Well what do you think she's implying when she's saying this?

MOTHER: Well she's—thinks perhaps she is like my sister you know, she thinks my sister was perhaps—she says, 'Was she normal, was she insane? Am I insane like her? Am I mad like— was she mad? Was it a mental thing?'—you know. She doesn't know what to—to put it on to.

INTERVIEWER: But she seems to be implying—there seems to be an implied reproach.

MOTHER: Oh yes. Oh yes.

INTERVIEWER: Do you know why she—

MOTHER: *She* probably thinks if I hadn't called her after my sister she wouldn't be ill.

INTERVIEWER: Mmm. She hasn't said that has she?

MOTHER: She hasn't said it in as many words but she inferred that.

INTERVIEWER: And is there anything else you have inferred from what she's said?

MOTHER: I don't think so. I don't think so.

INTERVIEWER: Why she blames you—there's nothing she's referred to?

MOTHER: No, no, no. No. When she's ill she doesn't like me to do anything for her, she wants to *try* to do things for herself, but she can't do them. I sort of take over, I do everything for her. Probably I've spoilt her a little while she's been ill, but she's so unable to look after herself and her hygiene—you know—that I do things for her, but she says, 'Don't interfere, leave me alone'. Well she can't be left alone. She can't be trusted to do anything.

INTERVIEWER: How did this disturbance start in the first place?

MOTHER: It was brought on by an unhappy love affair. She was going with a boy for a couple of years and she was then about eighteen-and-a-half, nineteen. She's always been a very sweet girl, a very easy child to rear—um—she wasn't a strong character but she was quite intelligent, she passed her eleven plus, I don't know if it was called that in those days, and she went to a secondary school, and she was quite a good-natured girl, a very clean, tidy girl, in fact she was a delight—she really was—until she met this boy. She was a popular girl, she always enjoyed herself and when she started a job I remember, she was there for about two and a half years, and this boy didn't want her to work there for some reason or other.

INTERVIEWER: How old would she be at this time?

MOTHER: She would be eighteen, eighteen and a half. And, um, she was going to leave and they were very upset about it. They pleaded with her not to. They trusted her implicitly. She used to open the shop you know, and—it was a dress shop—she was a salesgirl. That was the sort of thing she wanted to do. At one time she wanted to be a dress designer. Her brother, my son, is a writer and she always tried to ape him, you know, she wanted to be artistic like he was, she took a little course at—I'm trying to think what it's called now—it's um, a technical school, you know where they—she had some short training but she didn't stick it out. In those days she had the idea of being a dress designer or something like that. However, she gave that up and became a sales assistant and it was at that time that she met this boy, and—she wasn't particularly fond of him, he was terribly possessive. He would see her every single day, he practically lived in my house. He was a medical student at the time, and his parents resented that he'd taken up with a girl because they thought that he should continue with his career. He failed his exams on two occasions and I pleaded with him to finish with her. I said, 'You're both very young and you can always continue later when you've established yourself'. Oh no, he couldn't go on living without Ruth. This went on for two years and although his parents knew that he was seeing her and was coming to my house, he never took her home to his home and she was *very* humiliated. And she was—she was very sensitive. She was ashamed on our account, and she decided to give him up after being with him for two years. And I remember the night she came home and said that she was going to give him up and I said, 'Have you thought about it, two years is a long time?' She said, 'Yes, I've thought about it very carefully and I'm not going to see him any more,' and she finished with him completely. And from then on she became depressed and not herself at all. We couldn't put our finger on it. We didn't know what it was, in those days. I just couldn't understand what was wrong with her. I thought she was still upset about *him*. But she went out and about with girl-friends, went for her holiday, and when she came back from that particular holiday she'd put on quite a lot of weight, an enormous amount of weight for her because she was very slim in those days. I couldn't understand it. I think I took her to a specialist, a dietician, and I think she lost a little bit of weight but not very much, and then she began to behave rather strangely. She went to spend Christmas with a girl who lived in Manchester and came back after she'd been there two days, and I said, 'Why?' —'Oh I didn't like it.' And then a few weeks after that she was due to go to a girl's birthday party one afternoon, a twenty-first birthday, and she didn't turn up. And I remember that we were very distressed, well we were frantic. We didn't know what it was all about. And she came home that night—oh it was about ten o'clock at night, in a taxi, sobbing and crying, with her shoes—the heels of her shoes broken, and from then on we went from one psychiatrist to another.

What is particularly important to note, in this and other passages, is that the mother expressly states that *she pleaded with the boy to finish with Ruth*, and yet she expressly tells Ruth, and sometimes us, that she did not. Ruth does not know definitely the part her mother played in ending her love affair. Nor does her mother fully realize what she did. When Ruth accuses her mother of stage-managing its conclusion, she is simply told she is ill.

Her mother states:

MOTHER: Well I did—I was worried by it all the time—I was very worried by it all the time. And I think what hurt her more, after she'd given the boy up, about a fortnight later, she'd seen him somewhere with another girl and she was very very hurt, deeply hurt, you know, to think that she'd wasted two years with him and that he hadn't even sort of contacted her and asked her, you know, for her reasons and tried to sort of patch things up, because he'd professed such love for her. He couldn't live without her in those days and he'd quickly forgotten it. He was a very spoilt boy, a very indulged boy.

INTERVIEWER: Did she say—

MOTHER: *We* didn't approve of it *at all* but I didn't want to stop it because I didn't want her to reproach me.

INTERVIEWER: Your disapproval was because?

MOTHER: We disapproved because we didn't like the character of the boy. He was rather selfish, very spoilt, didn't work when he should have worked.

INTERVIEWER: And was there something about his manner that you found?

MOTHER: No, he was very respectful but, um, I felt he was treating it too lightly, and yet he was very possessive and he didn't feel at all ashamed that she was never taken to his home, you know, he had no shame about that at all. He *lived* in my house, never took her to his people.

INTERVIEWER: Did he say why he never did this?

MOTHER: He never ever spoke about it.

INTERVIEWER: Did you ask him?

MOTHER: We didn't—but we kept feeling that we *should*—we

should say something. We spoke to him on two occasions and we begged him to leave her alone and to wait until he'd made his career, until he'd passed his exams and until his parents were agreeable for him to have a girl friend.

INTERVIEWER: So you actually asked him to give her up.

MOTHER: We *begged* of him to give her up.

Her mother and father approached the boy, and his parents, unbeknown to Ruth.   At the same time they put pressure on her to give up the boy for his sake. But when he, for her sake, gave her up, they commiserated with her, because this showed he did not really love her!

Ruth still does not fully realize what happened at that time, and it is hardly conceivable how she could, from the information available to her.

RUTH: Well that's what's struck me as funny, because I can't remember why I wanted to break from him, and I never heard from him again. I saw him at various places but he never spoke to me. I collapsed one day outside a building, and I used to get funny feelings. I remember in the films one day I felt peculiar, but I didn't know what it was so my parents took me to a hospital—to a doctor.

INTERVIEWER: It was then that you started to feel that you had lost somebody or something important to you?

RUTH: Yes.

INTERVIEWER: And that was Richard?

RUTH: Yes. But it was all subconscious because I wasn't really consciously feeling I missed him. I remember when I was—I had an interview with a doctor and I started crying and talking about Richard and I'd never thought of him for two years you know. I just hadn't even thought of him. And it came sort of welling out of me.

INTERVIEWER: Yes it sounds as though you'd bottled it up, doesn't it?

RUTH: Yes, I'd bottled it all inwardly, that's why I had such a breakdown because I did bottle my feelings inwardly.

To this day Ruth does not know what 'really' happened.

At the time of writing she is living at home. Her parents are very happy with the present state of affairs.

MOTHER: We feel much as she does. I mean we do take her out—she doesn't—she's not indoors, you know, all the time. We take her to the cinema or wherever she likes to go. I mean our life is ruled by her these days.

FATHER: It is, definitely.

INTERVIEWER: You mean you don't do things you would otherwise do yourselves?

MOTHER: Quite, yes. We are very happy to do it.

Ruth, for her part, feels 'better'. She has given up the dress, the haunts, the friends, her parents disapprove of. She understands her parents love her, and know what is for the best.

Sometimes she has doubts. For instance,

RUTH: Over this matter I am a bit in the air. Not over all the things in the world, not over everything—not everything—but over this I am a bit sort of dubious, because most people sort of look down on beatniks and things like that don't they? I know my girl-friend wouldn't tolerate going out with them.

INTERVIEWER: Well it's a different point of view, isn't it?

RUTH: Yes, it's just a different point of view.

INTERVIEWER: But do you feel you have to agree with what most of the people round you believe?

RUTH: Well if I don't I usually land up in hospital.

FAMILY 8

The Heads

The investigation of Jean Head (née Jones) and her family began shortly after she had developed an acute psychotic breakdown of a schizophreniform type.

She was perplexed and self-absorbed when she was admitted to hospital. It was difficult to piece her story together because she spoke in a vague rambling way in the voice of a little girl, frequently talking past the point and stopping abruptly in the middle of sentences. Sometimes as she spoke she giggled incongruously, while at other times she wept, although without apparent depth of feeling. These expressions of emotion, however, were transient and her prevailing manner was that of a puzzled child doing her best to meet the demands of adults. There was a puppet doll-like quality about her, present not only with us but also with the nurses and members of her family. As she recovered it became less marked, but even when she was clinically 'well' and back to what she and her family said was her normal self, it was still present to some extent. Her story as it emerged was as follows.

About three years ago she had had a 'nervous breakdown' in which she believed that her parents and her husband (then her fiancé) were dead. She was treated in a general hospital and after a few weeks recovered. She remained well until three weeks

163

before her admission, when she began to feel an 'undercurrent' at the shop where she worked. She overheard snatches of conversation which indicated that a plot was afoot among her fellow employees in collusion with certain unknown persons to rob her as she carried money to and from the bank. She then began to feel that men in the street were watching and following her with intent, perhaps, to attack her sexually. These feelings gradually crystallized into delusions, and as they did so she began to feel that objects had a peculiar significance for her. Such an object, for instance, was the starting-handle of her car. Her anxiety mounted and reached a climax on the day of admission, when she suddenly 'realized' that her husband was dead. She sought police protection and eventually was admitted to hospital. On the day after admission the realization came to her that her parents too were dead.

To summarize, the following were the key features of Jean's psychosis.

1. A feeling of being the centre of some attention at her work, perhaps sexual, perhaps related to a plot to rob her of money she took to the bank.
2. A feeling that her husband was not her husband or was dead.
3. A feeling that her parents were dead.
4. The adoption of a girlish, pseudo-gay compliance, sometimes giving way to sarcastic mimicry of her mother, father, and husband.

Once again we shall address ourselves to the question:

To what extent are these experiences and this behaviour intelligible in the light of the praxis and process of this family nexus?

STRUCTURE OF INVESTIGATION

The investigation, begun immediately following her second admission to hospital, continued intensively through her psychotic phase (three weeks) and thereafter for seven months.

Her family consisted of Jean, aged twenty-four, her husband

(David) aged twenty-six, Jean's mother and father, and her brother, aged twenty-eight.

These were interviewed in the following combinations.

Interviews	Occasions
Jean	10
Husband	1
Mother	2
Father	1
Brother	1
Jean and husband	5
Jean and mother	1
Jean and father	1
Mother and father	1
Jean, mother, father and husband	2
	25

Also interviewed were a foster-brother and her employer.

This represents thirty-five hours interviewing time, of which thirty hours were tape-recorded.

THE FAMILY SITUATION

Both Jean and her husband are the children of fervent Non-conformist Christians of fundamentalist leanings.

Although they take up a somewhat more liberal stance in some respects than their parents, they are both very active church-workers and practising Christians.

They belong to that small minority of Christians who actively try to live according to their view of what are Christian ideals.

When one undertakes the task of conveying the nature of the praxis and the process, and particularly 'the atmosphere' or 'the spirit' of family life, every family in this series presents its own peculiar difficulties. The Heads and the Joneses are no exception. In this case, much of the difficulty arises from the fact that none of them, Jean (unless 'psychotic'), her husband, her mother or her father even think, much less express, any unchristian thoughts.

The reader who knows the active core of Nonconformist, fundamentalist ideology and way of life will have a background against which to set the specificity of this family and its members. We are not so much concerned with the theology *per se*, but the type of behaviour and the type of ideals, aspirations, thoughts, feelings, that good Christians of this kind and their children are expected to display and entertain.

There is probably no section of the community whose members expect more of themselves in certain respects than these people.

While living in families, and hence undertaking to have an active sexual life with their spouses, and to rear children, people such as the Heads and their parents regard it as sinful to have any sexual fantasies, even in relation to their own marital partners. It is completely taboo to entertain sexual thoughts about anyone else. Naturally, premarital and extramarital intercourse are completely forbidden, as are premarital necking and petting.

Typically, in the Jones family, the wearing of all cosmetics was unacceptable: Mrs. Jones had only once been to a cinema in her life—to see the coronation of the Queen; Mr. Jones had never been to a cinema. Neither had ever been to a theatre, or to a dance hall. Ballroom dancing was unacceptable because of the bodily proximity or contiguity it entailed. They had a wireless but not a television. Smoking was marginal. Mr. Jones used to smoke, but gave it up because it set a bad example. With this, as with the cinema, it might be all right in itself, but if he or his wife were 'seen to smoke or go to the cinema by a young person, it could be the beginning of his downfall', as Mrs. Jones said.

They did not, so they said, ever have arguments or get angry. On any and all matters they asked for God's guidance in joint and individual prayer.

Now, anyone attempting seriously to live according to these ideals is necessarily involved in very grave conflicts.

Man is created frail, yet commanded to be sound. It is better to marry than to burn with passion. Passion must be suppressed before marriage, and outside marriage, and to a large extent inside marriage, but sufficient passion must be left, and sufficient potency effectively preserved, to beget children. One must think only clean thoughts, yet one must handle dirty children. The chief end of life is to glorify God, yet children have to be educated in largely secular schools, and must develop secular and profane technological know-how in order to compete, as they are proudly expected to do, in a competitive society where Christian Love has little commodity value, even if it were a marketable product.

Although the Joneses were full-time Christians, they emphasized that their economic lot was not a happy one, and while holding to the fundamentalist interpretation about the rich man's difficulty in squeezing himself into Heaven, they encouraged their children to feel that there was much to be said for owning one's own house, being able to 'provide' for one's children, having one's own car, having decent furniture and other modest material features of lower-middle-class 'security', which they themselves had never possessed.

Mr. and Mrs. Head, particularly Mr. Head, were determined to have, unlike their parents, economic 'security'. They lived in a well-appointed house. As Jean's employer remarked, it looked more the house of an established business-man than that of a young couple in their early twenties and first few years of marriage.

But, as we have said, these dilemmas, conflicts, and sometimes contradictions, are the common denominator of many such families who, like the Jones, are the first to testify that it is beyond their unassisted capacity to live through these issues. They, in fact, expressly define their spiritual-carnal human condition as a double-bind. They are unjustified by anything except faith. They are saved by nothing else than Divine Mercy and Grace.

Such is the background. We must now study the way in which this family—mother, father, brother, sister (Jean), and Jean's husband live their situation in their own unique way, with our focus all the time on the intelligibility of Jean's so-called psychotic experience and action.

The Jones-Head family is a close-knit nexus. 'We are an independent family—we cling together', as her father succinctly states. The child born into such a group is born into the rights-obligations, duties, loyalties, rewards-punishments, already in existence, and much of his or her childhood training is necessarily taken up with parental techniques of inducing the interiorization of this whole system.

In the view of both parents this had been most completely accomplished. Jean had been a very happy, cheerful, good child, who was everything they wished or expected, at least until her first 'illness'.

This was truer, in a sense, than they realized. Jean said that until a point in our investigation, she had never ceased to feel controlled in what she thought, felt, or did, by her parents.

Now, we shall shortly see that Jean had been, it seems, living for years in a false position, which was at the best of times a barely tenable one. There was very little room for her to move, but she had achieved some measures of freedom by, as she put it, 'splitting' her personality.

She began to do this, as she recounted it, at the age of nine, when she first went to a cinema with a friend and her friend's parents without the knowledge of her own.

Having survived this, thereafter she began to live a double life. She had a life away from her parents of which she did not tell them. She wore make-up secretly, she went to the cinema, she went out with boys, and as a corollary to this division in her life, she cultivated a split between an 'inner' and an 'outer' self. However, her 'inner' self had very little room to breathe. She was, and remained, guilt-ridden by her duplicity. Although doing these things, she never freed herself from the inner control exercised over her, in particular, by her father, and would have felt deeply ashamed and in the wrong were he to have learned about these activities.

Her older brother, who described vividly his own technique of developing his own life, encouraged and supported her in this phase, especially from nine to eighteen, until he married and left home. She had become fond of a young man, with whom she had a sexually consummated love affair from fourteen to eighteen, but he had more money than she had been used to. He liked going to good restaurants, the opera, and the theatre, and she could not envisage ever reconciling her parents to him. She broke off the relationship, therefore, when he pressed her to marry him, and became engaged to David. She then had casual intercourse with various men, unbeknown, of course, to David, for four months, and then went into her first breakdown—the features of which were that she had a great feeling of tiredness, and the thought that her parents were dead.

However, she recovered from this within two months, reaffirmed her engagement to David, and shortly thereafter was married.

She had partly put herself into a false position with David, who knew at that time nothing about what was going on in her. She partially deceived herself in that she did her best to forget her own recent past and largely succeeded, only recalling it painfully and with considerable resistance, in the course of interviews with us, and in part she colluded with her husband in adopting the identity he allocated to her.

To some extent this identity resembled that accorded her by her parents, but it also contradicted theirs, was itself self-contradictory, and was almost totally disjunctive with her 'inner' feelings. Nevertheless, for four years she tried to reconcile in her own person all these contradictions. It is not surprising that, by, with, or without, the Grace of God, she collapsed under this impossible task.

David disapproved of his wife's failure to separate herself from her parents, on the significant ground that she was now 'a part of me, and not so much a part of them'. This we regard as one of the key findings in this case.

Although, through marriage, she had achieved some limited emotional detachment from her parents—she was at least able to tolerate being physically apart from them—it was at the price of becoming equally attached to her husband.

Neither David nor her parents recognized this. Although less afraid of him and more able to express herself to him, she felt that he was equally impervious to what she really felt. He treated her as 'not herself' when she expressed her 'inner' feelings, or he laughed them off as a joke. He attributed to her feelings and intentions he supposed her to have, often in total discord with the feelings and intentions she herself expressed, or, as she had learned to do, kept to herself. He denied intention or agency (praxis) to behaviour that was undeniable but disjunctive with his wishes, by attributing such behaviour to illness (process).

Further unavowed contradictions were clearly in evidence— for instance, over the issue of a baby. David told us frankly, 'I don't want a family myself and would be quite happy never to have one'. He justified or rationalized this (money, debt, the need for a house, for a car, etc. etc.) by a flood of words at an average of over two hundred a minute.

But to Jean, he said he wanted a baby as much as she did, though not yet. First of all they needed money for a house, a car, then more money to pay off their debts, then more for security . . . and then they could have a baby. But this was as far off as it had ever been. To bring it closer, however, Jean had taken a full-time job, installed two lodgers with full board, got up at six in the morning and went to bed exhausted at ten when she was not helping David till later in Church work three nights a week.

David insisted that, whereas there was need for more money if they were to have a baby, there was no need for Jean to be so tired.

DAVID: ' . . . well look, the only thing is, Jean, you've got to take things easily, if you're tired, for goodness' sake go to bed, if you feel you need sleep, get your sleep; if you need food, get your food.'

In his view, apart from lack of money and Jean's tiredness, everything was satisfactory and settled. He was sure that Jean agreed with him, taking as evidence for this a hollow compliance such as the following.

DAVID: If you particularly want to go back to work, but it's entirely up to you. Wait and see how you feel in a few weeks' time—last week-end you didn't particularly want to go back did you? (Jean: Eh?) Last week-end—remember—when we went out shopping you said you didn't even want to go past the place.
JEAN: Yes, but it doesn't worry me any more.
DAVID: Do you want to go back to work then?
JEAN: Yes, if necessary.
DAVID: It's not necessary, I mean—
JEAN: Well that's all right then, I won't go back!
DAVID: (Laughs) Well that's entirely up to you Jean, if you want to go back there you can do, if you don't want to—well go somewhere else. If you don't want to go back at all—you don't have to go back. You said you might want to have a part-time job anyway to have something to do—for a while.
JEAN: Yes, I'll go back there and work afternoons.
DAVID: Perhaps you could do that if you want to—anyway, we'll see.
JEAN: Yes, all right.
DAVID: I don't think you need worry about failing. Mr. Young was more than pleased, in fact he wouldn't have talked about making you head salesgirl there would he—mmm?
JEAN: No. No. No. (This last 'no' in a curious tone).
DAVID: What's the matter? Mmm?

He continued to suppose that she agreed with him, even when she made such statements as:

JEAN: Really and truly you talked me round to thinking all that because in myself I didn't really think—I never really have thought—I mean, I've *talked* that way. I've even said to you, 'Well yes it is best. I'll carry on working. I'll keep working. I'll get myself a good job', and I did get myself a good job, and I've always had good jobs since I got married. I used to travel up to town every day for two years. I mean because I thought that—and then I'd keep thinking, 'Well perhaps now', and then I'd say, 'Oh, I'm still having to go on, I'm still having to keep working!'

David maintains that when Jean is 'herself' she is bright and cheerful and sees things as he does. It is only when she is tired or ill that she says these things (above) that she does not really mean.

DAVID: . . . I think it is right for us to carry on just a little bit longer and try to get that little bit behind us so that we can give the kiddie a better start in life.

INTERVIEWER: She's been upset about it?

DAVID: Oh yes.

INTERVIEWER: Tell me, in what way?

DAVID: Well, when we've been talking about it she has cried, you know, once or twice while we were talking (laughing slightly). It sounds all very callous but it wasn't like that at all. This is while we've been discussing it she's cried inasmuch as being sad perhaps that she can't have one straight away. I mean I've said, 'Well if you really feel that badly about it Jean, fair enough, we'll have a family', and when I've said that she's said, 'Well no, your attitude about it is really right'. This is usually, by the way, very late at night, you know, after we've had a tiring day or something like that, when she's tired and she seems to get like this. When she's been tired, that's when I've noticed this has happened. And then tomorrow morning she's said, 'I know in the cold light of day I agree with you fully, it's just not worth our having a family yet', and it's only on the odd occasion when she has been tired that she's been upset about not having a family yet.

Thus, to David, his wife really agrees with him. If she disagrees it is not because she is using her mind but because she cannot use it by reason of exhaustion or illness. Disagreement therefore becomes a sign of illness.

According to David, his wife was, among other things, highly competent, but she took on too much and worried too much. She was so competent that the breakdown was a complete shock and surprise to him. But he said she need not worry about what he would think of her if she could not cope because he knew she could cope unless she was ill. He would not mind if she felt she could not cope because he knew she could. He set her no standards, but she was a perfectionist. He was proud of her. If he was not proud of her she would have cause to worry, but of course, he said, she need not because there was nothing she could possibly do to make him not proud of her. She did worry about untidiness. He himself liked things to be tidy, but she need not worry so much because the home was tidy anyway. Besides, he knew she was not perfect, although in his eyes she was. He had always accepted her for what she was.

David, like her parents, did not in his view set Jean ideals, since she already was ideal. How then would he, in such perfection, imperfection find? Only through sheer excess of perfection could she so worry, tire, exhaust herself, that she could not cope. But then she was not herself.

In this way they implicitly set her an ideal, deny that they have set it, then put the onus on her for taking too much out of herself in trying to live up to it, and thus breaking down.

FATHER: I think that's the one good thing that can emerge out of this experience. I mean people say, 'Now you've got to help yourself', and all this and that and the other, well that may or may not be the case, but in *this* matter, I believe that the power to prevent it occurring again is in Jean's hands.

The attribution of autonomy to someone who clearly is completely alienated from her autonomous self, by the persons who are perpetuating this alienation, albeit unwittingly, is surely most mystifying.

Jean was in a false, almost untenable, position, which she only fleetingly saw as such. If she argued when she was tired she was told she did so because she was tired, and that she should go to bed, which she did, and was repentant in the morning. Her husband and parents prayed for her in these circumstances.

Her 'recovery' consisted in return to the *status quo ante bellum*. During her 'breakdown' and before re-adopting the point of view of her husband and parents, she expressed her inner feelings in some measure, albeit somewhat frenetically and seldom directly. Her ways of asserting them were simply regarded as her illness, from which everyone prayed that she would recover as soon as it was God's will.

The following epitomizes the interaction when she was diagnosed as psychotic.

FATHER: Well you look a bit tired now, do you feel very tired?

JEAN: Yes.

DAVID: She's just been laughing and joking down there while you've been up here—and then she decided she wanted to go to sleep again and dropped off to sleep (smiling) didn't you?

FATHER: Let me sit by you and then perhaps you'll keep quiet will you? (Jean is sitting rigidly upright with eyes shut.)

DAVID: Wake up!

JEAN: Oh! Don't do that to me. (Very emphatically and distinctly, keeps eyes shut.)

MOTHER: You won't be able to sleep at night will you?

JEAN: Pardon, mmm?

MOTHER: I said you won't be able to sleep at night will you? If you sleep too much in the daytime—mmm?

JEAN: Won't you? Oh.

FATHER: We've got some biscuits and grapes.

JEAN: Have you? (Opens her eyes.)

FATHER: I say we've got some in the car.

MOTHER: And a shampoo. (David laughs. Jean shuts her eyes.)

FATHER: Well you'll be able to do your shampoo I expect when—(sighs).

DAVID: Oh dear!

MOTHER: She looks quite smart, David.

FATHER: Yes I thought that when I saw her.

DAVID: Yes, yes. I got her three pairs of pyjamas, a yellow pair, a coral pair and—(they laugh).

MOTHER: We've got to go in a minute or two, Jean.

DAVID: Have you?

MOTHER: Did you get my letter by the way?

JEAN: No.

MOTHER: Why not?

JEAN: (Inaudible.)

DAVID: Thank you for your letter by the way.

MOTHER: Oh I thought I wrote a letter to Jean too.

FATHER: Haven't you had a letter from Mum? Perhaps you'll probably get it Monday.

MOTHER: Well I didn't say much, but I thought you'd like to have a line from me. Do you remember you sent me a card?

DAVID: Pity she's just dropped off to sleep, down there—

MOTHER: Do you remember that card you sent me with—

JEAN: No I don't.

MOTHER: Oh don't you?

JEAN: No. I don't remember at all.

DAVID: She's been talking, chatting away down there, you know without saying much at all actually, just chatting away (slight laugh).

(Father, mother, and David try to attract Jean's attention.)

DAVID: Bo-ho! (whistles) You-hoo.

(Father leans over and takes her hand. She disengages herself.)

JEAN: Oh!

DAVID: Would you rather sit on the couch, it's more comfortable, would you like to, dear?

MOTHER: Come on dear, come and sit down.

JEAN: (Now begins to slope over rigidly, sits at an angle, eyes shut.)

FATHER: Well you'll fall off, you'll bang your head.

JEAN: (Crossly) I will *not* fall off the chair.

FATHER: Well you might bang your head.

JEAN: Why should I bang my head?

FATHER: On the fireplace.

JEAN: On the fireplace.

DAVID: I think she's just gone to sleep (slight laugh).

JEAN: I shall go to sleep again in a minute.

FATHER: Well you haven't said much to Mother yet have you?

JEAN: I haven't seen Mother yet.

FATHER: Well there she is.

JEAN: No. No it isn't her.

FATHER: Well who is it then?

JEAN: I don't know.

FATHER: Well who am I then?

JEAN: I don't know.

MOTHER: We've come quite a long way to see you, Jean.

JEAN: Have you! That's what you said before.

MOTHER: Yes. Well can't you just ask me anything?

JEAN: What would you like me to ask you? (slight laughter)—whether you're Faith or whether you're um—?

MOTHER: Who's Faith?

DAVID: She just told me she thought you were Faith. That's somebody at work (Mother and David inaudible).

FATHER: Well when did your mother come in to see you then?

JEAN: I don't know.

FATHER: What about your father?

JEAN: I don't know.

FATHER: He usually comes to see you if you're not well doesn't he?

JEAN: Beg your pardon?

FATHER: Father usually comes to see you if you're not well doesn't he?

JEAN: Mmm.

176

MOTHER: Have you seen television, Jean, since you've been here? Have you got the television?—Jean?

JEAN: (perkily) Yes, if you look out there you can see it.

MOTHER: I haven't seen it yet.

JEAN: Haven't you. Oh!

MOTHER: Which programme do you like best?

JEAN: Don't remember.

FATHER: What did you see on Saturday?

MOTHER: I thought I heard a wireless on just then.

FATHER: Well that may be the television I think.

MOTHER: I had to go up to London yesterday. I've been up to London twice this week for committees.

JEAN: Have you?

MOTHER: Mmm. Tuesday and Friday. Didn't meet you this time, did I?

JEAN: Didn't you?

MOTHER: Yesterday—you're here aren't you?

DAVID: Yes, she's just dropped off to sleep, she was really sound asleep, almost snoring just now. Probably come to in about five minutes (laughs nervously).

FATHER: Come over on the settee dear.

JEAN: No-oo. (crossly) Will you leave me alone please. Thank you.

FATHER: Well you needn't say—

MOTHER: Well you want to be nice to us while we're here, darling, because—

JEAN: (sarcastically) Yes, I must be, mustn't I, Mother dear! (pause) (David and father laugh simultaneously).

DAVID: Oh dear, oh dear.

FATHER: Have you been asleep?

JEAN: No.

Three weeks later her behaviour, though more sane clinically, gives her parents and David cause for sadness, since

FATHER: . . . there's never been *any* expression of thanks or thoughtfulness—well, apparently, it appears to us, the illness has reduced her to a state of non-awareness of other people, and an expression of thanks has largely been absent hasn't it? —At least it's *our* general observation.

A month later, she has resumed such attentions as expressions of thanks for her parents' and husband's thoughts, love, and prayers, but she is much more forthright than her usual self.

DAVID: Can you pinpoint what it is, because I can't—I'd like to know what it is if you've got any ideas as to what it could be (pause). Is there something in our relationship together that you know of Jean that you're not happy about?

JEAN: Only that I want a family, that's all.

DAVID: Yes I know—

JEAN: You keep saying, 'No we're not going to have one'.

DAVID: I keep saying 'no' you say?

JEAN: Well every time I suggest it you say we can't afford it.

DAVID: Well we haven't been able to afford it up till now. Could well be that this is one of the prime—that that is one of the things—I'm quite ready to accept that fact. I know whenever we've discussed this Jean has always been upset. And yet at other times—it all depends you see, at different times when we've discussed this it's been in the evening when Jean's been tired, as you might say, in the cold light of morning, then Jean has always said, 'No, we obviously can't afford it, we obviously want to get these different things first, we want to get ourselves established, let's get ourselves—'

JEAN: I think that's what you've drummed into me.

DAVID: Have I?

JEAN: Because when I first got married I thought we were going to settle down and have a family. I didn't know we were going to have . . . when we first got married I didn't think we were going to continue for several years, not really.

DAVID: Well we decided—decided that before we got married didn't we? (pause)

JEAN: Well I've always said to you, 'Other people can manage. Why can't we?' Your money's not that bad.

DAVID: But most other people have got something behind them or they've got parents who can help them out just that bit haven't they?

JEAN: There's no point in saying all the time—having that chip on your shoulder that we're never going to get a home together . . . is there?

As her husband says,
Yes, yes, oh it's definitely a problem. It's been a problem ever since we *got* married, without any doubt at all. This has been a problem for both of us. But as far as I'm concerned—I love kids. I always have done, I've always got on well with children.

Later still, as she gets 'better', she comes to adopt more completely her husband's point of view. They both agree that they will have a family when things are settled up. He wants one as much as she does. She is sometimes tired because she's overworked, and lets off steam a bit then, but she must watch herself that she does not overtire herself, because there's no real need for her to do so. She has a mind of her own, and is a highly contented and happy person, and so on.

The above discussion and extracts do not do full justice to the peculiarly Christian features of this family. This is not easy to characterize by specific, relatively short transcriptions—it is communicated much more in the manner of speech and in the visual pattern of movement.

The following passage, not specifically concerned with Jean, illustrates their practice of Christianity. They adopted a little boy to give him a good Christian home. This child (Ian) was a 'terrible handful'.

INTERVIEWER: Did he require to be smacked at times?

MOTHER: Oh yes, very often, yes.

INTERVIEWER: For?

MOTHER: Well for deliberately doing things we told him not to.

INTERVIEWER: Can you recall any particular occasion?

MOTHER: Well at the school he used to sit around in the playground and drag his shoes and all that sort of thing, you know, and come home with his shoes all worn out, and you'd tell him and he'd do the same thing again the next day. It didn't have any effect on him you see.

INTERVIEWER: He dragged his shoes?

MOTHER: Well, you know, various things that we told him not to do he would do, you see. I mean you don't expect children to sit in the playground in the dirt do you? And to crawl around on the playground and drag all their shoe-toes and all that sort of thing. That's the thing he used to do and do it deliberately you see, because we told him not to do it. That was the point.

He was a boy who would do things he was asked not to do.

INTERVIEWER: He'd had polio hadn't he?

MOTHER: He'd had polio, yes.

INTERVIEWER: Well—was he able to walk?

MOTHER: Oh yes—well when he came to us of course we used to have to carry him to school and back, but he got so much better that he was discharged from the hospital, although he's never been right. His legs have always been affected.

INTERVIEWER: His legs were affected?

MOTHER: Oh yes, very badly.

INTERVIEWER: In what way?

MOTHER: Well he was born with club feet and then the polio aggravated it. Every night he had to go to bed with irons on, you see. He had all the ligaments cut at the back and he used to have to go to bed with irons on and be pulled all up you see.

INTERVIEWER: Oh I see, yes, that's right.

MOTHER: So that he was—he was very handicapped really, so that I mean he needed more attention than our own children really.

INTERVIEWER: So he had club feet and he had his feet sort of deformed by the polio in addition?

MOTHER: Mmm, yes, that's right. His feet never grew. They were all clubbed up. So he was a cripple and needed care you see. That's why we say that Jean and Charles were marvellous because they just—she just used to patiently wait and bring him home ...

INTERVIEWER: How did this—well, so he wore his shoes out a lot did he?

MOTHER: Oh yes—that's only one little thing. It was partly his handicap of course and—but he used to do things that we used to ask him not to do, he would deliberately do just to get the attention we feel, you see.

INTERVIEWER: Yes, well surely ... this was why I was asking could you give me an example.

MOTHER: (thinking) Well I mean, at the table and various things like that—he—he always wanted the best of things and if you said—well—'No, no more' he used to make a scene, you know, and show off as children do.

INTERVIEWER: Would he say—you mean he would go into a temper tantrum?

MOTHER: Yes he would, yes, oh yes.

INTERVIEWER: Was he like that from the start?

MOTHER: Yes, yes he used to let off steam a lot.

INTERVIEWER: Do you know if he missed his mother much?

MOTHER: No, he didn't seem to miss his mother.

INTERVIEWER: Not at all?

MOTHER: No, he never asked for her.

INTERVIEWER: Did you wonder at this at all?

MOTHER: Oh I did, yes, rather. But I feel—you see they used to— they were very adaptable. They were so used to being in different circumstances and of course he adapted himself really.

INTERVIEWER: When he was five he came to stay with you?

MOTHER: Yes, just under five.

INTERVIEWER: What was he like? Was he very quiet?

MOTHER: Oh, no, no, he just enjoyed himself. I don't think he was old enough to realize you see. He'd been in hospital, and he'd been staying with other folk all round so—

INTERVIEWER: You don't think he was old enough to realize he had no mother?

MOTHER: No, no, not really. Well he knew he was coming to live with us you see, he was only quite a baby wasn't he?—Just under five.

Ian, according to mother, was quite happy, a bit forward, but not nervy. He did wet the bed and 'the other thing too' terribly, and was of course punished for that, and he bit his nails 'down to the bone', for which his arms and hands were put in bags and strapped to his body by attached cords tied behind his back.

However she said he has since realized what a handful he was and is very grateful.

Jean's parents and her husband show a notable inability to see the other person's point of view, and are completely unaware of this inability.

Only because Jean did not suffer from congenital clubbed feet and polio is it perhaps less obvious that her mother's picture of her is as impervious to her point of view as was the case with Ian.

She was 'quite normal', 'everything natural', 'a very good baby really', 'she never used to cry'. Although difficult to wean, 'we had a bit of a fight'. She had no transitional objects,[1] 'Well I never encouraged them to do too much of that because I thought, you know, you go to bed to sleep. I used to say, well, bed was bed and they should go to sleep and go to bed, that was my idea.'

Of the game of throwing things over the side of the cot, her mother says:

'No, I don't think it was a game, but I mean sometimes when you're out they do throw things over don't they, and you've got to pick them up (laughs) but quite a lot of children do

---

[1] 'Transitional objects'—those pieces of blanket or cloth, dolls, and so on, so dearly beloved by young children (described by Winnicott, D. W. (1951) 'Transitional Objects and Transitional Phenomena', in *Collected Papers*, London: Tavistock Publications, 1958).

that don't they? But I don't remember anything special about it. I mean they were just normal children.'

There was no jealousy at all towards her brother, and 'she was wonderful with Ian, no jealousy at all'.

According to Jean, however, she had had (since before she was five) nightmares of trees and horrible shapes, ominous and menacing. She awoke screaming and she was punished for this by her father. This happened repeatedly. One night she awoke screaming to see a big dog in her room. Her father hit her. She was always afraid of the dark, and is still.

At fourteen she began to feel frightened to be alone. When she was eighteen she worked in a large house which was surrounded by woods. She imagined men lurked there, and she was terrified but never showed it. She felt like a little girl and, although she never screamed at these times, she would run all the way along the road.

According to her mother, there had never been any disharmony in Jean's relationship with her. Of course she had not always agreed with everything her mother had said, but they had always got on very well together. Jean was very fond of her father, and she was very fond of her mother as well, really. There had never been any bad feelings between her and her parents, nor had she ever appeared to be fonder of her father than of her mother, because they had both tried to treat her the same.

Her father said that Jean used to get into 'a paddy'. Her mother added quickly, 'Well she'd get a bit worked up but not angry. I've never known her to be as *bad* as that really, have you?' Mr. Jones agreed. They agreed that she had never been angry because she had not an angry nature, although she had had one or two bursts when she had flung things, but that was nothing 'really'. She had always been balanced and a responsible girl.

They themselves never got angry with people 'really'. They could not afford it in their job and, besides, it was not Christian. Mr. Jones used to be sarcastic, but he had tried to cure himself of that. They did not get unduly angry. Naturally, they did get indignant, righteously indignant, at any injustice. Mr. Jones said that he had a reputation for plain speaking, but it was all a matter of balance. Balance was a matter of experience and young people were inexperienced, without anything to fall back upon, but not Jean. Jean was balanced, really. Like most of 'us' she would fight for the weaker person, but she never got angry. They came from a stock that tended to be quiet and hurt if they were injured, rather than to swear and show off. They would feel ashamed if they lost their tempers. They would have dishonoured their Christian faith. If anyone tried to harm them they would pity him and pray for him. They stood for a view of life that they considered ideal in a Christian way. They were fundamentalists, but we must not think they were fanatics. They represented a balanced religious view, and consequently they let their children go as they felt was right. The children did nothing under their, the parents', authority; for example, they had made their own home.

There is a complete taboo against entertaining or expressing any 'bad' feelings. One sees the husband struggling hard against, and finally being defeated by, this taboo in the following.

Asked about Jean and her mother he says:

'Um—(slight laugh)—um—well quite honestly I think she—I know she's always been extremely fond of her father, that's the usual relationship really I think when you get a mother, father, daughter, and son. Jean's mother is, I believe, extremely fond and worships her, you might say. Jean and her father perhaps hit it off better than Jean and her mother do. Jean and her mother also hit it off extremely well together. There's no— I don't think there's any real strain there at all, not that I know of.'

Mrs. Jones supposed Jean had been a bit afraid of the dark as a child, really, though no more than she herself had been when she was a child. She had never liked the dark herself, but she thought that was more or less normal, really, in a girl. She knew hosts of young people who did not like going out in the dark, and as Jean had got older she had not seemed too bad. Jean had never had nightmares or night terrors. After all, she had never had a light when she went to bed, so that showed she had not been afraid of the dark. She would never have let her scream in the dark. Quite definitely Jean had never had any nightmares. She had been very scared of dogs, but had never complained of any particular dog.

Jean and her brother had never wanted to stay out late. As Christians they did not reckon to go to theatres and cinemas. They had never been to a dance and Mrs. Jones did not think they had ever really wanted to. It was true that Jean had once said to her when she had been looking into a shop and saw evening dresses there, 'Oh Mummy, I shall never be able to wear an evening dress', but of course Jean was now going to parties since her marriage.

Jean had never worn make-up. She had not wanted to, not that her mother and father had ever stopped her from doing it. They did not like it, really, but they never interfered, but Jean knew how they felt about it. There had never been any quarrels over it, nor would there have been over going to the cinema. They would have been reasonable about it. They would not definitely have said she had not to go, really. There would never have been any row over it. They would never have quarrelled over her wanting to go to a dance, but it never arose because she had never really wanted to go to a dance. In fact she had not ever been to one really, she had never wanted to.

Jean was not very much of a reader. Her mother thought she had read quite a lot of magazines 'and that sort of thing', but she was not a reader, really. There had not been very much difficulty over books that they did not like, not that they would have stopped her. As for newspapers, well that had never worried Jean, she had never been a great newspaper-reader, though she might have been more interested in newspapers after she had left home at eighteen. They did not know what had gone on when she left home. They had no objection to her reading newspapers.

Nor had they had any objection to Jean and her brother having the radio on, but in fact they had never had it on very much because they had not wanted to. There had never been any trouble over this. Of course they had not had it on on Sundays, but apart from that they used to have on the news or Children's Hour, or if there had been something nice on. But they never interfered with her listening. Anyway she'd never had a lot of time for listening and there had never been any quarrels over music or over Jean putting on the radio at the wrong time.

There had been times when she had protested at being expected to do things, but nothing outstanding. The parents used to work together on these occasions. They tried not to go against each other, because if mother and father were divided it defeated their ends.

Jean had never smoked at home. She had smoked once, her mother thought, but she did not think she had made a habit of it, really. She did not think Jean smoked at all now. There had never been any trouble over smoking. She did not think Jean had wanted to. They would not have liked it if she had smoked, really. They would have stopped her. They had no objection to smoking as such, and so on.

Jean had been very popular with the boys. Her mother had been quite happy about this, after all, she had brought them home. She always used to bring them home. They had never stopped her doing this. As for possible boys that she had not brought home, well they never knew about those, really, but they would not have been so happy about them. There had been one or two she had brought home when she had been at the large house that they had not been pleased about. They had been of the worldly type and they had not fitted in well with their 'set-up'. They did not try to stop Jean going out with these boys. They did not lay down rules or regulations. Instead they had prayed about them because they felt that these things were overruled by the Lord. But they did say they hoped her boy friends would be Christians.

The following are some of her mother's statements about Jean and sexuality.

1. 'We never tried to stop Jean wearing cosmetics or going to dances. We never told her not to.'
2. 'Naturally we would be happier if she didn't, because we had to set an example.'
3. 'Naturally we wanted her to go out with boys and be attractive.'
4. 'It would have been difficult if Jean had wanted to go out with a boy, even if he were a Christian, if he belonged to a different denomination.' but
5. 'There was never any conflict because Jean never wanted to wear lipstick or to go out with boys who were not of the same denomination.'

Mr. Jones's picture of Jean is similar to his wife's. They have never kept her on strings. She is very capable, too capable. She is strong and independent. She is normally bright and vivacious. She was like that as a child also. She was rather highly strung as a child, and could be more difficult to discipline or control than her brother, although that was only an incidental. Generally and essentially there were 'no problems, no punishment, no discipline, in that sense'.

David's statements show the same structure:

These mystifications have to be set in the context of a nexus extending from her parents to include her husband.

She had been expected by her parents to be attractive, but not to promote her attractiveness in the usual way. David expected her to make herself attractive but not to be attracted to men. Not surprisingly, she became worried that she was being too attractive, that she was being followed. Unable to express, and inwardly forbidden to feel, dissatisfaction with, or disappointment in, her husband, she said he was not her husband. Not daring to reject or to defy her parents openly, she did so quite clearly but in a way that is 'schizophrenic'.

APPENDIX

SOME ATTRIBUTIONS MADE BY MOTHER, FATHER, AND HUSBAND ABOUT JEAN	JEAN'S SELF-ATTRIBUTIONS
Father and mother	
always happy	often depressed and frightened
her real self is vivacious and cheerful	kept up a front
no disharmony in the family	disharmony so complete that impossible to tell her parents anything
they have never kept her on a string	by sarcasm, prayer, ridicule, attempted to govern her life in all important respects
Jean has a mind of her own	true in a sense, but still too terrified of father to tell him her real feelings, still feels controlled by him
Jean never *wanted* to	
go to the cinema	she wanted to and did
go out with boys outside own denomination	,, ,, ,, ,, ,,
have sexual relations before marriage	,, ,, ,, ,, ,,
go to dances	,, ,, ,, ,, ,,
go to restaurants	,, ,, ,, ,, ,,
go to the theatre	she wanted to but could not
read books	she wanted to but was frightened to
Husband	
Jean is full of confidence and very capable	very unsure of herself
Jean and he see everything the same way	Jean sees many things differently

FAMILY 9

The Irwins

Mary is twenty. She is a plump, attractive girl, whose actions and words are slow and carefully chosen.

Her illness had followed the typical dementia praecox sequence. She had apparently been well until fifteen. Then she began to lose interest in her work at school and lost her position in class.

She had previously been happy and social. She became morose, and gave up her friends.

On leaving school, she could not decide what she wanted to do, but with prompting went into an office. She held the job for two years, then left because of lack of interest. Thereafter she did not want to do anything, but with prompting took another job. She was sacked after three months for incompetence. Over the next nine months she was sacked from two more jobs for the same reason. Shortly afterwards she was admitted to hospital for the first time.

About the time she left school she developed various 'habits', such as sniffing and coughing. She would sit or stand still for over an hour at a time. Later, in hospital, she would sniff, cough, or grimace, and sit or stand motionless unless prompted to move.

When seen by us she was being re-admitted for the third time, having spent twenty-two months of the previous twenty-four in two other mental hospitals.

189

During her stays in hospital, she had been in seclusion, had gained a reputation for smashing in states of catatonic excitement, had been tranquillized by daily electro-shocks, and 'maintained' by electro-shocks and Stelazine.

Since her illness her parents found her to be unmanageable at home. Although they wanted her to get better, they felt unable to cope with her illness until she had made a 'reasonable recovery'.

The list of schizophrenic symptoms and signs included thought-blocking and over-inclusion, vagueness, speculative woolly thinking about the meaning of life, inability to face life's difficulties and aggressively to overcome them.

Emotional apathy and affective-cognitive incongruence were noted, and delusions of persecution, for example, that her mother was killing her mind, were also found.

Her emotional apathy was said suddenly to give way to accesses of senseless and uncontrolled excitement and violence.

Various stereotyped movements, grimacing, catatonic immobility, negativism, occasional mild flexibilitas cerea, automatic obedience, and so on, were also recorded.

Her family history was negative, and no relationship was felt to exist between her various symptoms and her environment.

This case is particularly interesting in that the girl had been investigated especially closely from a clinical psychiatric point of view, because of a suspected encephalitic illness pre-dating the first psychotic manifestations. These investigations were negative for organic findings.

Her parents' view of this girl as 'ill' was essentially congruent with the clinical psychiatric gestalt.

We shall here present a radically different gestalt, in which the *attribution* of illness becomes socially intelligible. We shall see how this attributed illness comes to be taken as a fact, and how she is treated accordingly. Such is the spell cast by the make-believe of everyone treating her as if she were ill, that one has constantly to pinch oneself to remind oneself that there is no evidence to substantiate this assumption, except the actions of the others, who by acting in terms of this assumption conjure up a feeling of conviction that the experience and actions in question are the unintelligible outcome of process, rather than the entirely intelligible expression of Mary's praxis, in a social field where her position is untenable and where her 'moves' (her praxis) are explained on the presumption that they are generated by a mysterious, undubitable, yet indefinable pathological process.

Once more, we have to show to what extent the experiences and actions that are taken to be symptoms and signs of organic or psychic pathological process are explicable as social praxis within the context of the praxis-process of the social system of her family.

Here, as before, we are putting entirely in parenthesis the validity of any attributions of illness.

We shall review the experiences and behaviour of Mary, as seen through the eyes of her mother, father, older sister, psychiatrists, nurses, and ourselves; and, finally, as seen through the eyes of Mary herself.

STRUCTURE OF INVESTIGATION

The nuclear family consisted of Mary's mother, aged forty-six; her father, aged forty-eight; Angela, twenty-two; Mary, twenty; and a brother aged sixteen.

Interviews recorded and transcribed	Occasions
Mary	12
Mother	1
Father	1
Sister	1
Mary and mother	2
Mother and father	1
Mary and father	1
Mary, mother, and father	1
	20

This represents twenty hours' interviewing time, all of which was tape-recorded.

THE FAMILY SITUATION

According to her father, the trouble began when Mary was fifteen. She had always been very meek and cooperative, but then she started to question her parents and to show lack of respect for them. She became defiant.

INTERVIEWER: What was the first thing you can remember her being defiant over?

FATHER: Well one thing that sticks in my mind was—she was always very well-behaved and suchlike you know, and she came home from school this day—the children had to ask the teacher questions, and she'd asked the teacher if he thought it was right that teachers should be allowed to smack the children —something to that effect anyway it was—as her mate the day before had been smacked you know, at school. Well I was surprised at Mary's sticking up for that. You'd never have thought she would do anything like that before.

INTERVIEWER: Say such a thing?

FATHER: Yes.

INTERVIEWER: She told you this—that she'd said?

FATHER: Aye, she came home like and she told us. We never said anything at the time, but it just stuck in my mind at the time.

INTERVIEWER: You were quite surprised?

FATHER: I was. I was very surprised at it, because she was always so very meek and well-behaved. There's nothing wrong with that I suppose, but it was a bit impertinent to the teacher like.

This was the start. Then things went from 'bad' to 'worse'. They thought she might just be obstinate and stubborn, but the 'real start of it' was when she left school.

INTERVIEWER: Well what was happening then?

FATHER: Well I think she used to pick her head first of all, and she was always told to stop picking her head—that was the first thing. And she would sit and waggle her foot, you know —these sort of things, and she seemed to sort of do everything to try and annoy you. That was the start of it.

INTERVIEWER: Like picking her head and waggling her foot?

FATHER: Yes. She was told to stop but she wouldn't do it— sniffing when you spoke to her (sniffs twice). That's another thing you see.

Her father, however, has not got as good a memory as his wife. We have to place her mother's view in the context of her picture of herself and Mary since Mary was born. She feels that she and Mary were an ideal couple.

INTERVIEWER: Now Mary, when she was a baby, can you tell me about her? I mean what sort of baby would she be?

MOTHER: Happy. Just the kind of baby everybody wants.

INTERVIEWER: What would that be?

MOTHER: She was happy. She was no trouble. She'd eat anything you gave her. You couldn't look at her without having a smile because she was such a bonny baby, golden curls, big blue eyes, fat chubby legs. She was clean. She was beautiful. She went to bed half-past six to seven up till she went to school—never any trouble. She played outside, had fun, climbed walls—um—got her bottom smacked occasionally—but she was an absolutely normal child.

And of herself as a mother she says:

'I was always told I was the most wonderful mother.'

INTERVIEWER: Who would tell you this?

MOTHER: Just everybody I came into contact with. My husband's employer used to say, 'What a wonderful mother'. His wife said she'd never seen such beautiful children, they were so good and lovely. They were really good without any smacking or shouting at them or anything. They were just happy.

SANITY, MADNESS, AND THE FAMILY

Her mother currently addresses Mary, so it seems to us, as though she were about three years old, and it seems likely that she tended to treat her as a three-year-old both before and after she reached this age.

She says, for instance:

MOTHER: I used to think to myself 'How on *earth* will I ever get her trained'. But when we got in our own house I put her to bed and I talked to her, I sat beside her and I just let her cry and at first she cried for nearly two hours.

INTERVIEWER: This was between six and ten? (p.m.)

MOTHER: Yes.

INTERVIEWER: She woke up about eight o'clock did she?

MOTHER: No she woke up about half-past six—she just went off to sleep and woke up.

INTERVIEWER: She'd be about a year at this time?

MOTHER: She would be getting on for a year.

INTERVIEWER: So you sat beside her.

MOTHER: Yes. I said, 'Now be a good girl and go off to sleep', and she used to turn round to me and she'd say, 'Shut your eyes and go to sleep', and she'd cuddle down then, then she'd start again, crying. Well she said this *after* a while, when she started talking.

INTERVIEWER: I see. But you talked to her.

MOTHER: I'd talk to her firm and say, 'It's bedtime and Angela's sleeping'. And it gradually got less until after about three weeks of it she wasn't any more bother.

A further feature of Mrs. Irwin's attitude is that she treats Mary as a nurse might do. To her Mary is a little child who is ill, whom she has to see through a difficult, trying time, but it is her duty to do so.

Yet, according to her, Mary and she were alike in many ways —when Mary was well, that is to say.

MOTHER: We have the same sort of tastes, we like the same sort of colours and, um, well, until recently—And now Mary's tastes are different, she's gone for chunky jumpers and sloppy joes and I don't like those—but up to her being seventeenish, I could go and buy something for her or she could go and buy something for me and it would be just what we wanted, you know, exactly—that we'd both like the same thing.

All went satisfactorily until Mary became 'ill'. Then she started to 'shut herself off from me', she became selfish, defiant, too full of herself, and cheeky.

MOTHER: Now I'm completely haywire with her, I don't know what she's doing or what she's thinking. I've *got* to think she's ill or I wouldn't put up with it.

This is by now a familiar story. What Mrs. Irwin finds particularly upsetting is the developing distance between herself and Mary. They used to be the same, and now they are different. It is this difference that, for her mother, seems to be the essence of the illness. Signs of disjunction are met with negations or attributions of badness (selfish, defiant, cheeky, stubborn, etc.) or madness.

But this is not all. Mrs. Irwin had a 'dreadful old mother'. Although she hated her, she was terrified of her, and had managed to leave home only after a great internal struggle, to get married, when she was twenty-two. Her mother had always made out that she was ill, to get things done for her. She was selfish. Her father was strict, and had funny ways—he would say one thing when he meant another, but if you knew how to take him, as she did, you could get along with him very well.

She is proud to feel that she models herself in relation to Mary on her father, now dead. As a friend told her, ' . . . as long as you're there your father's still alive'.

Although Mrs. Irwin feels she is her father in relation to Mary (who, then, is Mary?), she, unbeknown to herself, behaves towards Mary like her own mother, and appears to encourage

Mary to see her as she had seen her mother, and to say and do to *her* what she (mother) had not said and done in relation to her own mother.

That is, Mrs. Irwin sees herself in relation to Mary as:

(i) a good mother—
   'I was always told I was a wonderful mother', etc.
(ii) a bad mother—
   'I feel it's me that's done something wrong.'
and
(iii) her own father.

In addition, she is identified with Mary, and induces Mary to see her as 'a terrible mother'.

The following are two examples of the confusing ways in which Mrs. Irwin acts towards Mary.

Mrs. Irwin says, as we have seen, that she is her father all over again with Mary: 'I'm aware of it with Mary, but not with anyone else.'

Now her father had a great sense of humour. An example of her sense of humour is the way in which she used to make fun of Mary and her boy-friend. She used to joke that he sniffed a lot and blinked his eyes. 'We had great fun with Mary and her boy-friends.' As she saw it, Mary thought it was fun too, but Mary said the very opposite. She resented her mother's 'fun' bitterly. This resentment was another sign of her illness that her mother hoped the hospital would help her to get over.

Another example given by Mrs. Irwin shows both her 'humour' and her way of 'encouraging' Mary. When Mary left hospital the second time she took a job in an office, but gave it up after a few weeks. In hospital the third time, she was frightened to take another office job because after two years in hospital she had become too used to hospital ways, and had lost confidence in herself.

MOTHER: We came to see her on Sunday and she was worried stiff about going out to work on Monday—'I won't manage it, I

196

know I can't do it. No, I won't do it right'. I said, 'No, that's right, you won't will you? You'll make a proper mess of it'. And I was trying to joke it off this way.

INTERVIEWER: Oh I see, you were sort of saying that in a jocular manner?

MOTHER: Yes, but she worries about everything.

We shall return to the interaction between Mary and her mother after we have gathered more about Mary's experiences and actions from Mary herself.

Mary says that what she is trying to do is to *establish herself as a person*, especially towards her mother. She feels that her mother is killing her 'personality' or her 'mind'. She resents her mother for this, but feels unable to get the better of her. She claims that her mother tells her to do one thing, and then asks her why she did not do the opposite. She feels that her mother muddled her about her boy-friend, and that her mother manoeuvred her into giving him up. She now feels that if she had known her own feelings at the time she would not have done so. Her mother is very kind, and has done a great deal for her, but she (mother) puts her under a debt of obligation for everything. She wants nothing more from her mother or from anyone like her, and is not asking for anything.

Her mother sees this as ingratitude and selfishness—another facet of her illness.

Mary says that her mother has always put thoughts into her head and had never let her have a 'mind of her own'. What she has been trying to do since she was sixteen is to keep her mother out. She feels that, although not entirely successful, up to a point she has held her own.

At school what she was really interested in was painting but 'this wasn't education' to her parents. If she could get back to that she feels she might discover her own life again.

Her parents agree that Mary did well at music and painting at school. But they have an explanation for this.

197

MOTHER: I think she got away with a lot did Mary, because she had such winning ways. Everybody took to her, everybody made a fuss of her.

INTERVIEWER: How do you mean?

MOTHER: Well, where the sort of tests—I don't mean arithmetic and English and things that *couldn't* be marked any other way but one way—but say art, composition—she might get higher marks than a less attractive child might get that was writing the same thing, because it was Mary.

INTERVIEWER: And did you think that at the time?

MOTHER: Yes.

INTERVIEWER: You thought that at the time?

MOTHER: Yes, yes.

INTERVIEWER: And your husband, did he think that at the time? —In other words, that she was being over-valued?

MOTHER: Yes, he did.

For Mary, her trouble with her mother had begun when she was eleven, after her mother had had an operation on her thyroid. According to Mary, her mother changed towards her after this operation. She picked on her and she went on and on at her. Instead of doing things, she just talked and talked. She could not stop her mother talking at her all the time, and her mother's talk began to get her muddled. She tried to stem her mother's flood of words by various stratagems. The following are some of them. We must remember that such obvious stratagems as *leaving* or telling her mother to *shut up* directly, were not feasible if our observations in the present are some index of the past.

1. She would go *rigid inside*

INTERVIEWER: Supposing you had an opinion, you see, and your mother puts forward the opposite opinion, and supposing—I mean it could happen that your mother's opinion could be right—supposing you saw that your mother was right—you could see that she really was right—what would you do?

Would you agree with her or would you still maintain your opinion?

MARY: I'd be too busy fighting to see that she was right. Tell you what I do, I sort of go rigid so that nobody can get at me.

INTERVIEWER: The whole of your body?

MARY: Yes, so that she can't get at me, nobody can, so that nobody can alter my opinion.

INTERVIEWER: Could you show me how you do that?

MARY: No, I can't show you because it's something I do so—

INTERVIEWER: Do you sort of go like this, or what—or what do you do?

MARY: I just sort of go like that. It docsn't show because—

INTERVIEWER: You mean inside?

MARY: Yes.

INTERVIEWER: Oh I see, inside—you stiffen up inside?

MARY: That's right.

INTERVIEWER: And does you mother not notice that?

MARY: No, I can do that now because she doesn't know, but I can't keep it up.

2.   She tried to *shut everyone out*

With her mother, and later with the nurses in hospital, she tried to be like them, but this was forbidden. So she shut everyone out.

MARY: I got to thinking—trying—being like the nurses, but I made everything too difficult, more difficult than it really was.

INTERVIEWER: In hospital?

MARY: Yes.

INTERVIEWER: In what way?

MARY: Well, I shut everything out then I had to get at it somehow again and I found there was a sort of bridge—I had to get out again.

3.   When she was about fifteen she began to see her mother as 'nasty'. She felt also that her mother was putting her (mother's)

SANITY, MADNESS, AND THE FAMILY

thoughts into her mind, and not letting her think her own thoughts. However, she was frightened to see her mother in this light, and, confused and ashamed, would deliberately muddle herself up.

To herself, she was not herself if she thought what her mother wanted her to think, and, to her mother, she was mad or bad if she did not.

The following passage occurs after Mrs. Irwin has been saying she thinks something was wrong with Mary.

MARY: What do you think was wrong with me?

MOTHER: Well I think your nerves were in a state. I mean to say then there might have been something bothering you that you couldn't tell me.

MARY: There wasn't.

MOTHER: Well you say there wasn't and that's it, but I'm only telling you what I thought then.

MARY: I've never—(pause)—Oh I see, yes. Well it was you that was bothering me.

MOTHER: (laughs)

MARY: And I didn't realize it.

MOTHER: You didn't realize it was me that was bothering you?

MARY: Yes.

MOTHER: Maybe, it could have been, but I think myself it was your job that was bothering you.

MARY: Yes of course—it wouldn't be you would it?

MOTHER: Now that is cheeky and not a thing I expect a mother to get. It's no way to speak to any mother, and you do cheek me nowadays.

4. Holding her breath, standing still, sniffing, and coughing were all means of countering what she felt as her mother's impingements.

MARY: I used to hold my breath because my mother used to go on so quick and (pause.)

INTERVIEWER: Moving you mean?

MARY: Yes.

INTERVIEWER: You mean your mother was moving about the house quickly?

MARY: Yes and everything.

INTERVIEWER: And what did you do?

MARY: Sort of stand like that.

INTERVIEWER: Can you demonstrate to me—sitting in a chair?

MARY: Yes. I just sort of (shows what she did).

INTERVIEWER: With your elbows?

MARY: I'd wait till she stopped talking and then maybe I'd be able to think again. She seemed to stop me from thinking.

INTERVIEWER: What was your mother doing?

MARY: She'd just go on and on about her jobs that she's got to do. She never stops and does them or goes on doing them. She talks about her jobs that she's got to do and talks and talks.

INTERVIEWER: How do you feel when she's doing that?

MARY: Well the jobs are nothing to do with me. She ought to get on with her jobs if she's got them to do shouldn't she?

INTERVIEWER: Sure, sure, but I mean, how do you feel inside yourself when she does that?

MARY: Oh, I don't know, she seems to stop me from thinking. I can't explain how I feel—sort of all upset, you know.

INTERVIEWER: And is it at this time you hold your breath?

MARY: Yes.

INTERVIEWER: Mmm.

MARY: Yes. To stop her from affecting me, you know. It seems to affect my head and everything you know.

Further evidence, showing that such so-called catatonic behaviour was praxis, is contained in two stories told by Mary's sister Angela and her mother respectively.

ANGELA: She had the habit of—um—going all stiff, and she wouldn't move, and she just would suddenly sit in the chair and she'd just go all stiff and rigid—you couldn't move her, you couldn't—you couldn't speak to her, get through to her at all.

INTERVIEWER: How long would she stay like that?

ANGELA: Oh she'd stay like that for half an hour or more. There was one particular time, I remember, she went through into the front room and stood with one hand on the settee and one hand on the chair, bent over like that, and she stayed there for —Oh I don't know, perhaps it was an hour. And she wouldn't move. And they had to get the doctor to her in the end because they thought perhaps there *was* something wrong (smiling). And meanwhile we were living in rooms in a big house, and the landlady came through into the front room, and when Mary saw her she stopped and you know, was quite natural. And as soon as the landlady went out and my father went into her again she started again (laughs).

INTERVIEWER: So that you feel this was something that Mary had control of?

ANGELA: Oh yes, yes. Oh it was definitely under her control. I'm *sure* of that.

Mother tells how Mary got 'better' for her sister's wedding.

MOTHER: Mary got better for the wedding and Mary was bridesmaid.

INTERVIEWER: She got *better* for the wedding?

MOTHER: Yes. Because it happened very suddenly. I went to see her on the Sunday, three weeks before the wedding, and I said to her, 'What about Angela's wedding, you always were going to be bridesmaid,' I said, 'Are you going to get better for the wedding?'—And this is how I tried to talk her out of that. 'Oh go on!' she says. I said, 'Well Mary, Angela's in a *difficult* position because,' I said, 'she'll need a bridesmaid,' and I said, 'Her friend is going to stand in for you if you're not able to be there,' and I said, 'If you are able Angela will have the two of you.' So either that night or the next morning she took

I don't know how many aspirin tablets, but I never knew of
that for a long long time.

INTERVIEWER: Tried to kill herself?

MOTHER: Yes. And when she came to, she was as right as rain.

INTERVIEWER: How do you mean 'she was as right as rain'?

MOTHER: Well she seemed to be perfectly normal to everybody.

So Mary was perfectly normal to everybody for the wedding,
and then went back to hospital immediately.

Mary, however, recognizes some of the consequences of the
perilous stratagems that she has used, since they are not always
easy to give up at will, and secondary consequences may ensue
which were not intended.

For instance, if you shut people off, and put things out of your
mind, you may come to a stop, feel empty, and necessarily fearful
of the inrush or implosion of reality in a persecuting form.

MARY: I'm scared I'm going to stop and then all that I've shoved
back will come rushing forward and hit me and knock me
over.

INTERVIEWER: How do you mean stop?

MARY: Well—well—that I won't be able to—(pause).

INTERVIEWER: You mean you're afraid somehow you will stop
living, or what?

MARY: That I won't be able to come to, or I do come to—Oh, I
don't know, I just can't seem to think any more, if you know
what I mean, and it's only because I—Oh, I don't know—
(pause).

INTERVIEWER: Only because?

MARY: Well, I—(pause)—put everything away from myself, I
can't go on putting it away from me can I? It gets to the point
when there is nothing more to put away I suppose, that is when
I come to a stop.

INTERVIEWER: You mean putting away your problems and so on,
or thinking about your problems, or what?

MARY: No, just people.

INTERVIEWER: Putting away getting on with people or what? Trying to shut people out of your life I suppose?

MARY: Yes.

INTERVIEWER: Mmm?

MARY: That's what I do—shut people out of my life and—(pause).

INTERVIEWER: Is that what you meant when you said putting things away?

MARY: I don't do it deliberately but em—Oh, I know what it is, what I mean is I stop putting good things away and then I meet bad things.

INTERVIEWER: You stop putting good things—

MARY: I get away from the—(pause). Oh I don't know, I have lost touch with reality, I seem to lose touch with reality. It's ridiculous (pause)—Is it right to think? You should think shouldn't you?

To come to a stop like this would be to die existentially if not biologically.

As has been partly shown so far, Mary was put in an untenable position, from which she could not make any of the more usual moves, for instance, leaving the field, controlling the others, identification, without the negative pay-off being too high. The only moves that it seemed feasible to make were of the order of coughing, sniffing, holding her breath, standing or staying still, going rigid inside, stopping her thoughts, shutting everyone out. But if she sees the whole world as her mother, she is liable to act towards everyone on the presupposition that everyone acts towards her in the same way as her mother.

In this she was at a disadvantage. Transference is a normal phenomenon. When she went from home to hospital, she could hardly be expected to discriminate between the two social systems. Her home was only too similar to a mental hospital, since her mother had defined their relationship as a nurse-patient one from an early age.

As at home, she had to ask permission to go out, she was

allowed no money of her own, she was told she was 'ill', and she was expected to get well. But to be ill is to suffer from obstinacy, defiance, and ingratitude. It is to lack emotions or to have emotions of the wrong kind. She was in a ward of women, and when she got fond of a male patient she was told not to get emotionally involved, and so on.

Our observations in this case extend over a period in which Mary was beginning to achieve some measure of genuine autonomy and independence. At every point this was met by the counter-attribution from her parents that what *we* take to be independence is selfishness and conceit.

MARY: My mother said it was wrong when I came home the first time but I was very happy then. I was happier than I have been—I really felt on top of the world, sort of thing and em—I felt confident as well, and, em, she says that I was too full of myself.

MOTHER: You know that's not what I mean Mary. You came home and you jumped immediately into a job.

MARY: When I was coming home for weekends you said that I wasn't well and that I was selfish and too full of myself, and all the rest of it.

MOTHER: Well you were selfish then Mary. It was because you were ill.

MARY: Sick.

MOTHER: Well that's how it appeared to us that you were selfish.

MARY: How was I selfish?

MOTHER: Well I can't remember now, but I do know that—

MARY: No, you won't tell me now, so I don't know how—so if I get better again I won't know if I'm right or wrong or when I'm going to crack up again or what I'm going to do.

MOTHER: Now that's what I call selfishness, thrusting your opinion on me and not listening to mine.

MARY: Well you were thrusting your opinion on me and not listening to *mine*. You see it works both ways.

205

MOTHER: I know.

MARY: But I always have to take it when I'm at home from you, because you're my mother. See—I can't be selfish—but if you're selfish that's not wrong. You're not ill because you're selfish, you're just my mother and it's right if you can do it.

MOTHER: I know what you mean.

INTERVIEWER: What was she actually doing when you thought she was either selfish or ill—what was she actually doing?

MOTHER: Well I can't remember.

INTERVIEWER: You can't remember?

MOTHER: But I mean I can remember saying she was selfish.

Investigation has failed to reveal in what way Mary is selfish, except that she no longer tells her mother everything, does not seek her advice or permission to do things, and so on.

It is hard for Mrs. Irwin not to see Mary as ill, for instance, when Mary tells her she feels in a rut at home, and would like to get away on her own.

MARY: I've told you it before haven't I?

MOTHER: Yes, you've told me it before, but it's *worse* now.

MARY: Well I wouldn't say it's worse.

MOTHER: Well it's stronger then.

MARY: I wouldn't say it's worse. I wouldn't count it as an illness that's got *worse* (pause). It's just something I *want*. If you want something it's not an *illness* that you want it. If you wanted to get married you wouldn't say you were ill would you?

MOTHER: No.

MARY: Well it's just like saying you want a career isn't it? You keep saying, 'Well wait till you find something that you really want'. I'll never find it will I? Folks say, 'Well don't just sit and wait for something'. You don't know what you're to go by.

MOTHER: I've said, 'Have patience till you're *better*'.

Again, Mary has been talking about being independent. This involves, she says, establishing herself as a person, finding out for herself what she wants to do with her life. It might even involve leaving home.

MOTHER: Well I think Mary's idea of being independent—it doesn't mean being able to do what you want to do, it means being able to model a course for your life—finding ways and means of carrying it out. But to be independent doesn't mean you walk out of the door and don't tell anybody where you are going, and you're worried stiff about where she is—that's not independence to me.

MARY: I didn't walk out thinking I was going to be independent —for goodness sake—

MOTHER: Oh I don't mean at the time you went away.

INTERVIEWER: But you wouldn't see that as inconsistent with being independent would you?

MOTHER: Well it may be independence of a kind but it's not the right kind of independence. She can be independent. She can make her arrangements and then say, 'I'll go away a week on Monday' or whenever it was—'I've got a nice job so-and-so' —and let's know and go decently.

INTERVIEWER: But supposing she didn't say that sort of thing to you?

MOTHER: Well if she didn't want me to know she could say, 'Well, look, Mummy, I'm going away, but I'd rather you didn't know or bother about where I'm going', I would say, 'All right then'. That's still the right way isn't it?

MARY: But when do I go the wrong way then?

MOTHER: When you leave us wondering how you are getting on and what you are doing.

MARY: When did I do that?

MOTHER: You've never done it, it's the way that you're talking about doing things—about independence.

MARY: Oh heck—I'm nothing of the kind.

MOTHER: Well you say you want to stand on your own feet and establish yourself, don't you?

MARY: I don't know whether I want to do that now (pause)—
Why I was going to leave home was because I just didn't think
I could get on with you.

MOTHER: Yes, well I've always advised you to go away from home
haven't I? Even when we were at Exeter we advised you—go
away. We tried to get you to join the Army and you wouldn't
hear of it.

One has to remind oneself that Mrs. Irwin is talking about
something that never happened. The most that happened was
that on one occasion Mary walked out after a row without
saying where she was going, and came back in a few hours. Her
mother is impervious to the point that Mary repeatedly makes,
that she does not want to be ordered to be autonomous.

FAMILY 10

The Kings

CLINICAL PERSPECTIVE

Hazel is sixteen. When admitted to hospital she was in a catatonic state. She said nothing, would not move, and would not eat. She looked very frightened. When she began to speak she said in whispers that she was afraid that her mother wanted to poison her, or otherwise get rid of her. She thought that the girls at school were saying she was silly and stupid, and that she wanted to murder her brothers.

Gradually, over three months, she recovered from this state, until she was what her parents regarded as her normal and usual self.

Our investigation extended through the period of relative recovery, a second less severe breakdown, and a second period of partial recovery.

STRUCTURE OF INVESTIGATION

Interviews	Occasions
Mother	2
Father	2
Hazel (16)	3
Brother (13)	
Brother (11)	

Interviews	*Occasions*
Mother and Hazel	2
Mother, father and Hazel	4
Mother's father (Mr. Brown)	1
Mother's mother (Mrs. Brown)	1
Mother's older sister and husband (Mr. and Mrs. Blake)	1
Mother's younger sister and husband	1
Mother, father, mother's mother and Hazel	1
	—
	18

This represents seventeen hours' interviewing time, of which fourteen hours were tape-recorded.

INTRODUCTION

The initial investigation of this family took two years. During this time we were continually making new discoveries about them. Only when the maternal grandparents and a maternal aunt and her husband were seen did an intelligible picture of the whole family situation constellated around Hazel come into focus.

To what extent are Hazel's schizophrenic experience and behaviour intelligible in the light of the praxis and process of her family situation?

The following is our synthesis of the multiple perspectives before us.

THE FAMILY SITUATION

This is a middle-middle-class family. Mr. King is a biochemist. He was born and brought up in Australia, where his whole family remains. Thus in this case the family nexus consists solely of Mrs. King's family.

For present purposes, Mrs. King's grandfather can be regarded as the founder of this section of the family. Of working-class origins, he amassed a considerable fortune, which he passed on to the eldest of his three daughters, there being no sons. This maiden aunt of the patient's mother now holds the family purse-strings. The maternal grandmother was the second eldest daughter, as Mrs. King was also. The maternal grandmother always felt put out by her older sister, and had little time for her own eldest daughter. However, a very close bond developed between her and Hazel's mother. We shall see below how extraordinary this bond is.

The maternal grandmother, although overshadowed by her older sister, has an empire of her own that includes her husband and the King family. Her husband has not worked for over thirty years, and is regarded by all the family as entirely in her emotional and economic control.

According to her own account, her husband's, and her older sister's, Hazel's mother grew up with an intense desire to outdo her older sister. Among other things, in line with her mother, she wished to divert the family fortune from the older sister's line (mother's aunt and grandmother's sister) to the line of the second oldest (she and her mother). This meant having the eldest male grandchild. With this in view, she indeed did marry *before* her older sister, and produced the first grandchild. Unfortunately, however, it was a girl, Hazel, and Mrs. Blake, who had married a few months after she did, produced the first male grandchild, a few months after Hazel was born, and before, of course, Mrs. King could produce her second child, who was a boy. Mrs. King and her mother continue to feel intensely what a bitter blow this was, and what bad luck they had. Mrs. King feels also that her aunt and her older sister have never forgiven her for getting married first, and that they (maternal aunt and Mrs. Blake) disparaged both her and Hazel, from the moment of Hazel's birth.

Such attributions, as far as we could gather from direct knowledge of Mrs. Blake, are without validity. Nevertheless, they continue to colour Mrs. King's and her mother's view of her. They keep all this to themselves, however, and Mrs. Blake appears to be quite unaware of the intense and mixed feelings that her mother and Mrs. King have about her, and the feelings that they suppose she has about them. Although Mr. King cannot help but be aware of the close tie between his wife and her mother, he is not aware that she married him, if she and her mother are now to be believed, largely for reasons of family intrigue. After their wedding, Mrs. King would not leave her mother, and so they had no honeymoon. Only on condition that her husband acquire a house *directly* across the street from her parents' house did she agree even to live with him. Her older sister believes that not a day in her life has passed when Mrs. King has not seen and does not see her mother. The neighbours have a joke about 'when is a tunnel going to be constructed between their houses'.

Mr. King has never been able to get his wife to come on holiday with him. He has the option of going on holiday with his wife and her parents, or by himself. He does the latter.

INTERVIEWER: Well then with your parents-in-law, how much is it possible to discuss problems like this, as I gather you really see them as rather interfering?

FATHER: Well they always *have* done to the extent that I can't get my wife to come away on holiday with me and the family, but she insists on going away with her father and mother, as I say, this is the second problem in a sense.

INTERVIEWER: Yes, it's really very important.

FATHER: It's an odd thing. I mean I did, after the war, go away with the whole bunch of them, but I decided later on that this was going a bit too far, that if she wouldn't come away with me and the children (laughing slightly) that I wouldn't go away at all with them, and in point of fact I don't usually do, although I'm quite willing to help as far as I'm able with their arrangements you know.

INTERVIEWER: And this means, does it, that you're simply left at home?

FATHER: That's right, yes.

It was made clear to him that it did not matter very much what he did.

In disgust he left for a while, but then returned because he felt an obligation to the children 'to try to save them as much as possible from the situation'.

Nevertheless, Mr. King was, as far as we could judge, unable to bring himself to intervene in any effective way. When it came to any point when he felt he might take a stand, he was always afraid to do so, principally, he said, because he felt that his wife would break down if he disrupted the family system which was so much based on his wife's desperately close relationship with her mother.

Our impression, comparing the families of schizophrenics with other families, is that they are relatively closed systems, and that the future patient is particularly enclosed within the family system. In no family was this so much the case as with the Kings.

The extent to which Hazel was kept within a set of relations comprising her mother, grandmother, and grandfather was remarkable. Even relations with her younger brothers and with her father were forbidden or discouraged.

Mr. King has never been allowed to go out with Hazel alone, because, according to Mrs. King and her mother, 'he cannot be trusted'. What they meant by this was left to the imagination.

Ever since she went to school, Hazel has been accompanied to and from the gates by her grandfather. This is one of his major tasks. He also takes her to and from Sunday school—the only other extra-familial situation allowed her.

She has never been so much as allowed out in the street unaccompanied in her whole life. She has never met any girls or boys except *in* school, or *in* Sunday school. She has never had a girl- or boy-friend into the house. As her mother and grandmother themselves talk to almost no one, the situation is virtually sealed off.

Mr. King thinks all this is not good for Hazel, but 'it is very difficult', and he does not see what he can do about it.

One justification that Mrs. King gives for this extraordinary situation is that it is what Hazel wants. She feels that she understands Hazel because she feels the way Hazel does. She feels no desire to break away from her mother, and assumes the absence of any such desire in Hazel. In her view, Hazel, like her, does not want friends: does not like to meet people, to go to or come from school either by herself or with other girls. She also supposes that Hazel does not like her cousin and is jealous of her.

These attributions are made quite imperviously to Hazel's own expressed views to the contary.

For instance,

FATHER: Yes, I have wondered whether we hadn't encouraged Hazel to mix enough, the family being sort of too closely knit, grandparents and cousins and so on, hasn't encouraged enough interest outside the family circle. I wondered whether that could have been a contributory cause. I think that Hazel has been rather over-protected, having adults or others with her— I think that's true isn't it Sybil?

MOTHER: Well I don't know about that. She never seemed to want to go out by herself like that, to my mind, I think.

FATHER: No, that's true, I mean when she came home from school on the bus, I mean your father would very often go—

HAZEL: I didn't like that.

FATHER: You didn't like that?

HAZEL: No.

Later:

FATHER: She was rather under the care of adults the whole time, being met by her grandfather—

MOTHER: (Interrupts) Oh she was. She liked it. I mean and it was —it was something for my father to do, I mean, you know. He likes a walk and a stroll, you know.

HAZEL: I didn't like it.

MOTHER: No—well.

FATHER: You didn't like him coming? No I felt perhaps the other girls might have thought it was rather odd if you were sort of met by a grandparent.

MOTHER: You said you didn't like coming by the bus by yourself.

HAZEL: Oh I didn't mind coming home.

Despite the way her mother and grandmother engulf her, and segregate her even from her father, their behaviour is at the same time contradictory.

Although not allowed to be with Hazel, her father was blamed both for giving her too much time and too little. For instance, he is said to spoil her.

INTERVIEWER: You were saying she was sulking. What did you do or what did your husband do when she sulked? How did you deal with that?

MOTHER: I'm afraid I left her alone I think.

INTERVIEWER: You left her alone. And your husband?

MOTHER: Well I think if anything he spoilt Hazel more than the boys actually. I think he used to sometimes go to her and deal with her but—

INTERVIEWER: How did he deal with her?

MOTHER: Well he tried to talk to her I think, that sort of thing really. Take her apart and sort of ask what she was sulking about.

Her father as well as her mother expressed intense ambivalance and disappointment in Hazel, in her presence, called her an ugly duckling, fat, awkward, without social graces or charm.

FATHER: She's not *entirely* without brains.

MOTHER: When all your family see so many faults in a child, it's difficult for it not to affect you.

Yet her mother says that she does not know where Hazel got the idea that she was not clever. Maybe it was because the girls at school called her silly. She and her husband had always told her not to worry about examinations, and they did not let her try for the eleven-plus, because they did not want to strain her.

MOTHER: Personally I think she is quite clever, but it hasn't come out—if you know what I mean (slight laugh). She's intelligent and her general knowledge and memory and things like that are very good. She's no good at arithmetic or anything like that.

Mrs. King had never thought Hazel was unhappy. Of course she got into sulky moods, but that was because she was always jealous of her younger brothers. Why Hazel should be like that her mother could not understand, because she had all the attention 'really'. In fact, she said, Hazel had been rather spoiled. Not that Mrs. King had spoiled her, since she had not spoiled any of her children. It was Grandfather who had spoiled her, and 'everybody else'. Hazel had perhaps been upset by her husband. He had never treated the children as a father should. Mrs. King had never been very close to Hazel. She was closer to the boys, but this was only because Hazel was such a difficult child to get anything out of. Often she cried quietly to herself and Mrs. King had then tried 'to get something out of her', but without success. Mr. King was closer to Hazel than she was.

Until ten Hazel had been rather disobedient, but since then she had had no trouble with her.

Mrs. King's attitude to Hazel reflected an ambivalence that was very disturbing to observers. Hazel, while so 'over-protected', was simultaneously ignored and treated with cold detachment.

While she was partially catatonic, the ward sister made these observations of mother, father, and daughter together.

SISTER: I felt the mother was terribly uninterested in Hazel's feelings this afternoon, and the father seemed quite immune. The child lay down on the bed and I wanted to comfort her myself. Mother sat bolt upright and just put her hand out, stretched out her arms more or less to the child to let the child really fondle the mother rather than the mother fondle the child.

The only time I saw her really animated was when she talked about her sons, which rather irritated me. Father—he talked in a monotonous voice as though he was reeling this off half of the time, and it was all just, well, you know, 'I've got to do something. The doctor wants me to talk', and unless the doctor prompted him there was hardly anything really different said. Mother didn't seem concerned when Hazel wouldn't eat, she was more concerned with the boys, she sat with the boys while they ate their meal, even in spite of Hazel being ill because she had—the husband said it was malnutrition and they didn't seem concerned because Hazel didn't eat. Mother gave a little laugh, she didn't really—at times she didn't seem at all concerned. I can't understand what she thought was funny. The mother said she couldn't sleep, she went into Hazel's bed, but couldn't sleep—How can a mother sleep if the child is ill and disturbed—I should want to be comforting the child. And she left her with Granny while she took the boys to Town, when Hazel was obviously ill, following her round looking strangely at her. Mother said she didn't like this—the way Hazel looked at her. And the father then rang his brother-in-law, and the brother-in-law said that she was ill, and that was his lot—he didn't seem to think he should do much about it. And when the mother sat with Hazel she sounded as though she was very brave to have done this while the child was so— feeling strange and looking strange.

Mr. King said that he thought that his wife was more upset at not being able to get another baby than about Hazel's illness. According to him, she had been blaming Hazel for this and other things that had gone wrong, and had now started to turn against her.

Mr. King, however, although appearing to be the rational one of the two, is hardly less contradictory and confusing in his statements than his wife. While speaking about his wife's desire for another child, he is extremely vague about the whole matter, even as to whether she might not have been pregnant recently. His wife may have had an abortion, but if she had, 'I was not consulted'. It all might have been arranged between his wife and her mother and her older sister. Anyway it was his wife's fault if she had not got four children.

Again, while saying that his wife has turned against Hazel, he reports that since Hazel's first 'breakdown' she has slept with her. She tells him she does this because Hazel calls out for her in the night. Mr. King doubts this, saying that his wife's behaviour was in answer to some need of hers, rather than Hazel's.

Mrs. King is grossly hysterical, giggly, dissociated, frigid, subject to multiple anxieties that she deals with by an extreme retrenchment of herself. For instance, she does not know whether she has had an orgasm or a climax, she is not sure whether or not her husband has 'proper' intercourse with her; she is not sure whether or not he uses a contraceptive, or whether he ejaculates inside or outside her.

Since her marriage she has hardly ever been outside the house unaccompanied by her own mother or father, apart from visits to the local shops. She has extensive fears of travelling, of meeting people. Her self-consciousness amounts to ideas that people look at her in the street, and that they make ridiculing remarks about her.

Both Hazel's 'breakdowns' become much more intelligible when placed in this utterly confused context, where each parent is simultaneously imputing and denying ambivalent feelings towards her, denying they are imputing them, and imputing that the other is denying them.

In some ways the most pathetic figure of all in this family is the grandfather. He was kept out of our way, and so it was only possible to see him once. As the grandmother said, 'Why do you want to see him, he can tell you nothing that I have not told you?'

But on one occasion when one of our team knocked on the Kings' door,[1] 'after a slight delay, the door was opened by an

[1] From report of home visit.

elderly man in a muffler and gaberdine raincoat. He seemed
hesitant about talking to me. Mrs. King was out shopping; she
would be back soon if I would like to come again later. To get
into the house, I asked to see Hazel for a moment. She heard
this and came out of the sitting-room, smiling, "Oh, it's you".
She hesitated as if unsure whether or not to continue and then
with a smile at me she turned round and went back into the room.
The grandfather, who had been completely ignored, said sadly,
"She won't stay in the same room with me now. It's terrible,
terrible; but if that's the way she wants it, I try not to let her see
how much I mind. I've always tried to put up with everything
for their sakes". He didn't wipe away the tears that ran down the
lines of his small round face—as though perhaps he was too used
to having them there to notice. At one time he must have been
a cheery, robin-like little man, with bright colouring and eyes.
He still has red cheeks and a red moustache, possibly not natural
but dyed with smoking. He didn't sit down or ask me to, and
my impression was that he had been standing like a sentinel in
the cold hall, in outdoor clothes, since entering. Although I knew
Hazel could hear everything I said (her grandfather is slightly
deaf but speaks softly himself), this opportunity to speak to him
seemed one not to be missed. I asked him why Hazel didn't want
to be in the same room as him. "She thinks it's me that keeps her
a prisoner. I think they've told her something—something that
makes her hate me and feel it's all my fault. She was my little
bird, my whole life, and now they've taken her away and keep
her shut up. She should be out in the sun and the fields. She
should learn to use her wings. She used to sing so sweetly, my
little bird. She was so gay, so alive. And then gradually she became
quiet. Things happened I didn't understand. She used to tell me
everything: she was my whole life but she began to get frightened
and now she doesn't want me any more. She says she hates me.
No one will ever know what I feel, know what I go through.
I ask myself why she should hate me, why she should be frightened
to talk to me now. I only know she should be free to try her wings,

but they use me to keep her a prisoner." He had to stop to blow his nose copiously, and having done this, went quiet, answering only, "I try not to say anything", when I asked him to go on. Perhaps Hazel might want friends of her own now? He replied he wouldn't mind *anything* if she would only talk to him again.

I had probably been alone with him for only ten minutes when Mrs. King could be seen through the hall windows hurrying up the other side of the road and into her mother's house. Mr. Brown, now calm, commented, "She'll be going to ask about your visit". She was there about five minutes before reappearing to cross the road, home. She entered ignoring her father, who left at once. We went into the sitting-room. Hazel who was there was sent off into the kitchen. She went unwillingly but obediently rather like a child going up to bed.'

FAMILY 11

The Lawsons

Past History

Agnes Lawson, a plumber's daughter, entered mental hospital for the first time when she was nineteen. There she was diagnosed as a paranoid schizophrenic and given fifty insulin comas. Six months later she was discharged 'apparently well'. Over the next two years she was seen as an out-patient, and then discharged finally.

She took a job, but worked only intermittently. A year later she was referred again to the out-patient clinic, where she was diagnosed as relapsing. Tranquillizers were prescribed. She improved clinically for a time, but relapsed again, and one year after her re-referral she was readmitted to hospital. She was twenty-four.

Again she was given fifty insulin comas, and four months later she was discharged.

She remained at home for a year doing no work, and then got herself a job, but one month later she again began to 'relapse'. She was readmitted. She was now twenty-five. Six months later she was discharged, having been treated this time with tranquillizers alone. For the next two years she attended the out-patient clinic, and for most of this time she remained clinically improved, although making no more attempts to work. However,

221

after a year and a half she began to relapse, and six months later was readmitted for the fourth time. She was now twenty-seven.

Recent History

During the six months before her fourth admission, Agnes had frequently complained to the out-patient psychiatrist that she felt her father did not want her and wished to get rid of her, and that her mother colluded with him. She said also that she was frightened and lonely, insecure and rejected and could easily imagine voices again. Shortly before her admission she said she was hearing the voice of an electrician who had been working in her house. At this time also her mother complained perplexedly that Agnes had turned against her father 'and it is very hurtful, Doctor'.

Clinical examination at the time of admission revealed the following features. Auditory hallucinations, paranoid ideas (e.g. people were saying unkind things about her and could read her thoughts; the hospital was not interested in helping her; her parents did not want her and were ganged up against her), impulsive aggressiveness, thought-disorder (inconsistent, woolly rambling), and incongruity of thought and affect. Her manner was childish, and she was shy and over-sensitive to the presence of others, being afraid to mix with people. She showed volitional defect, in that she was unable to work or support herself, and she was preoccupied with religious ideas.

She was again diagnosed as suffering from paranoid schizophrenia, and tranquillizer therapy was instituted.

Three months later Agnes, although from the clinical point of view still paranoid, with only partial insight into her persecutory delusions and into the fact that she had been ill, was regarded as fit enough to leave hospital and to try to train as a shorthand-typist. Arrangements were made for her to attend a local College of Further Education. At the same time her parents were told that she was now fit to leave and informed of these plans. It became very difficult, however, to arrange for her discharge.

Agnes complained that she felt her parents did not want her at home, while her parents in turn said that she was very difficult to live with. This was put down to Agnes's paranoid attitude. The possibility of her going to a hostel was considered. However, there was no hostel available, and we felt that this was an appropriate point to start the main body of our investigation, and a series of interviews was arranged.

Her parents refused to be interviewed alone, and they would not agree to a home visit (although at one point in the investigation her father invited us to visit their home and to interview all the neighbours because, as he said, he had nothing to hide). However, we do have statements by her mother to us, although not at formal interviews. Advantage was taken of the fact that she came up to the hospital to visit Agnes, and later accompanied her as an out-patient; on these occasions one of us had a few words with her. In this way we managed to gather some valuable items of information.

STRUCTURE OF INVESTIGATION

The family here consists of father and mother and three children. Father is fifty-nine; mother is fifty-seven; Shirley, the oldest, is thirty-six; Jimmy, the son, twenty-eight; and Agnes twenty-seven. Both the brother and the sister are married.

Interviews	When held	Form of record
Agnes and her mother	0	written report
,, ,, ,, ,,	0 + 6 dys	,, ,,
Agnes	0 + 16 dys	tape-recording
Agnes and her mother	0 + 17 dys	,, ,,
Agnes and her father	0 + 19 dys	,, ,,
Mother and father	0 + 20 dys	,, ,,
Agnes, mother, and father	0 + 20 dys	,, ,,
Mother	0 + 1 yr	written report
Agnes	0 + 1 yr 4 mths	,, ,,

Interviews	When held	Form of record
Agnes	o + 1 yr 4 mths 1 wk	tape-recording
Agnes	o + 1 yr 4 mths 2 wks	,, ,,
Agnes's brother and		
sister-in-law	o + 1 yr 4 mths 2 wks	,, ,,
Agnes	o + 1 yr 4 mths 3 wks	,, ,,

This represents fourteen hours of interviewing time, of which ten were tape-recorded.

PRESENTATION OF DATA

We shall present our description of the interviews in the following order:

Agnes
Agnes and her mother (derived from all three interviews)
Agnes and her father
Mother and father
Agnes, mother, and father
Mother
Agnes (derived from the series of four interviews)
Agnes's brother and sister-in-law

We start with a description of the first interview with Agnes alone, because although two interviews with Agnes and her mother occurred before this, the investigation of the interaction between them was not completed until the third, and these three interviews are best treated as a single series.

Agnes, as we have seen, had been attending the out-patient clinic for six months before her admission, and in the out-patient records there are frequent notes that she felt that her father did not want her, that he wanted to get rid of her, that her parents were ganged up against her and had told her to get out of the house and get back to hospital. She had also said that she felt very frightened and lonely, anxious and rejected, and could easily

224

imagine voices again. About a month later there was a note which consisted of two parts: a statement from Agnes that she was now hearing the voice of a man, an electrician who had been working in the house, and a perplexed statement by her mother that Agnes had turned against her father, 'and it is very hurtful, Doctor'.

We shall now go on to describe under various sub-headings the first interview with Agnes alone.

AGNES

Incongruity of thought and affect
Agnes giggled frequently and laughed in an embarrassed way when she spoke of sexual matters. This lessened as the interview went on, as she became less shy.

'Thought disorder' and 'lack of insight'
Examination of this interview shows that her 'thought disorder' was highly selective and present only over certain issues. The vagueness and contradictoriness described clinically seemed the expression of conflict between a desire to think things out for herself and her uncertainty over the validity of her perceptions and evaluations. Throughout the session she constantly sought validation of her point of view from the interviewer, and when this was not immediately forthcoming she tended to retract what she said. When her opinion was endorsed she tended to stand by it and restate it more firmly.

The illness
Her problem, as she described it, consisted of imagining up things; quarrelling with her parents, particularly her father; not telling her parents what she was thinking; not being grown up; wanting attention; and not mixing with people.

Although she said that this was part of her illness, she was also doubtful whether, in fact, she had been imagining things. Although she did not expect the interviewer to be able to say whether or not these events had occurred, she constantly sought from him confirmation that they were possible. They were:

1. Hearing the voice of a man in bed at night, making love to her and asking her to marry him. Sometimes the voice threatened to kill her, in a tone of love and affection, so that she could never be sure what his true feelings were for her. This hallucination had been present on each admission, although in each case it had been a different man; but in every case it had been the voice of a man that she was acquainted with and had spoken to, and who she felt had shown affection for and interest in her. On this last occasion it was the voice of an electrician who had been re-wiring the house. He had been there about three or four days with a helper, a boy of sixteen, who had started talking to her. He asked her if she were married, and told her that the electrician was not. The electrician then spoke to her, and he told her about himself, for instance, that his girl friend had recently broken off their engagement. She felt this man was interested in her, and she was attracted to him, and felt the boy was encouraging her interest. The electrician asked her how she spent her spare time, whether she went out much, and when she said no, he offered to take her out to a club. Before he left he promised to write. She was very thrilled. Later that day, walking down the street feeling excited, she began to wonder if this was her 'Mr. Right'. Then something funny happened inside her, something she could not clearly describe, but that night while lying in bed she heard him speaking to her.

2. Perceiving that different men at her place of work found her attractive. Again, she was not sure whether this was imagination or not. However, she felt it must be, because she was too dowdily dressed and too immature to be attractive to any man. It had usually been the voice of one of these men that she had heard at night.

3. Imagining that people at work had criticized her.

4. Imagining that her parents did not want her at home.

5. Quarrelling with her father because she imagined he disliked her.

6. Imagining her parents did not want her to get married.

She was also worried about imagination in another way, although she was unaware that she was using the word in two different ways. At night in bed she became sexually excited, and imagined (not hallucinated) erotic scenes. This worried her because she felt it caused her to hear voices. Since childhood she had masturbated when she felt lonely, and was afraid she had damaged herself.

Comment

Items 2 to 6 had been labelled as delusions from the clinical point of view. From our point of view such a judgement is not possible without first investigating the relevant social field. For example, in the case of item 3, she described an incident where she had been sacked for being slow, but she so lacked confidence in her perceptions that despite this she still felt uncertain of her impression that her workmates had been criticizing her for slowness. In the case of item 5, she felt she had been unnecessarily rude to her parents in the past, and had caused them to worry. She decided she was not going to be rude in future, although she said it would be difficult not to be because her father had such a temper. She felt great concern for her parents, even though her father had accused her of thinking more about outsiders than about them. Although she did not think this was true, she did think perhaps she was a bit selfish. In respect of item 6 she described an exchange with her parents as evidence that she was really imagining that they did not want her to get married, but ironically, the exchange, as she described it, was an excellent example of mystification on this issue. She, of course, failed to perceive this. It was clear to us, therefore, that this girl had the greatest difficulty in evaluating cues of other persons' behaviour, particularly those indicating sexual interest or hostility. Her hallucination, with its sexual content, and the threat made in a loving tone, illustrated this. It was also clear that she was afraid of her sexual feelings and of becoming sexually excited.

Further features which she regarded as expressions of illness

She felt she had not grown up, and this was because she had no boy-friend
She was ill, she said, because she dressed dowdily and could not attract, far less hold, a boy friend.

She said she wanted to be the centre of a boy's attention, but this was illness because it meant wanting to be 'in the limelight'. Thus it was illness not to be able to attract a boy-friend, and it was illness to want to attract one, demonstrating again her difficulty in evaluating her sexual feelings. She was aware of this problem, and thought it an important factor in her 'illness', but she was unable to work out its ramifications. For instance, she knew that she felt anxious when she was attracted to a man, but she was unable to explain why. The reasons she gave were contradictory, and she ended by saying uncertainly, 'I suppose it's not quite a nice thing to have sexual feelings, is it, do you think?'

She felt that part of her illness was that she kept things to herself, but she was extremely vague about this, and about when it started. She thought it must have been when she was nineteen, but she could not say what she was keeping to herself, because actually, she said, she found it difficult to keep anything to herself because she talked too much, and besides she thought people could read her thoughts. As a child she had always been open with people because she had wanted to be like Jesus, straightforward and above-board, but she found that people were underhand; so she started keeping her thoughts to herself, when she was about nineteen perhaps. Another reason for keeping her thoughts to herself was that people were nosey. They were always trying to pry into her affairs, her relatives for example, although not her parents. She supposed it was true that her parents wanted to know all she did, but she did not think they were nosey, because after all it was only natural for them to want to know all about her as they wanted her to get better. However, she said, she did not discuss sexual matters with them, but she was vague about her reasons for not doing so. She seemed to imply both that it was her fault, because she felt they were broadminded, and that it was their fault, because they had had a strict upbringing and would not understand.

She felt that not mixing with people was another aspect of her illness, and that she was to blame because she was not a good mixer. However, the clinical record showed that on earlier occasions she had blamed her parents for this, complaining that her father in particular had been discouragingly strict about her mixing with people. Recently, she said (the record continued), he had begun urging her to go out and enjoy herself, but she felt she now lacked the necessary self-confidence.

However, during the past year she had been going to church and mixing better. This was her only extrafamilial activity, and she was very keen on it. She felt Jesus was helping her and she now wanted to help him. Accordingly, she said her prayers each night and went to church three times on Sunday and every Wednesday evening.

To summarize, Agnes lacked confidence in her perceptions and evaluations of the cues of behaviour, particularly those of sexuality and hostility. She was unable to evaluate attitudes over these matters, and she was unsure of the validity of her sexual feelings and of her desire for privacy and autonomy.

AGNES AND HER MOTHER TOGETHER

We shall now summarize some of the issues that arose in the interviews with Agnes and her mother.

In the following passages we shall condense sections of tape, preserving as far as we can the speaker's own words and idiom.

Attributions, implicit injunctions, unrecognized contradictions

MOTHER: They had been such a close family until Agnes's 'illness', which had come to them as a terrible shock. She believed

Agnes had been given an inferiority complex at the hairdresser's where she had been apprenticed, because they lived in a council house. Agnes had never been the same after that. She had always been bright and happy-go-lucky, kind, generous, and obliging, until unaccountably she had changed. She became hard, irritable, and rude, particularly when her parents told her to do anything. She began to think she knew better than them, and refused to do as they said. This had become worse in recent years because of the hospital which had just encouraged her to get ideas of her own.

The present breakdown had been coming on since Christmas, and Mrs. Lawson had had a bad time of it. There had been a big improvement in the last fortnight, and she was more like her old self, but before that you could hardly speak to her. You had to choose your words very carefully. For instance, when Agnes was sitting by the fire putting some cream on her face before going to bed, and—well, she knew they had a funny chimney, and she threw the greased paper on top of the fire. Her Dad had said, 'Oh do be careful', and Agnes had just gone off the deep end, real rude and nasty-like. But definitely this last fortnight there had been an improvement. Yes, they would be prepared to have her at home now, but she did not think she was well enough to do any work yet. Yes, they would be prepared to have her home. They would do anything to help, definitely. It was a great worry but they would do anything in their power to help her, and they did. Well she didn't know about her getting better as she got older. The hospital really had no idea how difficult Agnes was to live with at times, because they never saw how badly she behaved. In fact no one saw how she behaved. Even Agnes's aunt (Mrs. Lawson's sister) who was a frequent visitor to the house had said that she would never have thought there was anything wrong with her. It was only when she was alone with her parents that it was obvious that she was ill.

AGNES: Yes she did get irritable and rude, she supposed, really.

But she had got better as she got older really, hadn't she? Yes the breakdown had been coming on since Christmas, but she'd fought against it all the time. Yes she was different in front of other people because she couldn't show off. Outsiders wouldn't think there was anything wrong with her—it was definitely with her parents. Perhaps they got on each other's nerves a bit.

MOTHER: Agnes told her mother that she would like to find herself a job. Mrs. Lawson agreed that this was a good idea, but not yet, because Agnes was not well enough, but perhaps she would be in two or three years' time. After all, she said, Agnes should remember what had happened in the past, how she always broke down after two or three days at work. Anyway she thought Agnes was going to abide by what the doctor said. And besides, look how bored she got with everything. She couldn't settle to anything or finish anything. Look what happened at home. She couldn't settle to sewing or ironing, and in any case, she was always forgetting things. She should be honest and admit it; tell the doctor. She really didn't know what she wanted to do.

AGNES: Yes, she would probably go queer again if she found herself a job and it was true she did get bored, though she did think she was a lot better, but perhaps she really ought to wait a bit. She really didn't know what she wanted to do.

MOTHER: Mrs. Lawson had no objection to Agnes going to dances or going out with boys—she should go out, but Agnes had never been one for doing so. However, she wouldn't like Agnes to be like some of the types today. As for the boys, she didn't mind what boy she went out with provided he intended to marry her and was not flighty. She had never objected to Agnes kissing boys. It was natural, provided it wasn't done openly, but that was Agnes's business. She would not interfere, unless he wasn't Agnes's type.

As for sexual feelings, it was a normal thing, she supposed. It was all right to have them provided Agnes didn't do anything wrong. On the other hand she didn't think it was quite right either, really. Well she didn't know what to think. Besides, Agnes had never been one for going out. They'd tried their hardest to make her go, and in any case Agnes had kept all her doubts about her feelings from them—she'd never spoken to them about them. She seemed to feel embarrassed about sex altogether. Anyway *she* hadn't known a thing when she got married (at twenty-one). She hadn't even known what a period was. She'd been brought up strict and she wasn't ashamed of it—it hadn't done her any harm, but nowadays that's all you heard. They never talked sex at home. Mind you, she had a friend, her best friend, who was very open about that. The way they talked in her (friend's) house—well, she'd horrified them sometimes—she'd tell dirty jokes, but they'd never done anything like that in their house; she liked to feel she'd got a few ideals left. Mind you, this friend was a wonderful woman—she'd had eight children, but she embarrassed you at times. Not that she took any notice of what her friend said. And Mr. Lawson didn't like it either. But her friend was a wonderful woman.

As far as wanting to get married was concerned, Mrs. Lawson said she thought it was a normal thing, but there again—she'd always thought it was religion that was Agnes's problem. However, she had never stood in Agnes's way, but where was Agnes going to meet someone she liked? Men nowadays didn't come up to her (Mrs. Lawson's) standards. Anyway, how could Agnes look after a baby properly with her bad memory? She couldn't even remember to do the errands and she never finished anything she started. She started to sew something and she didn't finish it, she started knitting and she didn't finish that. She wasn't opposed to Agnes getting married, but she was too ill at the moment. And besides marriage wasn't everything. Lots of girls would rather have a career, like she would have done if she hadn't married her husband. After all she'd never been interested in boys herself. Her husband had been the only boy she'd known and she'd married him only because she had been living at home and was unhappy with her stepmother,[1] and if she hadn't had him she wouldn't have had anyone. But she'd never regretted anything, they'd been such a close, family until Agnes's illness.

AGNES: There wasn't any harm in feeling attracted to men, was there? Perhaps she oughtn't to talk about it. She hoped people didn't think she was sexy, but maybe it was because she was a bit passionate or something. Sex was a lot of her trouble, and her mother did embarrass her, probably because she was embarrassed herself. She would like to get married but it wasn't easy meeting the right one. She thought marriage would make a difference to her, although she agreed with her mother that you couldn't know for sure, it might lead to trouble. Still, sex was in the background of her trouble, but it was true she had been getting very religious. There again, she did think she'd be better if she were married, but she didn't know anybody. Boys usually liked to get friendly before they asked you to marry them, but there were lots of girls who would rather have a career than be married, weren't there?

MOTHER: Another issue between them was that Mrs. Lawson accused Agnes of keeping herself to herself. Mrs. Lawson was acutely embarrassed when Agnes spoke of sex. However, when Agnes told her that she felt embarrassed talking about sex to her mother, and that was why she never spoke to her about it, Mrs. Lawson replied that she couldn't understand why she felt like that. When Agnes then tried to tell her about masturbating, her 'stunt'[2] as she called it, and told her that she (Mrs. Lawson) had seen her doing this as a child, Mrs. Lawson's embarrassment became even more acute. First she denied knowing anything about it, then she said there never had been anything like that, then she said of course she knew what Agnes was talking about, then she said she didn't really know what it was, and then that

[1] Mrs. Lawson was ten when her mother died of T.B., and was herself in hospital with T.B. at the time.
[2] Crossing her legs tightly.

233

she'd never seen her do it, anyway, and ended up by saying that Agnes was always keeping things from her.

MOTHER: The way young people dressed today was disgusting. She didn't know what Agnes meant when she said she'd like to dress more attractively. Agnes may think she was drab, but she didn't think so, and besides she had to remember she'd done no work for three years. As for wearing jeans and slacks, well she didn't think Agnes wanted to dress like that. But it had nothing to do with her how Agnes dressed, although she wouldn't like her to be a Bohemian. But then as she said—but she didn't think Agnes was a Bohemian.

AGNES: She agreed it was shocking the way some young people looked, although they thought they looked attractive. She couldn't remember saying yesterday she wanted to be more attractive—but she would like to look more attractive really, she supposed, if she could—well more smart anyway, because she did feel so drab. Of course it was true she hadn't worked for three years. As for jeans and that, well they were rather mannish, though men did seem to find them attractive, and Shirley and Betty did wear them. To tell the truth she would like to wear them, but she hadn't the nerve because people would be thinking she was a bit Bohemian and she didn't think she was.

MOTHER: Agnes thought everybody was against her and there was no reason for her to think like that. It wasn't true that people weren't being kind to her or that something had happened in her childhood. As for always getting the blame for things in the house, that wasn't true either. They'd been a very close family, and Agnes had been spoiled more than the other two. She was always thinking she was left out of things. For instance, when Mrs. Lawson's sister came up and she and Mrs. Lawson sat talking together without bringing Agnes into the conversation. Agnes thought it was a slur on her and it wasn't. She was always imagining atmospheres and it was very trying.

AGNES: The feeling that people were against her had really got worse this. time. She often masturbated when she felt people weren't kind, or maybe it had something to do with her childhood. But it was true she had been spoiled more than the others. It was probably because she had been too spoiled that she'd done it, probably because she'd had too much affection showered on her. She hadn't really always been blamed for things at home. She'd really been spoiled. She could see that now. She did tend to sense atmospheres with people but really it was imagination. Mum had always said that.

MOTHER: Yes, she knew how Agnes felt and that it was all imagination. She emphasized that she knew Agnes's feeling about hostile atmospheres was all imagination since she was quite sure it was. Besides, she knew all about atmospheres herself because she was very quick to detect whether she was wanted or not. *She* could read what people were thinking very quickly.

MOTHER: She thought that religion was Agnes's trouble because that was all they'd had from her. She was always on about Jesus and all that, and someone had said that they didn't think it was right for her to speak about it all the time. After all, Mrs. Lawson knew about religion. She'd been a Sunday-school teacher. She'd been brought up religious, and she'd brought up her children that way. Even now they went to church on Sunday morning, Agnes and she, but . . .

AGNES: She felt that going to church had helped her a lot, partly through being in contact with religion and partly through mixing with people. She felt she had achieved something. Really religion was her trouble. She'd got too religious. She liked to say her prayers every night and she read the Bible most nights if she wasn't too tired, and she found comfort from that, and she'd always believed in Jesus, even as a child. Jesus had helped her a lot, but she really felt He was too much in her life. He drove her too much and it got on her nerves.

Mrs. Lawson explained that she was very worried about Agnes's memory. She believed it was bad and continually told Agnes so. Agnes believed her. They both believed this was part of the 'illness'. (In fact, it seemed to us that her memory was perfectly good, and it had at no time been regarded as faulty by any doctor who had examined her.) Mrs. Lawson, however, was able not to remember events uncomfortable to her, while at the same time accusing her daughter of imagining them. For instance, Agnes said she had told her mother something. Mrs. Lawson denied it. Agnes agreed that she must have been mistaken, and put it down to her tendency to keep things to herself and to imagine things. Mrs. Lawson endorsed this with, 'That is Agnes's trouble, she does forget so'. A few minutes later, however, when Agnes began to tell her about the event she cut her short with, 'Yes, I know, you did tell me that'.

Mrs. Lawson, in her description of Agnes's 'illness' completely omitted to mention her hallucinations. When she was explicitly asked about them, she dismissed them as not worthy of comment or alarm.

INTERVIEW BETWEEN AGNES AND HER FATHER

In this session Mr. Lawson invalidated every activity or interest of Agnes's that might have helped her to establish her autonomy. Agnes tried to argue with him, but she was unable to maintain her point of view. To do so she would have had continually to make metastatements[1] of a highly sophisticated kind.

Imagining her parents dislike her—madness or badness
The following statement by Mr. Lawson shows how determined he was to see Agnes's behaviour as process rather than praxis. His ill-concealed (to us) anger was barely held in check.

FATHER: He couldn't understand this irritability of Agnes's, but she did get irritable and that was a fact, and she probably

[1] Metastatement: a statement about a statement.

236

made them (him and his wife) irritable with her. Sometimes, he said, he wondered whether she wanted to go somewhere and she didn't. But they'd never stopped her from going out and Agnes knew it. She went to church now, but you could have too much of church really. And little things worried Agnes. Things often upset him too, but he'd never let them worry him. *He'd* forget about them but not Agnes. She'd keep on about it. She kept on and on about things, like Jesus and this, that, and the other. It got on his nerves and she knew it. He didn't mind admitting it. He just couldn't stand that irritability. He wasn't used to it. She wanted to pull herself together. Mind you, he tolerated it, but at times he felt like shaking her—if he thought it would do any good. But if it wasn't going to do any good, well naturally he wouldn't do it. But there was something wrong with Agnes, deep down, and God alone knew what it was. He had another two, a boy and a girl, and nothing seemed to worry them. They were just like normal persons. Why Agnes should be like this he'd no idea. She thought they'd neglected her, but she'd had the same upbringing as the other two. He believed in fact they'd made too much of a fuss over her, but they'd never stopped her from going anywhere or doing anything. There was definitely something wrong with Agnes or she wouldn't be in hospital really, would she? That's what he had to remember. But for the life of him—. Well, she didn't even look vacant. And this last two weeks there'd been a wonderful improvement, but she still wouldn't do anything or go anywhere. Even if she went to church she wanted her mother to go with her. She always got worked up to a point, to a pitch, and she'd become ill again, and naturally she came back into hospital. When Agnes came in this last time she was ill. There was no doubt about it—and she looked ill. Now what would make her ill physically? Only worry he thought.

AGNES said she didn't know why she worried so. She just got so irritable and edgy. Perhaps she was just sensitive. It wasn't true she'd said her parents had neglected her. In fact she'd always said they'd made a fuss of her. And it wasn't true that she thought nobody liked her. She used to think that, but not any longer, because she was better. She didn't think her father was wicked. It was just his temper that annoyed her. He'd always picked on her more than the others, even when she was a little girl he used to say she caused the rows in the house. As for saying she caused them when she was first ill, she couldn't see how he could say that because if she was sick, how could he blame her? She didn't like her father to go at her, you know, raising his voice, because then she thought he really meant it.

The following list of attributions made by Mr. Lawson about Agnes indicated, according to him, that she was ill.
  1. Being irritable at home.
  2. Getting on his nerves.
  3. Worrying about things.
  4. Going on about things.
  5. Not going out or mixing with people.
  6. Going to church and church socials.
  7. Not mixing with everyone and anyone.
  8. Talking about religion in a simple manner.
  9. Saying that her father was picking on her and criticizing her.
  10. Thinking that her parents didn't want her home.
  11. Not going out to work.
  12. Worrying about not working.
  13. Feeling herself excluded by people.
  14. Forcing herself on people when people don't want to talk to her.
  15. Not telling her father her thoughts.
  16. Laughing to herself.
  17. Not pulling herself together.
  18. Not going out with boys and thinking he would stand in her way.
  19. Liking a boy and not knowing whether or not she was in love with him.

20. Thinking no one likes her.
21. Not being cheeky the way a normal person is cheeky, but going on and on about it.

As far as we can see, the only feature that these attributions have in common is that they all irritated Mr. Lawson. A more detailed examination of some of them, and of other statements by her father, throws further light on Agnes's uncertainty over those issues which are so important to her.

FATHER: All he wanted was for her to be home and to be able to go to work and enjoy herself.

AGNES: She couldn't work being as she was.

FATHER: She needn't worry about work.

He said he wasn't an angry man. He was a disappointed man. What had he to be angry about? Angry with life, that was the only thing. He couldn't be angry with her, really, because she couldn't help it. But he was disappointed in her because she ought to be normal—living a normal life. Instead she'd been ill for nine years—nine years was a long time—she was always saying she suffered terribly inwardly. But he wasn't always quarrelling with her, though it was disappointing. There was nothing he'd like more than for his daughter to go to work. There was nothing nicer in life than to come home from a hard day's work and relax and sit down and listen to the wireless or television, with a nice fire. That's what he wanted for her. It was all right for her to say she watched television, but she didn't come home from work to do it, did she? No. She'd been to work two or three times since she'd first come to this hospital, and each time she'd been a failure at it. Oh he knew others had had more jobs than she had, but they kept going to work. Not that he was blaming her. He'd hoped Agnes would have got married and lived a normal life like his other two. It was disappointing but it wasn't Agnes's fault, from what he could make out. But he hoped she realized that she would have a terrible time finding a job. They just didn't give them jobs coming from these places. He could tell her that.

He didn't mind Agnes being cheeky, but she wasn't cheeky like other people. His other children, if they thought he was wrong, told him off about it and that was the end of it. But not with Agnes, she just went on worrying about it. It was all very well for her to say she worried because she wanted to keep friends with her mother and father, but why did she have to try to be friends with her mother and father? You didn't have to make friends with your own parents. He just could not make head or tail of it.

Agnes remained silent.

He and his wife had never stopped Agnes from going out or doing anything and Agnes knew that. She was going to church now, but you could have too much church really. She didn't seem to want to go out anywhere. And she was choosey who she mixed with. She should mix with everyone like he did. He'd mixed with some uncouth people in his time.

AGNES: No, her parents had never stopped her from going anywhere. She just didn't want to go out and mix with people because she was nervous of mixing. But she did go down to the church now, although that was the only place she'd been to. But it had helped her a lot going down there. She didn't think you could have too much of church—well, maybe she was having too much.

FATHER: Mr. Lawson said they'd never stopped Agnes from doing anything and having a fellow. Agnes could do exactly as she wanted to. He'd never stood in her way, and he was sure her mother hadn't, but he wouldn't like her to go out with anyone from the hospital for a start like a lot of them did. That was fair enough, wasn't it? But she could please herself. One was enough in the family coming from these places.

AGNES: Well, there was no one there she was interested in.

FATHER: Mr. Lawson said he felt Agnes was old enough to know whether or not she was in love with the electrician. But there you were. How could he cope with that sort of thing—wondering what the electrician had meant? True enough there was no harm in *that*—for a normal person.

AGNES: She promised she wouldn't do it in future.

FATHER: Wherever Agnes went she always imagined people didn't like her, like at church socials—or people didn't want to talk to her. The trouble with Agnes was that she was jealous and she was always forcing herself on people when she wasn't wanted.

AGNES: Well, she wasn't the only one to think people didn't like her. That's what people were like. Her father also thought things like that about people. He thought she didn't like him. Still, maybe she was unkind. She didn't think things like that now, and she wouldn't force herself on people when she wasn't wanted. Though she was puzzled because if people at church didn't want her why did they ask her to help?

FATHER: Agnes was always miserable, never happy. She really wanted someone to dislike. And there was another thing, she was always laughing to herself. She'd be sitting by the fire and all of a sudden she'd give a silly grin or a laugh, and he'd say, 'Well, what are you laughing at?', and she'd say, 'Well, thoughts', and she'd never tell—she'd never once told him her thoughts.

AGNES: She hadn't done it since she'd been in hospital.

FATHER: Agnes was so irritable and she was always saying he'd picked on her even as a child. She was always feeling picked on. It wasn't true that he used to tell her as a little girl that she caused all the rows in the house, and anyway she probably did cause all the trouble that time when she was becoming ill. Look at that case with the piano. He'd had her taught the piano although she hadn't been very successful. Three years she'd been at it. Three years was a long time. Now he could read music although he wasn't a pianist. He could read music, and he could tell when Agnes was going wrong, and so he'd tried to put her right. But, no, that was no good. He didn't know anything. 'What do you know? You don't know, Dad', and she'd slam the piano down. He'd think to himself, 'Well I don't know Agnes, you're a funny sort of girl. You won't be told anything', and she wouldn't. She always knew, and he was just big-head and suchlike. Of course, looking back on it now he could see it was her illness coming on all the time.

But he also said that Agnes was never nasty or aggressive. She would never do anyone any harm. She was gentle, too gentle really and quiet—at least she was quiet at home. He didn't know what she was like in hospital, but at home she was quiet and slept a lot or lay on the couch. Unless, of course, it was because she thought she could do as she liked at home. Perhaps he ought to make her get up and sit about. But then if he did that she'd say he was a bully.

AGNES: Three years is nothing to become a pianist. It takes at least seven years. Anyway, she didn't know at the time he was trying to help her. She didn't know what to think. It just annoyed her being picked up all the time. It was true she didn't like anybody telling her, but she had thought she was doing right. She hadn't liked him telling her she was wrong, and of course he had only been trying to show her, but she couldn't see that at the time. That was because she hadn't been well.

FATHER: Sometimes he thought Agnes hadn't grown up. Look how childish she talked at times, dead childish, about religion, 'Jesus loves me. Jesus is with me'. Only little kids talked like that. It was blooming childish. Not that he had anything against religion: he was religious himself, up to a point, but to say that Jesus was the only one that cared about her in front of her father and mother. Well that was all right with him, he wasn't against

Jesus. He didn't mind her having faith in Him provided it did her good. It didn't seem to.

AGNES: She felt going to church helped her, but it was a silly thing to say about Jesus, really, because her Mum and Dad did care for her as well, though at times it had seemed that Jesus was the only one because she felt she was away from everybody. Still she had had a relapse so it showed it hadn't done her any good.

Paranoid ideas: (a) imagining her parents didn't want her home
(b) saying the hospital hadn't helped her

FATHER: Agnes shouldn't think she'd never get properly better. He'd sooner Agnes was at home and normal. Why didn't she do what she was told and stop there? It was up to Agnes. She talked about getting better, but it was not as if she could just jump up and say, 'Oh I'm all right now', and forget everything. She was still morbid about it. It was true that she'd been wonderful this last fortnight, and if Agnes had been like that all the time he wouldn't mind her being home, but let's hope she stayed that way. They talk about advancements—well he didn't like to say this, but he guaranteed there was hardly a person gone out of there that hadn't come back, and Agnes would probably be coming in and out of those places for the rest of her life. That wasn't very nice for a parent to have in the back of their mind. He'd never given Agnes the impression that he'd resented her being in hospital to that extent. It was disappointment he felt. After all, she'd been ill for nine years. She'd failed every time she'd come out. He didn't know what help she had been getting, but whatever it was it didn't help her. It was all very well to say she shouldn't be bitter, but she was entitled to be.

AGNES: She wondered if she'd left it too late to get better. She was very anxious to get herself right. She'd been in three months now and felt a lot better, but maybe she was still morbid, though she had thought she was nearly better, really. However, it was true she did worry because she had visions of coming back before she'd even left. She knew she shouldn't think about that, but she didn't know what to make of it. She wasn't bitter, really, but she felt she hadn't been helped the way she ought to have been.

MOTHER AND FATHER
'Imagining her parents don't like her'—nasty and ill—how her parents see her:
Agnes, they said, was a very sensitive girl and shy, and she didn't want to mix. She was afraid, though why she should be they did not know. They'd given her every encouragement. And many a time she'd spoiled an outing by refusing to go out at the last moment—just to be awkward. They didn't want to make it blacker for her than it was, but she had deliberately done it to be awkward, but not when she was with other people. Nobody else would dream there was anything wrong with Agnes. But when she was with them she was deliberately trying and nasty. She'd been like that since she was ill but it had been worse in the last two or three years. She hadn't been like that before she fell ill. She had been more—well it was difficult to describe, she'd been very irritable with her father. Over the piano, for instance, and over the bicycle. He'd tried to teach her to ride a bicycle and she'd got so irritable with him. She won't let him tell her. If only she could have conquered that not being told and knowing she's right. Well they didn't know whether she really thought she was right. But she definitely didn't like being told—not by them any-way—she might with other people, but not them.

Later they said she hadn't ever been nasty or aggressive. She really was a lovely girl but she was always under the impression that nobody liked her and nobody wanted her, and yet if anyone spoke to her she probably said she loved her Dad and loved her Mum. She was so changeable. She wanted to be shaken out of it.

To her parents, Agnes's criticisms made no sense. For instance, she criticized her mother's cleanliness and competence in washing up. And as for her father, he might just be combing his hair at the table, and she'd make sure that everything was away from

244

him. She'd be waiting for him just to make that slip—'Oh don't do that, Dad, it's not right'. Or with the bathroom—he mustn't use another towel, or if he used someone else's flannel—'That's my flannel'. Well they didn't want to be told that all the time did they? Normal people would use a towel and soap and that would be the finish of it. And anyway, they always did use their own towels and flannels and things.

They felt Agnes was spoiled. Actually her father had spoiled all of them. They had loved their children. They couldn't think of anything that could have caused this illness. Well, Mr. Lawson could remember something—perhaps—he could remember saying once or twice or three times—they both could remember him saying to her as a little child that they had found her on the doorstep or in the street—only in fun. He wondered if that may have had an effect, because not being like the other two she may have taken it to heart. Although she didn't seem to take it seriously—well, she talked about it, 'You didn't really, Daddy, did you?' But she didn't seem upset. When he reassured her she was okay, that settled it. Of course he hadn't stopped at that. He'd said it again. He'd said it another night, like one did with children—for fun.

They'd never stopped Agnes from going anywhere or doing anything provided it was right. And when she was out he didn't know whether she was doing right or wrong, did he? Unless she came back with her trouble, but they had had no fear of that.

They both said she had been a wonderful baby and a wonderful child. Never a moment's trouble. She was the best of the three. The others had cried, but not her. She had been wonderful right up until she was nineteen, though her father at least used to wonder—used to think to himself a lot about her, 'You're a funny-tempered girl'. But it never occurred to him she was ill. She didn't look as if she was ill. She looked just as normal as anyone. She was no different from other children. There was never any trouble about her going out or mixing with people.

She used to go out to the pictures with her sister and her sister's two friends, or roller-skating. Agnes was as good as gold.

Imagining people don't like her and feeling excluded[1]
However, there had been something Mr. Lawson had not liked about Agnes. Before she came into hospital she worked in a hairdresser's,[2] and she used to come home and think that the girls were against her and were snooty and snubbed her, and he used to think to himself, 'Well I don't know, is it them or is it you?' He came to the conclusion that it was Agnes. Don't ask him why, and don't ask him why she's like that because he didn't know. At this point his wife intervened to make the only dissent of the session. It was true about those girls. They had been snooty because Agnes had lived in a council house and they had got their own houses, and Agnes had taken it to heart because she was very sensitive. You could hurt her as easy as anything. She had always put the illness down to that because she had changed then. It seemed to have given her an inferiority complex because they had lived in a council house.

The early years
All three children were born at home.

The Lawsons had had some very upsetting experiences with their two older children. Their eldest child, Shirley, nearly died of starvation and malnutrition because they said Mrs. Lawson's doctor had insisted that she breast-feed her. For three months she had kept it up while the infant had been simply fading away, until one day Mr. Lawson told her to go out and buy a bottle of Nestlé's food. From then on the child picked up. When the next child, Jimmy, was born, five years later, Mrs. Lawson had had a terrible time. He was born asphyxiated. They tried to revive him, but after a time the midwife had said, 'It's no good fighting for the child, let's fight for the mother'. But Mrs. Lawson's mother happened to be present and she said, 'Don't tell her, have another

---

[1] Clinically viewed as a delusion of reference on her first admission to hospital.
[2] Her first and only job before her first admission.

go at the baby for goodness sake', and they'd had another go and they saved him also. Jimmy was fed on the bottle but he was very fretful for eighteen months until he was circumcised.

At that time the Lawsons were in bad circumstances. They were cramped, living in a very small house—bedroom, living-room, and scullery, and it was the time of the Depression, with Mr. Lawson out of work a great deal. In addition, Mrs. Lawson, who had suffered from pulmonary tuberculosis as a girl, was in poor health from the effects of the pregnancy and confinement. They decided they should not have any more children, but, to Mrs. Lawson's dismay, nine months after Jimmy's birth she found herself pregnant again. At first she wouldn't believe it. She decided that it was the anaemia that she was suffering from that had caused her to miss a period, but her doctor eventually confirmed that she was pregnant. She'd never had such a miserable pregnancy, and she'd had a severe haemorrhage after the birth, and for a year afterwards she was ill—she felt awful and had no energy. But although they hadn't wanted another child, the moment she was born they loved her. In fact, they had made more of her than of the others. But it had been a great strain bringing up a family in those days. They'd tried to do their best.

MOTHER, FATHER, AND AGNES

Agnes was unsure what to think about herself (was she good or bad, well or ill?), about the hospital (was it a good or bad place?), about her parents (were they ganged up against her or not, did they want her or not?).

Mystifications were maintained over all these issues, and over what her madness or badness consisted in, over the validity of her perceptions of hostile and sexual cues, and over how to evaluate her own sexuality and her parents' attitude towards it.

Ambiguous feelings about hospital and her parents

The ambiguity of her parents' attitude was clear. Mr. Lawson, as we now know, is highly ambivalent about his daughter's treatment in hospital, and in the interview with Agnes he both expressed bitterness and enjoined her to feel bitter for not being helped or cured. In this session he spoke differently.

Agnes said that she wanted to come home because she felt well. She 'admitted' that she didn't think she was completely cured, but then she didn't think there was a complete cure.

Both Mr. and Mrs. Lawson reproached her for having such doubts. They tried to show Agnes that she was still ill in various ways—e.g. that she was still imagining things when she said she wasn't liked by other patients (the nurses indeed observed that patients did not like her), by failing to validate her memory that when she had left hospital last time she had been very well (the hospital records described her as 'very reasonable'), and by failing to endorse her view that although she asked to leave hospital herself last time, her doctor would not have agreed if he hadn't thought her well enough (the doctor concerned remembered, and the hospital records confirmed, that she left hospital with consent, and not against advice). They did not refuse in so many words to have her home either at this time or later, but their attitude remained ambiguous and discouraging.

This pattern of 'demonstrating' that she was ill, of telling her to have confidence in the hospital, and that she should stay in hospital until she was better, was repeated throughout the session, while Agnes protested that she felt well enough to go home, but agreed she was ill and that perhaps she should stay until she was told to go.

Evaluation of Agnes's own sexuality and of sexual implications in the behaviour of others
Over the question of her sexuality, her parents' joint attitude was as mystifying as it had been in the previous interviews. Their statement also shows how they have been mystified by the clinical point of view—'otherwise she wouldn't be in here'.

They said Agnes's mind didn't work like a normal person's, otherwise she wouldn't be in hospital. Her illness was that she was liable to imagine that men or some men found her attractive and/or her illness was caused by imagining this. Anyway she wanted to be careful with men, although it was her illness that made her careless, though she should have been careful just the same with the electrician because she was ill, though she hadn't been ill at the time. Anyway, he might have thought she was easy to seduce because she was mentally ill, though Agnes wasn't like that, but it could happen to any girl, and besides, Mr. Lawson knew what workmen were like and men too, because he was a man himself. Not that he had met the electrician, so he didn't know what he was like, but how did they know whether Agnes could control herself? After all, you couldn't be behind her all the time. Not that they knew if Agnes was man-mad or whether her illness was caused by that, though it probably was. But they hadn't stopped Agnes being interested in men or going out with them. Besides, lots of girls weren't married. Marriage wasn't everything.

Mr. and Mrs. Lawson, as far as we could gather, had never suggested she invite her boy-friends home so that they could vet them and tell her what they thought of them in a straightforward way. Their help seems to have consisted in uttering vague but ominous general warnings—'You want to watch yourself'. She was expected to apply this generalized advice to particular individuals and to be able to tell whom she could trust.

Agnes said she found it difficult to talk to her mother about sex. She thought her mother was a different type of person from herself. Her parents attributed this belief to her illness. She said it embarrassed her to talk to her mother about sex. Her father's response was to imply that she had no reason to let it embarrass her (her parents had said a few minutes earlier that they were embarrassed by it), and to order her not to let it embarrass her in future. Her mother's comment was that the young people of today were very complicated.

Agnes explicitly stated that her parents' attitude caused her to lack self-assurance because they refused to validate her perceptions and evaluations. Her father ridiculed this by asking whether, if Agnes were to say that she wasn't ever going to get well, he was then supposed to agree with her.

For the most part, however, Agnes complied with her parents' point of view, agreeing with them for instance that her memory was bad, that she was unable to work because she couldn't concentrate, that she had headaches, that she hadn't got headaches, that she imagined headaches, that it was not pleasant in hospital, that it was pleasant in hospital, that she imagined her parents didn't love her, that her illness made her imagine this, that her jealousy made her imagine this, that her illness made her jealous, that her jealousy made her ill, and so on.

MOTHER ALONE

Mrs. Lawson believed as much as Agnes that people in the district were talking about her being in hospital, but because this worried Agnes she told her that no one knew about it.

Her mother said that they disapproved of Agnes's attendance at the hospital out-patient social club because it wasn't 'nice' to mix with ex-patients. They told Agnes so. Consequently she had attended only once since her discharge from hospital.

However, they continued to complain that Agnes did not mix enough. Mrs. Lawson said they disapproved of the hospital encouraging her to attend socials, where, she implied, sexually loose behaviour was allowed, and she also complained that the hospital had encouraged Agnes to go to work before she was fit.

AGNES ALONE

A series of four interviews with Agnes at weekly intervals sixteen months after the start of the investigation showed her to be as mystified as ever, although clinically recovered.

Her illness, she said, boiled down to not getting on with men. She did wonder, however, if she was too sexy, and if there was something wrong with her because she thought so much about having a boy-friend and getting married. She thought she was sexually frustrated, but she wasn't sure how she could tell. She wanted to get married and have intercourse because this changed a woman. She noticed how much nicer girls looked after they were married. But she didn't know how to meet a boy or how to keep him interested in her once she'd met him. Supposing you wanted to marry him and he started going out with someone else, what did you do? Did you try to keep him or did you leave him or did you let him go? She'd always been worried about boys and how she appeared to them. Not that she'd ever been warned about going out with boys. In fact her mother had never told her anything about them, and had always appeared to think that marriage was not for her. She had always been too frightened to bring a boy home, although probably her parents wouldn't have minded as long as he was all right. But even when she was sixteen her parents used to say, 'Shirley will get married but not Agnes. She'll never get married'. If she asked, 'Oh I wonder if I'll ever get married? Who should I invite to my wedding?', her mother would reply, 'What are you worrying for? It's not everything, marriage. You're better off single'. And recently her mother and her sister had both said the same thing. She found this very puzzling, because after all they were married and had had babies. No one had ever spoken about marriage to her in a nice way, 'Oh one day, Agnes, perhaps you'll get married.' However, she didn't think her parents would mind if she found a nice boy, although her mother had said, 'You've got to go a long way to find a nice fellow today. They're all rogues round here.' She was afraid she was getting ill again because she was now thinking a lot about a boy she'd met, and whenever she played a record on the gramophone at home she thought of him, and when this happened she'd feel restless and get up and dance to the music. That, she felt, wasn't normal. Normal people didn't behave in that way, although she had seen girls doing it, but . . .

Really her trouble was she didn't get on with people and imagined they had a grudge against her, for instance, the girls at the hairdresser's where she'd worked before her first breakdown, though they had been snooty because she and her family lived in a council house and voted Labour while they owned their houses and voted Conservative. She *was* inclined to be nasty and rude and over-fastidious, like cleaning out the bathroom regularly or clearing the food and dishes away when her father combed his hair over the table, or turning funny if he used the same towel as her, and demanding one of her own. But that had been in the past. She didn't mind sharing towels now. She'd only been like that because she'd been ill at the time. Her parents were very good to her. They were lovely. Her father bought her presents at Christmas and for her birthday. He really thought a lot of her. He'd gone terribly grey through worrying over her, so he'd told her. But they often quarrelled, and he said hurtful things to her, and her mother always took her father's side. It was really because she was inclined to be sloppy over little things that they quarrelled. For instance, if she tried to be friendly and went up to him and kissed him he'd tell her off. He'd tell her to get away and stop slopping over him: but still he did let her wash his hair, and put cream on it and comb it for him. This, however, was an old custom. Until she was fourteen she would sit on her father's knee and comb his hair while he told her fairy stories. It was because she was attracted to hair that she went into a hairdresser's, but now she was afraid to have her hair styled and look attractive.

She remembered her parents telling her that they'd found her on the doorstep. She'd taken it to heart although she didn't know why. Maybe it was because she hadn't known the facts of life. But her parents really loved her. Her mother thought the world of her and worshipped her, although by the way she talked at times she sometimes wondered. Her mother was inclined to worry too much about her and nag her and tell her off, and she got irritable and told her mother off. But that was because she didn't really like being told, because she always wanted things her own way. As her mother said, 'If you let people tell you what's right, you'll be all right'. Still perhaps they did fuss too much and treat her like a baby. Her trouble was she lacked confidence and relied too much on her mother, and perhaps their fussing had something to do with that, because she sometimes felt they stopped her from going to work. And once when she'd been admiring a friend's baby and said she wished she had one, her mother replied, 'You, you wouldn't be able to look after a baby'.

Another thing about herself was that she was liable to talk too much. She was always telling people her business. Her mother was always telling her off, 'You're always telling people things and they don't tell you nothing'. The other night as she left to go down to the church her mother had said, 'Be careful what you say down there. Don't tell them about your illness.' People were so nosey and she was liable to blurt out that she hadn't been sleeping too good.

AGNES'S BROTHER AND SISTER-IN-LAW (JIMMY AND BETTY)

They confirmed that Agnes and her father had always been very close. She had sat on her father's lap while he read stories every evening until she was fourteen years old.

Agnes, they said, insists on her mother washing her hands and cleaning under her finger-nails before she kneads the dough for making pastry, and this annoys her mother.

They feel Mrs. Lawson fusses too much over Agnes and confines her unduly. Her brother felt that his mother had over-protected him also. It was the Army that helped him break out. His mother would never let Agnes travel any distance, nor go shopping on her own, although when Agnes had stayed with them she had gone shopping by herself perfectly well. Mrs. Lawson would not believe this. She would not let Agnes do the washing up or the housework, although she had done it when she had stayed with them. Agnes, they said, had little confidence in herself. When she doubted her ability to do something her mother would say, 'Well perhaps you'd better not'. She needed somebody to encourage her.

Like all the patients described in this book, Agnes is extremely confused about how she experiences herself and how others experience her. Moreover, once again this confusion reflects the mystifying situation in which she has lived for many years.

The standard psychiatric interview is not an instrument that brings this social situation to light. Hence, in the absence of discernible gross external traumata, and in the absence of so-called internal psychogenic factors, Agnes and the other patients we have studied have all come to be regarded as suffering from some meaningless pathological process. By building up a picture, however, of the actual situation in which Agnes has been living for years, we begin to see that she is struggling to make sense of a senseless situation—senseless at any rate from her position within it.

By seeing Agnes's situation simultaneously from our point of view and hers, we can now begin to make sense of what psychiarists still by and large regard as nonsense.

APPENDIX

O = start of investigation
W = written record
T = tape-recording
(all tape-recordings transcribed)

MAYA ABBOTT

Interview No.	Interviewee(s)	Time of Interview	Method of Recording
1	Maya	o	W
2	mother and father	o	W
3	mother	o	W
4	father	o	W
5	Maya and mother	o + 2 dys	T
6	Maya and mother	o + 6 dys	T
7	Maya and mother	o + 9 dys	T
8	Maya and mother	o + 13 dys	T
9	Maya and mother	o + 17 dys	T
10	Maya and mother	o + 4 wks 3 dys	T
11	Maya and mother	o + 5 wks	T
12	Maya and mother	o + 5 wks 3 dys	T
13	Maya and mother	o + 6 wks	T
14	Maya and mother	o + 6 wks 3 dys	T
15	Maya and mother	o + 7 wks 3 dys	T
16	Maya and mother	o + 8 wks	T
17	Maya and mother	o + 9 wks 3 dys	T
18	Maya and mother	o + 11 wks	T
19	Maya and mother	o + 12 wks	T
20	Maya and mother	o + 12 wks 3 dys	T
21	Maya and mother	o + 13 wks	T
22	Maya and mother	o + 13 wks 3 dys	T
23	Maya and mother	o + 14 wks	T
24	Maya and mother	o + 14 wks 3 dys	T
25	Maya, mother, father	o + 15 wks	T
26	Maya and mother	o + 15 wks 3 dys	T
27	Maya, mother, father	o + 16 wks	T

255

MAYA ABBOTT—*cont.*

Interview No.	Interviewee(s)	Time of Interview	Method of Recording
28	Maya and mother	0 + 16 wks 3 dys	T
29	Maya, mother, father	0 + 17 wks	T
30	Maya and mother	0 + 17 wks 3 dys	T
31	Maya, mother, father	0 + 18 wks	T
32	Maya and mother	0 + 18 wks 3 dys	T
33	Maya, mother, father	0 + 19 wks	T
34	Maya and mother	0 + 19 wks 3 dys	T
35	Maya, mother, father	0 + 20 wks	T
36	Maya and mother	0 + 20 wks 3 dys	T
37	Maya, mother, father	0 + 21 wks	T
38	Maya and mother	0 + 24 wks	T
39	Maya and mother	0 + 39 wks	T
40	Maya and father	0 + 40 wks	T
41	mother and father	0 + 41 wks	T
42	Maya	0 + 1 yr 2 mths	W
43	Maya and mother	0 + 1 yr 2 mths	W
44	Maya, mother, father	0 + 1 yr 7 mths	W

LUCIE BLAIR

Interview No.	Interviewee(s)	Time of Interview	Method of Recording
1	Lucie and mother	0	T
2	Lucie and mother	0 + 3 wks	T
3	Lucie and mother	0 + 3 wks 4 dys	T
4	Lucie and mother	0 + 4 wks	T
5	Lucie and mother	0 + 5 wks	T
6	Lucie and mother	0 + 5 wks 4 dys	T
7	Lucie and mother	0 + 6 wks	T
8	Lucie and mother	0 + 8 wks	T
9	Lucie and mother	0 + 9 wks	T
10	Lucie and mother	0 + 10 wks	T
11	Lucie and mother	0 + 11 wks	T
12	Lucie and mother	0 + 12 wks	T
13	Lucie and mother	0 + 13 wks	T
14	Lucie, mother, father	0 + 2 yrs 4 mths	W
15	Lucie	0 + 2 yrs 7 mths	T
16	Lucie	0 + 2 yrs 8 mths	T
17	Lucie	0 + 2 yrs 9 mths	T
18	Lucie	0 + 2 yrs 10 mths	T
19	Lucie	0 + 2 yrs 11 mths	T

CLAIRE CHURCH

Interview No.	Interviewee(s)	Time of Interview	Method of Recording
1	Claire	0	W
2	Claire and mother	0 + 7 dys	T
3	mother and father	0 + 2 wks	W
4	mother	0 + 2 wks	W
5	father	0 + 2 wks	W
6	Claire and mother	0 + 5 wks	T
7	mother	0 + 6 wks	W
8	Claire and mother	0 + 6 wks	T
9	Claire and mother	0 + 7 wks	T
10	Claire and mother	0 + 8 wks	T
11	Claire and mother	0 + 10 wks	T
12	Claire and mother	0 + 11 wks	T
13	Claire and mother	0 + 12 wks	T
14	Claire and mother	0 + 13 wks	T
15	Claire and mother	0 + 15 wks	T
16	Claire and mother	0 + 16 wks	T
17	Claire and mother	0 + 17 wks	T
18	Claire and mother	0 + 24 wks	T
19	Claire and mother	0 + 25 wks	T
20	father	0 + 2 yrs 6 mths	W
21	mother	0 + 2 yrs 6 mths	W
22	Claire	0 + 2 yrs 6 mths	T
23	Claire	0 + 3 yrs	T
24	Claire and mother	0 + 3 yrs 1 mth	T

SARAH DANZIG

Interview No.	Interviewee(s)	Time of Interview	Method of Recording
1	Sarah	o	W
2	Sarah	o + 3 dys	W
3	Sarah	o + 4 dys	W
4	Sarah	o + 3 wks 2 dys	W
5	Sarah	o + 3 wks 5 dys	W
6	mother and father	o + 3 wks 5 dys	W
7	Sarah	o + 4 wks 1 dy	T
8	Sarah	o + 4 wks 3 dys	W
9	Sarah, John, mother, father	o + 4 wks 5 dys	T
10	mother	o + 4 wks 5 dys	T
11	father	o + 4 wks 5 dys	T
12	John	o + 4 wks 6 dys	T
13	Sarah and mother	o + 4 wks 6 dys	T
14	Sarah, John, mother, father	o + 4 wks 6 dys	T
15	Sarah and father	o + 4 wks 6 dys	T
16	mother and father	o + 4 wks 6 dys	T
17	Sarah, John, mother, father	o + 4 wks 6 dys	T
18	Sarah and John	o + 4 wks 6 dys	W (unsuccessful recording)
19	Sarah, John, mother, father	o + 4 wks 6 dys	T
20	Sarah	o + 7 wks	W
21	Sarah	o + 11 wks	W
22	general practitioner	o + 12 wks	W
23	Sarah, mother, father	o + 17 wks	W
24	Sarah, mother, father	o + 19 wks	T
25	Sarah, mother, father	o + 21 wks	T
26	Sarah, mother, father	o + 22 wks	T
27	mother and father	o + 8 mths	W
28	Sarah, mother, father	o + 8 mths	W
29	Sarah	o + 8 mths	W
30	Sarah and John	o + 8 mths	W
31	Sarah	o + 8 mths	T
32	Sarah, mother, father	o + 8 mths	W
33	mother and father	o + 8 mths	T

SARAH DANZIG—*cont.*

Interview No.	Interviewee(s)	Time of Interview	Method of Recording
34	Sarah	0 + 1 yr 2 mths	T
35	Sarah, mother, father	0 + 1 yr 2 mths	T
36	John	0 + 1 yr 2 mths	T
37	John and Sarah	0 + 1 yr 2 mths	T
38	Sarah	0 + 1 yr 2 mths	T
39	Sarah, mother, father	0 + 1 yr 2 mths	T

APPENDIX

RUBY EDEN

Interview No.	Interviewee(s)	Time of Interview	Method of Recording
1	Ruby	o	W
2	Ruby	o + 1 wk	W
3	Ruby, mother, aunt	o + 1 wk 5 dys	W
4	Ruby	o + 2 wks	W
5	Ruby	o + 12 wks	W
6	Ruby and aunt	o + 14 wks	W
7	Ruby, mother, aunt	o + 25 wks	T
8	Ruby and mother	o + 28 wks	T
9	mother and aunt	o + 33 wks	W
10	mother	o + 34 wks	W
11	uncle	o + 34 wks	W
12	mother and uncle	o + 34 wks	W
13	mother, uncle, aunt	o + 34 wks	W
14	mother, uncle, aunt, cousin	o + 34 wks	W
15	Ruby	o + 36 wks	T
16	mother	o + 38 wks	T
17	Ruby	o + 41 wks	T
18	Ruby and mother	o + 45 wks	T
19	Ruby	o + 48 wks	T
20	aunt	o + 50 wks	W

APPENDIX

Interview No.	Interviewee(s)	Time of Interview	Method of Recording
1	June	0	W
2	June	0 + 7 dys	T
3	June and mother	0 + 7 dys	T
4	June, mother, father	0 + 7 dys	T
5	mother	0 + 9 dys	W
6	June	0 + 2 wks 3 dys	T
7	June	0 + 2 wks 3 dys	T
8	mother and Sylvia	0 + 4 wks	T
9	mother	0 + 6 wks	W
10	mother	0 + 8 wks	W
11	June	0 + 10 wks	T
12	father	0 + 11 wks	T
13	June and father	0 + 11 wks	T
14	mother	0 + 11 wks	T
15	Sylvia	0 + 12 wks	T
16	June and Sylvia	0 + 12 wks	T
17	mother	0 + 12 wks	W
18	June, mother, father	0 + 13 wks	T
19	Headmistress	0 + 13 wks	W
20	June and mother	0 + 14 wks	W
21	June	0 + 14 wks 3 dys	W
22	general practitioner and assistant	0 + 16 wks	W
23	mother	0 + 18 wks	W
24	mother	0 + 21 wks	W
25	mother	0 + 27 wks	W
26	June	0 + 27 wks	W
27	mother	0 + 31 wks	W
28	June	0 + 31 wks	W
29	June	0 + 34 wks	W
30	June	0 + 35 wks	W
31	June and mother	0 + 35 wks	T
32	June	0 + 36 wks	W
33	mother	0 + 36 wks	W
34	June and mother	0 + 36 wks	T

JUNE FIELD—*cont.*

Interview No.	Interviewee(s)	Time af Interview	Method of Recording
35	June	o + 41 wks	W
36	June	o + 43 wks	W
37	mother	o + 44 wks	W
38	June	o + 46 wks	W

APPENDIX

RUTH GOLD

Interview No.	Interviewee(s)	Time of Interview	Method of Recording
1	Ruth	0	T
2	mother	0 + 18 wks	T
3	mother and father	0 + 18 wks	T
4	Ruth	0 + 44 wks	T
5	Ruth, mother, father	0 + 44 wks	T
6	brother	0 + 48 wks	W
7	mother	0 + 51 wks	T
8	Ruth	0 + 1 yr 4 mths	T
9	mother and father	0 + 1 yr 4 mths	T
10	Ruth	0 + 1 yr 4 mths	T
11	Ruth	0 + 1 yr 5 mths	T
12	Ruth	0 + 1 yr 5 mths	T
13	Ruth and mother	0 + 1 yr 5 mths	T

APPENDIX

JEAN HEAD

Interview No.	Interviewee(s)	Time of Interview	Method of Recording
1	Jean	0	T
2	father	0	T
3	Jean and father	0	T
4	Jean	0 + 2 dys	T
5	David	0 + 2 dys	T
6	Jean and David	0 + 2 dys	T
7	mother	0 + 2 dys	T
8	Jean and mother	0 + 2 dys	T
9	mother and father	0 + 2 dys	T
10	Jean, David, mother, father	0 + 2 dys	T
11	Jean	0 + 1 wk 4 dys	T
12	Jean	0 + 2 wks	T
13	Jean and David	0 + 3 wks	T
14	Jean	0 + 3 wks 5 dys	T
15	Jean	0 + 4 wks	T
16	Jean	0 + 4 wks 1 dy	T
17	Jean, David, mother, father	0 + 4 wks 2 dys	T
18	Jean	0 + 4 wks 4 dys	T
19	Jean and David	0 + 5 wks	T
20	Jean	0 + 7 wks	T
21	Jean and David	0 + 8 wks	T
22	mother	0 + 8 wks 2 dys	T
23	Jean's employer	0 + 9 wks	W
24	Jean and David	0 + 13 wks	T
25	Jean's brother	0 + 14 wks	W
26	Jean's foster-brother	0 + 17 wks	W
27	Jean	0 + 19 wks	T

265

MARY IRWIN

Interview No.	Interviewee(s)	Time of Interview	Method of Recording
1	Mary	o	W
2	Mary	o + 1 dy	T
3	Mary	o + 3 dys	T
4	Mary	o + 6 dys	T
5	Mary	o + 10 dys	T
6	mother	o + 11 dys	T
7	Mary and mother	o + 11 dys	T
8	father	o + 2 wks	T
9	mother and father	o + 2 wks	T
10	Mary	o + 2 wks	T
11	Mary	o + 2 wks 3 dys	T
12	Mary and father	o + 2 wks 4 dys	T
13	Mary, mother, father	o + 2 wks 4 dys	T
14	Mary	o + 3 wks 6 dys	T
15	Mary	o + 4 wks 1 dy	W
16	Mary and mother	o + 4 wks 4 dys	T
17	Angela	o + 5 wks	T
18	Mary	o + 8 wks	T
19	Mary	o + 12 wks	T
20	Mary	o + 19 wks	T

HAZEL KING

Interview No.	Interviewee(s)	Time of Interview	Method of Recording
1	Hazel	0	T
2	Hazel	0 + 1 dy	T
3	Hazel and mother	0 + 2 dys	W
4	mother	0 + 2 dys	T
5	Hazel, mother, father	0 + 5 dys	T
6	Hazel	0 + 13 wks	T
7	Hazel, mother, father	0 + 14 wks	T
8	Hazel, mother, father	0 + 25 wks	W
9	Hazel and mother	0 + 39 wks	T
10	father	0 + 40 wks	T
11	Hazel, mother, father	0 + 41 wks	T
12	father	0 + 49 wks	T
13	mother's older sister and brother-in-law	0 + 1 yr	T
14	mother's younger sister's husband and mother's mother	0 + 1 yr 1 mth	W
15	mother's mother	0 + 1 yr 1 mth	W
16	mother's younger sister's husband	0 + 1 yr 1 mth	W
17	mother's father	0 + 1 yr 1 mth	W
18	mother	0 + 1 yr 1 mth	W
19	Hazel, mother, father, grandmother	0 + 1 yr 2 mths	T

INDEX

sexual control, diminished, 36, 52
delusions, 118, 164
feelings, condemnation of, 85, 91,
166, 232; confusion over, 228,
233, 249 ff
ideas, imposed, 35
'things', imagining, 26

silence, need for, 53
sleep, inability to, 15
sniffing, 189, 200
solitude, fear of, 183
splitting, 26 n, 168
spontaneity, and role-fulfilling, 85
stratagems, 198 ff
structural changes, absence of, 3
suicidal state, 146
suspicion, 28, 103 f

telepathy, 23
television, 95, 119
'thinking', disapproval of, 114
thought-blocking, 131, 190

thought control, 16, 23, 27, 28 f, 197,
200
thought-disorder, 43, 61, 131, 146,
222, 225, 254
thoughts, vagueness, 35
vocalization of, 26
woolly, 190
tiredness, 169
transference, 204
transitional objects, 182 n

unreality, feelings of, 146

vagueness, 35, 131, 190; see also
thoughts
violence, outbursts of, 61
voices, 16, 25, 30, 95, 118, 131, 222
see also auditory hallucinations

will, weakness of, 50, 222
withdrawal, 20, 28 f, 95, 101, 131,
139, 152
see also autistic